ADDICTIONS

TRUTH FOR LIFE®

THE BIBLE-TEACHING MINISTRY OF **ALISTAIR BEGG**

The mission of Truth For Life is to teach the Bible with clarity and relevance so that unbelievers will be converted, believers will be established, and local churches will be strengthened.

Daily Program

Each day, Truth For Life distributes the Bible teaching of Alistair Begg across the U.S. and in several locations outside of the U.S. through 1,700 radio outlets. To find a radio station near you, visit **truthforlife.org/stationfinder**.

Free Teaching

The daily program, and Truth For Life's entire teaching archive of over 2,000 Bible-teaching messages, can be accessed for free online and through Truth For Life's full-feature mobile app. Download the free mobile app at **truthforlife.org/app** and listen free online at **truthforlife.org**.

At-Cost Resources

Books and full-length teaching from Alistair Begg on CD, DVD, and USB are available for purchase at cost, with no markup. Visit **truthforlife.org/store**.

Where to Begin?

If you're new to Truth For Life and would like to know where to begin listening and learning, find starting point suggestions at **truthforlife.org/firststep**. For a full list of ways to connect with Truth For Life, visit **truthforlife.org/subscribe**.

Contact Truth For Life

P.O. Box 398000 Cleveland, Ohio 44139
phone 1 (888) 588-7884   **email** letters@truthforlife.org
 /truthforlife   @truthforlife   truthforlife.org

ADDICTIONS

A Banquet
in the Grave

Finding Hope
in the Power of
the Gospel

EDWARD T. WELCH

P&R
P U B L I S H I N G
P.O.BOX 817 • PHILLIPSBURG • NEW JERSEY 08865-0817

Page design by Tobias Design
Typesetting by Andrew MacBride

Printed in the United States of America

Library of Congress Cataloging-in-Publication Data

Welch, Edward T., 1953–
    Addictions : a banquet in the grave : finding hope in the power of the Gospel / Edward T. Welch.
        p. cm. — (Resources for changing lives)
    Includes bibliographical references and index.
    ISBN-10: 0-87552-606-3 (pbk.)
    ISBN-13: 978-0-87552-606-5 (pbk.)
    1. Alcoholics—Religous life. 2. Addicts—Religous life. I. Title.
II. Series.
BV4596.A48 W45 2001
248.8'629—dc21   2001036858

To Ben Ferris,

a wise and insightful co-worker

Bound as I was, not with another man's irons, but by my own iron will. My will the enemy held, and thence had made a chain for me, and bound me. For of a froward will, was lust made; and a lust served, became custom; and custom not registered became necessity. By which links, as it were, joined together (whence I called it a chain) a hard bondage held me enthralled.

Augustine, *Confessions, Book 8*

Contents

Illustrations

Figures

Tables

Acknowledgments

At this point in my life, I know I am simply writing down other people's ideas, most of which my poor memory prevents me from citing. But there are some contributors I remember well. John Bettler, David Powlison, Winston Smith, and Paul Tripp—my colleagues at CCEF—continue to be chief catalysts, instructors, and examples. They teach me that attentiveness to biblical doctrine and a life of love are inseparable.

To write this book, I was freed from my regular duties at CCEF through the generous and sacrificial support of Dee Miller, a person who has a vision for biblical counseling. This person's financial support and godly life have blessed me in many ways.

Sue Lutz is listed as "Series Editor," but behind this title is a job description that includes theologian, practitioner, coach, friend, and pages more. She has been devoted to bringing out the best in me. Thank you.

When you spend time with people who have struggled with addictions, they all change you in some way. The men and women I have known have often caused me to grieve, but they have also reminded me that the triune God loves addicts and delights in setting them free. I have valued my time with them immensely.

My wife, Sharon, has a hand in everything I do. This project is no exception.

Preface

There is an accepted tradition among those who struggle with addictions that goes something like this: helping yourself will help others, and helping others will help yourself. If an alcoholic learns to "take his soul to task," it will bless family, friends, co-workers, and probably many others. If that same alcoholic looks out for the needs of others, and goes out of his or her way to serve another drinker, then that person will most certainly be blessed in some way. With this in mind, the material that follows will examine both ourselves and those we want to help. It might seem awkward to think about our own struggles in one paragraph and then focus on other people in the next, but in a book that considers the human heart and the Christ of Scripture, there can be no other way. Preachers must preach to themselves before they preach to others. Counselors are always counselees.

You will probably come to this book with a particular role in mind. For example, I came with the idea of helping others. But as I dug into Scripture's teaching on the reckless nature of the human heart and its rich teaching on self-control, it made me see that I *needed* help as well. So thinking about your own struggles is the best way to start. Be sure to look for addictions in your own heart and life. Even though the focus of this book will be primarily on drugs and alcohol—prototypic addictions—the basic ideas are relevant to all kinds of sins that are not easily cast off. (Are there any that are?) Look for the activities or substances that entice you, leaving you wanting to come back for more, even though "more" may not be wise, godly, or legal. Look especially at the activities that provide you with a fairly rapid bodily experience. Scripture targets sex, alcohol, and food, but there are others.

What is the basic point of this book? Theology makes a difference. It is the infrastructure of our lives. Build it poorly and the building will eventually collapse in ruins. Build it well and you will be prepared for anything. The basic theology for addictions is that the root problem goes deeper than our genetic makeup. Addictions are ultimately a disorder of worship. Will we worship ourselves and our own desires or will we worship the true God? Through this lens, all Scripture comes alive for the addict. No longer are there just a few proof texts about drunkenness. Instead, since all Scripture addresses our fundamental disorder of worship, all Scripture is rich with application for the addict.

What follows will, I hope, seem radical. Rightly understood, Scripture should always seem radical, leaving us amazed and a bit off-balance. But a Christ-centered perspective on addictions should definitely be revolutionary. We are living in a culture where the theory and language of addictions are presently controlled by secular categories. Words like *disease, treatment,* and even *addiction* convey the idea that these problems have their ultimate cause in the body rather than the soul—a commonly accepted view that is at odds with clear biblical teaching. Given the domination of this secular perspective, careful biblical inspection will most likely reveal many layers of error in our thinking about addictions that will take years, and the insights of many people, to uncover. Thinking biblically about these difficult problems will require much more than redefining words or making Jesus the higher power. Instead, everything must be open to biblical inspection. Since we live in a culture that assumes a sub-biblical position, we must realize that it affects us more than we think.

For those who have been keeping track of cultural trends, what follows might not seem that radical. There are more and more probing and insightful voices—secular and Christian—that are questioning the legitimacy of current views on addiction. So this book is certainly not alone. I hope, however, that it can contribute wisdom and practical help to this very important area of debate and spiritual struggle.

The woman Folly is loud;
    she is undisciplined and without knowledge.
She sits at the door of her house,
    on a seat at the highest point of the city,
    calling out to those who pass by,
    who go straight on their way.
"Let all who are simple come in here!"
    she says to those who lack judgment.
"Stolen water is sweet;
    food eaten in secret is delicious!"
    But little do they know that the dead are there,
    that her guests are in the depths of the grave.

PROVERBS 9:13–18

PART 1
Thinking Theologically

1 | Practical Theology

Jim had been sober for a year—an amazing feat for someone who had been drunk about half his forty-five years. It seemed like a good time to meet for lunch so we could remember and celebrate. But when he walked into the diner, I could see that something was bothering him.

"I am getting angry at God for giving me this problem with alcohol," he said as he slid into the booth. "Most people in the world don't have to struggle to stay away from the next drink every day of their lives. But I do. It's just not fair."

He went on to say that he was losing interest in his church because it just wasn't speaking to his needs. He was finding his help and companionship in his daily AA meetings.

I had known that my friend's thinking about his alcohol abuse was not always shaped by Scripture. Instead, it had been informed by an eclectic combination of AA, Scripture, and the chip he had carried on his shoulder for years. But why quibble about fine points of doctrine when the important thing was his sobriety?

Scripture, however, says with good reason, "Watch your life and doctrine closely" (1 Tim. 4:16). At the moment Jim said that he was angry with God, I realized that doctrine, or theology, makes a difference.*

---

*Theology has a narrow and a broad sense. Narrowly, it is the study of what Scripture says about the triune God. Broadly, it is the study of what Scrip-

- The only way he could have been angry with God was if he believed that his genetic constitution was more to blame for his history of lies and alcohol abuse than he was himself. Cravings, in particular, were assumed to be outside his control.
- Added to this was a theology that allowed him to think that spiritually he was a pretty good guy. As a result, God owed him.
- Why had he become less involved in his church? Is it possible that his eclectic theology defined him more as an alcoholic than as a Christian, and therefore his real family was the family of recovering alcoholics?
- Shouldn't Jim have realized that growing in godliness is not an overnight process? His theology must be telling him that the Christian life should be easy and change should be quick. The doctrine of progressive sanctification, however, cautions us that spiritual growth is going to emerge gradually, with some bumps and bruises along the way.

What was odd about Jim's thinking was that he knew good biblical theology. He was a seminary graduate who was well educated in the Scriptures. He had studied some of the great church documents, creeds, and confessions of faith, and he agreed with them. In fact, he taught theology in his church. How, then, could he believe correct theology and at the same time not believe it? How could his everyday theology—his actual or practical theology†—be so contrary to what he recited in church on Sunday?

---

ture as a whole, rather than one or two specific passages, reveals about a broad array of topics, addictions being one of them.

†Practical theology is simply theology in action. It is the application of theological teaching to life. It is asking "So what?" of our theological propositions. What difference does it make that I am united with Christ? What

WE DON'T KNOW WHAT TO BELIEVE

One reason Jim operates out of two contrary systems is that he doesn't know what to believe. He *has* no practical theology. Yes, he knows basic theological principles that are true. He knows that we are sinners. He knows that Jesus died on the cross and rose from the dead. But these truths are silent when he struggles with temptations. They do not seem very relevant or practical to him. His theology tells him that there is a heaven, and he is hoping to get there, but it doesn't tell him how to live. He sees no present benefits to the cross of Christ. Without Scripture to guide him in the details of his life, other beliefs will.

We tend to look to Scripture for the life to come, but, since the psychotherapeutic revolution of the 1960s, the Christian community has tended to look to secular psychotherapies for guidelines on how to live successfully *now*. For example, biblically unsupervised principles about self-esteem, individual rights, and the alleged centrality of personal success and significance quietly exert their influence on our thinking, casting shadows on the truth.

In the realm of addictions AA controls the discussion, even within the church. This might sound like good news to many Christians, since AA is certainly founded on moral principles, has years of experience, and seems to be a good steward of practical wisdom. Its material, however, is not Scripture, and AA doesn't claim to be Christian. Although it has roots in what was called the Oxford Movement, and there were some fine Christian participants in that group, Bill Wilson wanted a system that would be available to everyone. To do

---

does it mean that people are idolaters? What difference does it make that I am created in God's image? All theology is practical theology, but some theological statements are still waiting to have many of their applications unpacked.

that he and his colleagues developed principles that could be comfortable anywhere. (However, I don't think that even Bill Wilson could have foreseen that his material would eventually be amenable to atheists.)

The result is that what really guides the thinking of many people who struggle with drugs or alcohol is a syncretistic set of beliefs that combines AA, pop psychology, pieces of Scripture, and miscellaneous features of American culture. These beliefs are not all bad, but they certainly need to be examined. Like every humanly designed program, it should be examined, revised, and improved to bring it closer and closer to the truth of God's Word. But, even more importantly, we need to go back to basic biblical teachings—teachings that are generally accepted by the majority of evangelical churches—and make them practical. When Scripture talks about the slavery of sin, what does that mean for us today? What about idolatry and lust? How are they relevant to addictions? What does it mean to be filled with the Spirit rather than an intoxicating substance (Eph. 5:18)? When we encounter clear biblical teaching, we must say, "So what?" "What does this mean for how I live and how I fight insatiable cravings?" That is how we do practical theology.

Here is the question: Do you have a good grasp on the wealth of biblical material that speaks precisely to the modern problem of addictions? Can you go through any book in Scripture, even if it doesn't mention alcohol, food, or sex, and see how it speaks to addictions? Think about it. If addictions are really as prevalent as they seem, we would think that Scripture would be preoccupied with this struggle. And it is.

WE DON'T BELIEVE WHAT WE BELIEVE

When it comes to addictions, Jim does not have a day-to-day, practical theology. Scripture does not come alive for him when he tries to apply it to his daily battles. Instead, his struggle with alcohol is disconnected from his knowledge of Scripture. He does not persevere in asking, "What does this passage (sermon, hymn) have to do with my desire to drink?" But there is another reason why Jim's theology doesn't always impact the way he lives. Sometimes it is not so much that we are poorly taught or are unaware of what Scripture says, but it is that we don't want to believe the truth we already have. Even when we know the truth, we don't always want it to guide our lives.

Consider, for example, the most fundamental theological statement in Scripture: Jesus is Lord. Jim has sung this, said it, and taught it. Maybe he even ventured an "Amen" on occasion when this truth was preached. But when it came to the things he desired, like alcohol, "Jesus is Lord" was not his practical theology.

When our desires conflict with Scripture, human beings do not always live according to what we say we believe. We can say we believe one thing, but our lives betray other allegiances. A husband can say that he loves his wife, but his actions reveal that he loves his pornographic habits or flirtatious work relationships. A single woman may be an avowed follower of Jesus, but when she feels alone, she pursues sexual relationships to satisfy her sense of emptiness. Her life reveals that, at the core, she is a follower of her desires. Jim may sing "Jesus shall reign," but his drinking indicates that he wants Jesus to reign only when his desires and God's commands do not conflict.

Is there anyone who has not experienced this battle within? It is as though we have partitions in our minds where contradictory beliefs and behaviors live in separate compartments and never meet. It is the Sunday Christian phenomenon. On Sundays a person might be a vigorous worshipper of the true God, but every other day of the week he or she lives a spiritually reckless life, seemingly without pangs of conscience, as though the triune God does not exist. Such partitions often take years to build as we work diligently to keep the truth at bay, but, once erected, they can be very effective.

All this is aptly described in Scripture. In Romans 1, the apostle Paul says that we all know many things about God and his law, but we suppress those truths when they interfere with our wants and desires. As a result, it is as if we practice two different religions. We believe one thing, but *really* believe another. One set of beliefs says that Jesus is the Son of God who has risen from the dead. He is Lord, and he deserves our devotion and obedience. The other says that we prefer a certain degree of independence in our lives. *We* can make the laws we live by, not God. In fact, we can develop a religion that frees us from walking humbly and gratefully before God and instead authorizes us to demand certain rights from God—if, in fact, God is even part of our religious system.

How can you detect these false beliefs? Start by looking at the things you do in private. Do you live very differently in private than you do in public? Do you permit your imagination to indulge itself in ungodly fantasies? If so, even though you know that God sees everything, you are experimenting with an alternative theology that says that there are some places where God can't find you.

Jim's two sets of belief were clearly in conflict. When he slipped into the booth for lunch, he might have been able to give an orthodox statement of his theology, but his behavior and speech indicated that he was a devoted member of Jimism, a religion that justified his anger and judgment of God.

Yet Jim didn't see that all these things were going on just beneath the surface of his conscious awareness. He could still, in good conscience, sign his name to the most orthodox of theological statements. His real beliefs—the ones that were the actual moral rudder of his life—preferred to stay hidden below the surface. There they could deceive him and avoid being confronted by the truth.

Here is one way to ask the question: Are you willing to truly consider what it means, especially in reference to addictions, when you read, "You are not your own; you were bought at a price" (1 Cor. 6:19–20)?

OTHER PEOPLE CAN HELP

The idea of sin being able to deceive us, suppressing truth so that we believe a lie, should send shivers down our spines. It is one thing to deceive other people. That is scary enough. It is even more frightening when we realize that each lie we tell leaves *us* more self-deceived. All practiced sin teaches us to believe lies. We don't often consider the boomerang effect of our deception. In the end it will get us.

The good news, however, if we are willing to receive it, is that God uses other people to help us see. As we have undoubtedly witnessed in others or ourselves, we might be blind to our own hearts, but other people can often see our problems very clearly. Other people can sometimes spot our self-deceptions and *real* beliefs better than we can ourselves. This is true for everyone, but it tends to be especially obvious with drug or alcohol addiction. The addict's enslavement may be painfully clear, but the addict has an alternative system that preaches, "I can stop any time I want"; "I am in control"; "They are wrong, I am right." This is one reason why it is so critical for each one of us to be accountable to others, and to have people in our lives who are willing to say hard things to us. We need people who know us and speak the truth to us in love, like the prophet Nathan did to King David (2 Sam. 12:1–14).

How would this apply to Jim? In his situation, speaking the truth in love to him would *not* mean confronting his alcohol use *per se*. After all, Jim had been sober for a year. Instead it would mean confronting his false religion, which exalted his own comfort and desires. Jim fits the AA description of the dry drunk, who is no longer drinking but hasn't really changed. Jim's actual use of alcohol had changed but all the beliefs that motivated his drinking persisted. True change was going to have to go deeper than sobriety.

GOD HAS TOLD US ALL WE NEED TO KNOW

This is where theology comes in. Practical theology protects us from the deceptions in our hearts and the competing "isms" of the world. It sets the boundaries for our lives. Better yet, accurate theology is a kind of treasure map: it guides us and compels us to relentlessly search Scripture for more and more relevant, penetrating, enlightening, life-changing truth. Scripture, after all, makes bold claims. It says that it provides "everything we need for life and godliness" (2 Peter 1:3).

At first glance, it doesn't seem as though Scripture has all the answers for our out-of-control appetites. As a result, we turn to the sometimes shaky observations of "experts" in the mental health communities. But if 2 Peter 1:3 is true, there are probably many new insights and principles of human life and liberation still available to us in Scripture. Scripture is crammed with truth and meaning. In the same way that people can read Scripture repeatedly and still find something new, so it is likely that an ongoing examination of Scripture *as it is applied to addictions* will yield more and more relevant teaching. Our God is certainly not stingy in revealing himself and his truth.

Don't expect, however, to find this revelation in the form of a theology textbook. Instead, expect it to be in the form of an autobiography. Yes, there will be principles and mottoes, but we shouldn't expect anything that ends up looking like the Twelve Steps. Instead, Scripture points us to Jesus Christ. It is his story. Our liberation comes through a person, not a system of ideas and principles. "Everything we need for life and godliness" ultimately comes "through our knowledge of him [Jesus Christ]" (2 Peter 1:3). The principles that follow reveal the character of Christ. They are enacted in our lives by way of the Spirit of Christ, and the reason we pursue them is for the glory of Christ. Anything else would not be truly Christian.

A WORD ABOUT ADDICTIONS

As we begin, remember that we are moving into a realm in which people can easily talk past each other. Sin, disease, spirituality, God, and many other seemingly common words can have many different definitions, making dialogue especially difficult. This means that definitions and clarity with language are essential. The first word to consider is the word *addiction* itself.

In popular use, *addiction* has become a very elastic and ambiguous category that contains everything from the frivolous (addicted to the six o'clock news) to the grave (addicted to alcohol). It also includes the unequally yoked categories of disease and sin. Given its ambiguities, there is growing sentiment that we need a different word. Yet since there is no agreement on new terms, I will continue to use the term *addiction,* though carefully.

As used in this book, *addiction* will be used to *describe* certain experiences and behaviors. At least initially, I will try to distinguish *descriptions* of behavior from *explanations* for behavior. We can all agree on the actual description of addictions, but we tend to have differences about actual explanations. In common use, the word *addictions* tends to be one in which the description is quietly attached to a biological explanation. As the chapters of this book unfold, a biblical view of addictions will also begin to carry an explanation with it, but it will differ from its secular counterpart.

DESCRIBING ADDICTIONS

What is a description of addictions? How do addicts feel? Addicts feel as if they are trapped and out of control. They feel like abject worshippers, devoted to something that can be very dangerous. They feel desperate hunger and thirst for something. They feel like they can't let go, clinging even when the addictive behavior yields very few pleasures and a great deal of pain. They feel like they are in bondage. Addicts feel out of control, enslaved, stuck, and without hope for freedom or escape. Something or someone other than the living God controls them, and the controlling object tells them how to live, think, and feel.

For example, alcohol tells you to place your own desires above the interests of your family. Pornography and other forms of adultery tell you that the immediate pleasures are worth it, and you probably won't get caught anyway. Gambling tells you that you might hit it big on the next spin of the wheel, even though there is also a chance that you will be broke for the rest of the month. Food says, "One more serving; you can always purge."

Since we live in a culture that encourages self-indulgence, it should be no surprise that addictions are everywhere. Scripture emphasizes sex, food, and alcohol (a category which would include modern mind-altering drugs) as the most common addictions, and these appetites remain the most prevalent. Yet the list of potential taskmasters is always growing. Addiction was once a term used for the chronic heavy drinker, but over the past two decades its turf has expanded dramatically. Now the list of addictive substances and desires is limited only by our own imagination, as we see here.

alcohol	exercise	sex
anger	gambling	caffeine
love	nose drops	shoplifting
weightlifting	cocaine	lying
sleep	work	chocolate
nicotine	sports	risk
pain	sugar	success/winning
TV	people	pornography

What unites these and most other activities or substances described as addictions is that they deliver a bodily experience. With them we feel more alert, more calm, less shy, or more powerful. Furthermore, most addictions change our physical experience and they do it quickly, working within seconds or minutes rather than days or weeks. As a result, people are rarely addicted to vitamins, which take months of steady use to produce measurable changes, but they will be addicted to the rapid-onset bodily feeling associated with Valium, alcohol, sex, or even pain.

Some criticize the widening scope of addictions, claiming that when a category expands too much it loses its meaning. But God's Word anticipates the way the term is being applied to more and more behaviors. The thing that drives addictions can be found in every human heart. For example, we all have had experience with unruly desires that don't take no for an answer. If we are afraid to admit it, we can take our cue from the apostle Paul who said, "I have the desire to do what is good, but I cannot carry it out. For what I do is not the good I want to do" (Rom. 7:18–19). Indeed, "the addiction experience is the human experience."[1]

This broader view of addictions is important because it challenges us to examine what drives addictions instead of focusing on the particular drug of choice. What is it about our humanness that leaves us susceptible to being overtaken by certain desires? Why do alcoholics, drug addicts, compulsive shoppers, and secret indulgers in pornography crave things that are wrong or unwise? Why do we inordinately desire things that, in themselves, might be legitimate (money, approval from others, comfort) but then become too important to us? Why do we have a hard time saying no to our desires? Since the answers to these questions strike at the core of our humanness, the biblical teachings are relevant to us all.

PRACTICAL THEOLOGY

At the end of each chapter, you will have the opportunity to hone your practical theology skills. Ask yourself, *What other biblical teaching could be added to this?* Ask *So what?* of every doctrine: *So, what does this have to do with life?* If Scripture is applied in the chapter, think of twenty other applications. Our goals are to make Scripture come alive and to be changed by the ways the Holy Spirit applies it to our lives.

As You Face Your Own Addiction

1. Scripture always stretches categories so that they include us all. For example, the Sermon on the Mount indicates that we are all murderers. The only difference is that some people use guns while others use their tongues (Matt. 5:21–22). What can own you besides Christ? When do your own appetites for food, sex, or drugs grow to the point where they can control you?

2. What illustrations do you have from your own life where your attempts at deceiving others went hand in hand with self-deception?

3. Consider the place of Scripture in your own thinking. Does it provide oversight for everything? When talking about addictions, Scripture is too often put next to AA rather than over it. Let's do with AA and addictions research what we do with work, leisure, marriage, singleness, and the rest of life: allow them to be interpreted by Scripture.

As You Help Someone Else

1. Having seen our own tendency to be ruled by certain desires, it is easier to be patient with people whose struggles are even more apparent than our own. Do you need to confess your own impatience or lack of love to someone who struggles with addictions?

2. There are already hints that addiction is slavery. Since it takes spiritual power to be released from slavery, do you see how prayer is central when we offer aid to an addict? Are you praying? How?

2 | Sin, Sickness, or Both?

Jesus replied, "I tell you the truth,
everyone who sins is a slave to sin."

JOHN 8:34

As we build the theological framework for understanding addictions, the doctrine of sin is foundational. This doctrine is not necessarily the most important doctrine in Scripture—that distinction would be reserved for the doctrine of Christ. But it is a biblical concept that currently arouses significant differences of opinion. These differences might seem academic at first—technical points that matter only to a theological scholar. But ideas have consequences. Like the first of many dominos, your position on this doctrine will affect everything that follows. It is an unavoidable place to begin to understand addictions.

"Unavoidable" sounds like "unpleasant but necessary," and in some ways that is true. When anyone talks about sin and addictions, and raises any questions about, or suggests refinements of, disease-oriented perspectives, people head for the exits. Some people leave because the very mention of sin is evidence to them that the speaker just doesn't get it. Others leave because they get angry that anyone would add spiritual condemnation to the self-loathing an addict already experiences.

Yet the topic should not be quickly dismissed. *The Twelve Steps and Twelve Traditions* of Alcoholics Anonymous (AA) speaks very frankly about "vengeful resentments, self-pity, and unwarranted pride."[1] The AA literature has never been shy to talk about what Christians call sin.* Furthermore, there have always been religiously oriented writers who have tried to bring sin into the discussion of addictions.[2] They are now being joined by more and more secular authors who suggest that the disease approach is incomplete at best, and that further discussion—or even a paradigm change—is needed. (Keep remembering that, except for Scripture itself, *every* system of thought is in need of further development. Nothing is a finished product.) The idea that "you aren't responsible for the cause, but you are responsible for the cure" doesn't always fit the data, and the near-exclusive reliance on the disease metaphor can stifle discussion. With this in mind, Scripture and its teaching on sin can be called on to sharpen and guide our thinking.

WE SIN—THAT'S JUST THE WAY IT IS

Many of the reactions against the word *sin* are certainly understandable. Even in conservative Christian churches, the subject is often raised apologetically. "OK, in a few minutes I am going to use the *s*-word. Please don't leave. After I get it out of the way, I will try to end by saying something positive." If churches are sometimes embarrassed to discuss sin, how can it ever enter the public discourse on addiction?

The mention of sin tends to immediately polarize. In a culture where self-esteem and high views of self-worth are con-

---

*Still, it is one thing for an alcoholic to say these things to another alcoholic. It is another for a person who has never struggled with heavy drinking to speak accusingly about sin to those who have.

sidered psychological essentials, talking about sin seems to be an attack on mental well being. It conjures up images of dour Puritans and preachers screaming damnation upon those who don't repent. It feels like judgment without mercy, tearing down rather than building up.

Sin, however, is simply a reality. Without doubt, some people are nicer than others, but no one consistently treats others—in word, thought, and deed—as we ourselves want to be treated. In fact, the more ethically careful we are, the more we tend to be aware of our own faults. In other words, the nicer folks are usually the ones who think they are the least nice. They are quick to acknowledge their own faults or sins.

To talk about sin defined as a violation of the Golden Rule is not cruel, condemning, or judgmental. It is simply stating the truth about the way we are. In fact, to ignore something wrong in ourselves would be to practice self-deception, and this, especially when we talk about addictions, is exactly what we want to avoid. Furthermore, one of the great problems in our culture is a failure to admit that we do wrong. Do our wrongs offend our sense of self-worth? Perhaps. But we can't coddle an unrealistic self-concept when the price we pay is self-deception and its destructive consequences.

As a culture, we are leaving behind the days when we avoided moral judgments about our own or other's behavior. When sexual abuse came into the public eye, "You do your thing and I do mine" was no longer an option. It became clear that our decisions could have immense consequences for others, and we had to be held responsible for them. Of course, in any discussion of right and wrong there is a danger that one group will claim exclusive rights to set the moral standard for others. They become self-appointed judges, yet allow no one to evaluate them. Such an attitude is reprehensible and deserves judgment itself, since these judges have set themselves above the law of God instead of submitting themselves to it. If we say that someone is wrong, we must be willing to confess any comparable wrongdoing in our own lives, thereby limiting self-righteous, hypocritical, condemning judgment. Such self-evaluation is by no means easy, but we have no choice. To forsake the hard work of moral examination is to forsake a core element of humanness itself.

These observations are, for the most part, self-evident. Why then is there such a reaction when we talk about sin, especially when it comes to addictions? One reason might be that Scripture insists that sin is even more than a violation of "do unto others as you would have them do to you." Sin is ultimately against God. It is any failure to conform to the law of God in either action or attitude. While some people are simply frightened by this and prefer to avoid it, others feel like it doesn't really apply to them. They have no awareness that what they are doing has anything to do with God. The problem, they believe, is simply within themselves. It is neither against God nor others. It is one thing to acknowledge that we occasionally do wrong; it is something else to acknowledge that what we did was sin—it was against God.

Scripture, however, doesn't stop there. It teaches that we sin much more than we think, and it teaches that sin is our *primary* problem.

SIN IS *DEEPEST* PROBLEM

Even among Christians, sin is not always seen as our deepest or primary problem. For example, if I were to reflect on the problems of my day, they might include my finances, children, wife, health, weight, reputation, lack of lasting contributions, car, leaky faucet, or environment-endangering lawn mower. Even when I am an obvious wrongdoer, I still can think that sin is *not* my primary problem. It is one of those problems that come up occasionally; it is not, I feel, a core feature of my very being.

Yet the fact that I do not *feel* like sin is my primary problem does not prove anything. Sin by its very nature is more often quiet and secretive than loud and public. For every overt episode of rage, there are dozens of jealousies, manipulations, white lies, and malicious thoughts, none of which immediately register on the conscience. And, according to Scripture, the greatest sin of all is even more covert: I do not love the Lord my God with my whole mind and heart. If our failure to consistently worship the true God is the key feature of sin, we are sinners all.

Notice what happens when we lose sight of these biblical teachings. If sin is not our core problem, the gospel itself—the thing of first importance—is marginalized. The good news that Jesus proclaimed and offered is that there is forgiveness of sins, not through our own attempts to please God, but by placing our confidence in Jesus himself, in his death and resurrection. If sin is not our primary problem, then the gospel of Jesus is no longer the most important event in all of human history.

So what is the deepest problem of an addict? The answer, if we are going to be informed by God's Word, is clear and indisputable. The deepest problem is sin.

So far, this is theologically straightforward. What we are saying about an addict's heart is what we say about everyone else's. Yet there is something incomplete in this. For example, the deepest problem of both the murderer and the diabetic is sin, but that doesn't mean that diabetes is sinful. Are addictions themselves sinful?

SIN AND ADDICTION

With such a question, Scripture must be the guide. Among Christians, this rule usually goes without saying. But on the topic of addictions there are thoughtful people who believe that Scripture is true, yet they don't rely on it to shape their view on addictions. Their thinking is that Scripture speaks about the perennial problem of drunkenness but not the modern diagnosis of alcoholism or addiction. Addiction-as-disease data were not available during biblical times; therefore, they believe, Scripture is relatively silent on addiction for much the same reason that it is silent on computer chip technology. In these areas, the popular thinking goes, our primary guidance comes from science. With this in mind, let's first consider some of the basic passages of Scripture that seem relevant to this discussion.

Biblical Teaching

Since the history of drunkenness extends back to the beginnings of recorded history, the writers of Scripture were very familiar with it, probably even more than we are today. The biblical view of drunkenness—the prototype of all addictions—is that it is always called sin, never sickness. Drunkenness is against God and his law. Scripture is unwavering in this teaching and relentless in its illustrations. Noah (Gen. 9:18–27), Lot (Gen. 19:30–38), Elah (1 Kings 16:9), and Nabal (1 Sam. 25:36) all portray the moral foolishness of being mastered by alcohol. Proverbs 23 offers a timeless, frightening description of the heavy drinker (and a warning to him as well).

> Who has woe? Who has sorrow?
>> Who has strife? Who has complaints?
>> Who has needless bruises? Who has bloodshot eyes?
> Those who linger over wine,
>> who go to sample bowls of mixed wine.
> Do not gaze at wine when it is red,
>> when it sparkles in the cup,
>> when it goes down smoothly!
> In the end it bites like a snake
>> and poisons like a viper.
> Your eyes will see strange sights
>> and your mind imagine confusing things.

You will be like one sleeping on the high seas,
    lying on top of the rigging.
"They hit me," you will say, "but I'm not hurt!
    They beat me, but I don't feel it!
When will I wake up
    so I can find another drink?" (Prov. 23:29–35)

It's all there: the captivating appeal, the irrationality, the cravings that seem irresistible, and the fact that bad consequences do not reform the drinker. Indeed, the Old Testament is very familiar with the experience of addiction.

The New Testament continues with the same resoluteness as the Old. According to the New Testament, a pattern of drunkenness is no different than sexual immorality, thievery, greed, or selfish ambition (1 Cor. 5:11; 6:9–10; Gal. 5:19–21). Like these other sins, it is called immoral or an act of the sinful nature. On the one hand, this means that drunkenness is not singled out as a sin that is worse than selfish ambition. On the other, although the New Testament had a clear theology of sickness as contrasted with sin, drunkenness is always placed in the category of sin.

But why is this, especially if we maintain the orthodox view that sin is against God? Isn't drunkenness "only hurting ourselves"? How is it against God?

When you look at it closely, drunkenness is a lordship problem. Who is your master, God or your desires? Do you desire God above all else, or do you desire something in creation more than you desire the Creator? At root, drunkards are worshipping another god—alcohol. Drunkenness violates the command "You shall have no other gods before me." Heavy drinkers love alcohol. They are controlled by it as if they were its subjects and it was their ruler-lover. This alcohol-worship, however, is actually a form of self-worship. We worship people and things to get what we want. Those who worship money do so in order to get what they want. Heavy drinkers drink neither to glorify God nor to love their neighbor. They drink to indulge their own desires, whether those desires are pleasure, freedom from pain, alleviation of fear, forgetting, vengeance, or a host of others.

Drunkenness also interferes with our God-given task of subduing the earth. Drunkenness leads to dereliction of duty in the marketplace. Industrial accidents, lateness, and absenteeism are commonplace for the heavy drinker. Unemployment is too familiar. As Proverbs indicates, the norm for drunkards is poverty (21:17; 23:21).

Relationships are disrupted too. "Wine is a mocker, and beer a brawler" (Prov. 20:1). All heavy drinkers leave a wake of broken relationships and victims. In fact, students of alcohol abuse estimate that each heavy drinker leaves a wake of pain for at least ten people. The pain does not always come by way of fistfights, but through car accidents, harsh words, neglect, broken promises, and unwise decisions. Heavy drinkers inevitably hurt others deeply.

But this accumulation of proof texts is not persuasive to everyone. "You are talking about drunkenness, I am talking about alcoholism. Alcoholism is a disease. The alcoholic has a disease, not a moral flaw, and the only hope is never to take that first drink again."

How does Scripture respond? Your answer will have many practical consequences. Make concessions here and your biblical foundations will start to erode. If you say that Scripture is unaware of this allegedly modern problem, on what other problems will you say that it is silent? Anorexia? The host of psychiatric diagnoses? And how can we be sure that Scripture's teaching on adultery or anger is analogous to the problems we have today? Perhaps these teachings are not relevant to our modern situation either.

Is there a difference between a drunkard and an alcoholic? Scientifically, no. There are no medical tests or brain scans that distinguish them, and their behaviors are identical.

Both terms refer to those who have been repeatedly intoxicated and show a loss of self-control with alcohol. The main difference is that *drunkard* is an old-fashioned word and *alcoholic* is a more recent word that implies its cause is biological. The behaviors, however, are indistinguishable.

"Yes," agrees a disease-oriented spokesperson, "technical precision among the categories of drunkenness, heavy drinking, and alcoholism is difficult, but, as you say, loss of control is the issue. An addict is helpless before alcohol in the same way that a sick person is helpless before an invading disease."

In other words, how can we suggest that something is sin when we didn't choose to do it? Sin is usually thought of as a self-conscious choice, and an addict certainly does not feel as if he or she is making a choice. Instead, the drink makes the choice. Maybe there was a time, years ago, when there seemed to be a choice, but no longer. Now the drug makes the choice. When we sin, however, we intend to sin. We know what we are doing. Our entire legal system is based on this view of moral responsibility. If a legal violation was involuntary and beyond control, then there is no real culpability. In such cases, a person is not guilty by reason of insanity or mental defect and is hospitalized rather than imprisoned. How can people be held responsible when they are not in control?

Choosing My Addiction

The concept of loss of control is the critical issue when deciding whether to look at addiction through the lens of sin or sickness. Here is the majority opinion on it. If we do something wrong and we do it purposefully, self-consciously, and in control, then it is sin. If we do something that might be considered wrong, but we do it without apparent intent or even in spite of our intent, then it is a disease. Therefore, drunkenness, heavy drinking, or alcoholism—*whatever* we call it—is a disease. We might grant that it started as sin but quickly transformed into a disease.

The theological dilemma is this: how do we reconcile the out-of-control nature of addictions and the apparently self-conscious, intentional nature of sin? The two seem incompatible with each other and categorically different. Therefore, we opt for the only model available: addictions are diseases. There seem to be no other choices.

But the disease model doesn't fit as well as we might think. The cravings and desires at the core of the addictive experience are not quite the same as an invading virus. If you catch a virus, you have no choice. You don't want it, and you would be glad to be rid of it. Heavy drinking, however, doesn't just happen to us. Instead, the drinker feels there are payoffs—however temporary—to drunkenness. (There are for any sin.) In other words, addicts make choices to pursue their addiction.

As one experienced drinker observed, "When the desire for drink hits me, I feel like I am being pulled in different directions by two teams of horses."

"Which team wins?" asked a friend.

"Whichever one I say 'giddyap' to."

Even with all the associated misery, people drink because on some level drinking does something for them. Their drinking is purposeful. It may allow a brief opportunity to

- forget,
- punish ("drinking at" people),
- cure self-consciousness and timidity,
- avoid pain,
- fill holes in one's self-image,
- manage emotions,
- fit in with others,
- prove to yourself that you can do what you want (no one can tell you what to do),
- keep loneliness at bay.

This is not to deny either the feeling or the reality of being taken captive by an addictive substance or behavior. It is just to say that, for the addict, slavery with the object of desire is sometimes preferable to freedom without it. At first, this seems to fly in the face of the scientific data. For example, one of the more commonly cited genetic studies examined adoptions in Denmark and suggested that biological children of heavy drinkers had a three to four times greater chance of being heavy drinkers themselves, even if they had been adopted at birth into a nondrinking home.[3] Such data certainly seems to confirm a disease hypothesis, and it is the kind of evidence that Jim (chap. 1) was using when he claimed that God was ultimately the author of his drinking problem.

But such data is subject to interpretation. There are many difficulties in this kind of research, including problems in the definition of an alcoholic, deciding who is a problem drinker and who isn't, and determining the quality of the adoptive homes. Even if we ignore these technical difficulties, the scientific data still cannot support the disease approach. For example, it doesn't account for identical twins (with the same genetic makeup) when one twin is a heavy drinker and the other is not. It doesn't account for the fact that there is no clear biological difference between a heavy drinker and a nondrinker, other than the biological problems that stem from the drinking itself. It doesn't account for the way lower socioeconomic status is associated with both greater abstinence and greater addiction.[4] Clearly, something more than genetics is at work.

Most researchers are quick to point out that the biologically oriented studies suggest that genetics can *influence* people, and with this Scripture has no dispute. People can be physiologically predisposed to enjoying a particular drug, food, activity, or physical experience, but there is a categorical difference between being *influenced* by genetics and being *determined* by it. Possible physiological tendencies do not mean that self-control is impossible or that personal responsibility is diminished. They simply mean that some people must be more vigilant in situations where that sin can be easily provoked.

The reality is that physiological studies that try to establish cause and effect links between brain differences and addictive behavior are either inconclusive or, at best, suggestive that addictions can be influenced by biological factors. Careful researchers will acknowledge this. Why, then, is the disease model so entrenched? It is not the claims of science that persuade people that addictions are best understood as a disease. The disease theory persists because there are no other readily available explanations for why people can feel out of control.

Thousands of heavy drinkers give testimonies of uncontrollable cravings. They can leave home in the morning with the best of intentions, committed to abstinence, when suddenly, a smell or memory triggers a craving that seems overpowering. The next thing they know, they find themselves in the local bar. If Scripture is going to be relevant to struggling addicts, it must offer an explanation for this experience.

Cravings

There can be no argument that people experience cravings. They are real. They feel like itches that must be scratched. But that does not necessarily mean that either the craving or the addictive behavior is fundamentally a genetic predisposition.

First, consider the different types of cravings. They can come at three different times:

(1) while abstaining and sober,
(2) after taking the first drink and then wanting more, and
(3) when physically dependent on the substance.

Cravings while sober. When cravings come as unpredictable urges for alcohol even when a person is "clean and sober" and there is none around, it certainly seems to suggest a biological culprit. After all, there was no conscious intent. How can the person be morally responsible when the craving came automatically? This kind of craving, however, is more commonplace than we might think. If we really like something, our entire person will desire it—we will feel the desire physically. Also, these desires can be dormant sometimes and then stirred up for no apparent reason. Usually, however, there *is* a reason.

For example, if we are very attracted to a particular substance, such as sweets, the desire for food can be triggered by almost anything: boredom, happiness, good conversation, the sight of the kitchen cupboard, loneliness, and so on. The person who has struggled in the past with pornography might abstain without craving for months. Then, when he goes through an airport on a business trip, the desire is overwhelming. Why? Because there is availability without accountability.

With drugs or alcohol, anything that has been associated with the beloved substance—the smell of cigarettes, a marital argument, the sound of a bottle being opened—is enough to provoke more intense desire. In these cases, we have been reminded of once-loved items. Like the scent of an old flame's perfume, these cues can provoke vivid memories, nostalgia, and desire. They are, however, much more than genetic tendencies exerting themselves. They are more like the conditioned responses of Pavlov's dogs. These animals salivated not only when they encountered real food but also when they encountered anything *associated* with food.

These cravings can also be provoked by our own imagination, even when there is no reminder or trigger from the world around us. These come about because clean and sober people might still love the object of their past desire. Although they may have been away from the alcohol, the drug, the pornography, the illicit lover, or the food binges for years, there are still times when they sit back and bask in the memory of the past "relationship." They remember how quickly they could wash away the pressures of the day or get chemical courage. On the heels of such imaginations come desires that don't want to take "no" for an answer. "No," of course, is possible but very difficult. It becomes even more difficult if there is the opportunity to indulge without accountability. This is when cravings seem nearly impossible to contain. For example, the desire for pornography will be more intense when you are alone in a motel room with cable movies than it will be when your family is with you. Desire will be greater in an airport where no one knows you than it will be when your boss is meeting you. A heavy drinker will feel less desire to get drunk when eating lunch with Billy Graham than when meeting friends who love to drink. Such desires feel physical, but they are better explained by our desires than our genetics.

Cravings after the first drink. The second kind of craving is triggered by the addictive behavior itself. With heavy drinking, this has been simplified to the motto, "One drink, one drunk." That is, once you take the first drink, your craving for the second will be irresistible. This motto has been canonized as gospel in many quarters but it is not as simple as it seems. For example, every person who struggles with heavy drinking will be able to remember times when he or she had just one drink. Even though it is wise advice to avoid the first drink, it is just plain wrong to say that the first drink will inevitably and irresistibly lead to the second. In fact, some have suggested that this motto has backfired, in that problem drinkers assume they will *have* to continue to drink if they drink just one. The reality is that in order to drink to intoxication, there must be time, resources, and a context where drinkers feel they have permission to continue. Drunkenness is *not* inevitable after one drink, nor is the craving for more *always* present after one drink.

Cravings when physically dependent. The third kind of craving accompanies heavy, daily drug or alcohol use, and is a result of physical dependence on the addictive substance. If the body becomes accustomed to the drug, it will gradually come to believe that the drug is a normal requirement for optimal functioning. Then, when blood levels of the substance fall too low, the body asks for more. If deprived, the body registers its complaints through nausea, temporary sickness, and, in some cases, fairly intense withdrawal symptoms. Without doubt, withdrawal can be difficult. Although it is not a chronic disease, withdrawal is a real physical problem that can be painful and, at times, dangerous. It is one of the ways sin brings greater and greater tragedy as it is practiced.

In these situations, the physical problem is primary. To focus on the underlying spiritual problems would be like reading Scripture to someone who has just cut her wrists. God's Word certainly brings hope to the hopeless, but when someone is bleeding, you bandage her wounds and seek medical attention. With actual physical addictions, spiritual ministry begins after the person has medically stabilized or weathered the physical storms of detoxification.

Biblical approaches to addictions do not deny that the physical body is part of the addictive process. We are, after all, embodied souls. Everything we do is physical. Where Scripture brings more precision into this discussion is in its teaching that the physical body can't make us sin. It can make our lives miserable, it can leave us vulnerable to certain temptations, and sometimes it should be the focus of our attention, but it can't irresistibly force us to violate God's commands.

Why all the fuss about the disease model? Perhaps it seems that I am splitting hairs and overreacting to the mislabeling of heavy drinking and other forms of enslavement. But these labels have a profound effect on our corporate opinion. Theology really does make a difference. Words such as alcoholism, treatment, symptoms, disease, therapy, and even addiction itself, eventually communicate that the ultimate cause is in our body rather than in our heart. There is a dramatic difference between seeing drunkenness as a victimizing physical weakness versus an expression of a self-focused heart.

- A physical weakness is not changed, only tolerated and controlled. A self-centered, idolatrous heart can be transformed by sanctifying grace through the Holy Spirit and can receive spiritual resources to fight a winning battle.
- A physical weakness does not motivate us to engage in spiritual battle. Knowing that we have a self-centered heart should *compel* us to examine ourselves and repent.
- A physical weakness limits Jesus Christ's role to that of helper. The person convicted of a self-centered heart cries out to Christ the Lord, Redeemer, Shepherd, Conqueror, and King.

Voluntary Slavery

Yet there is still more to the addictive experience that must be biblically examined. Heavy drinking still *feels* like a disease! It feels like some gene or virus has taken over and you are no longer in control. To say "stop it" seems powerless and irrelevant. "Just say 'no'" may seem effective to the person who was never captured by addictions, but it is a joke to those who have fallen victim to it. Indeed, the disease model forces us back to the theological drawing board. Where does Scripture discuss experiences so difficult that they feel like diseases, though the real problem is even deeper? Where does Scripture speak of being controlled and dominated by something?

If we think of sin only as overt, calculated disobedience, we will not find what we are looking for in Scripture. But sin is more than self-conscious rebellion against God. It is also a blinding power that wants to control and enslave us. Sadly, over the last fifty years the church has neglected this aspect of sin. As a result, the church has been unprepared to address experiences that seem to happen without conscious intent. It has been unable to respond to Freudian models of the unconscious or disease models of addictions.

But it has not always been this way. In 1524 Martin Luther wrote *The Bondage of the Will,* a book that created a stir in its day and still has its detractors. Nevertheless, it is an insightful guide to the topic of addiction. In it, Luther emphasized that our will is powerless apart from the power and grace of God poured out on us.

Sin is more than conscious choices. Like a cruel taskmaster, sin victimizes and controls us (John 8:34). It captures and overtakes (Gal. 6:1). In fact, there are times when we intend to do one thing but sin causes us to do things we don't want to do. Even though we may really want to change, it can seem like an overwhelming or impossible task to actually do so. As the apostle Paul said, "I do not understand what I do. For what I want to do I do not do, but what I hate I do. . . . As it is, it is no longer I myself who do it, but it is sin living in me" (Rom. 7:15, 17). In other words, *sin feels exactly like a disease.* It feels as if something outside ourselves has taken over. In fact, one of Scripture's images for sin *is* disease (e.g., Isa. 1:5–6).

Yet this is where it is important to be a theologian who sees all of Scripture, not just isolated texts. The slavery of sin, which everyone has experienced in some way, is similar to slavery and diseases in many respects, yet there are also some critical differences. As with all images or metaphors, there are limitations on how far to extend it. For example, if someone "runs like the wind," there are ways that the person is both like the wind and unlike it. Similarly, there are ways sin is like a disease and ways it isn't.

The main difference is that the slavery of sin is one for which we are responsible, and we can be empowered by God's grace to turn from it. As Luther says,

Man . . . does not do evil against his will, under pressure, as though he were taken by the scruff of the neck and dragged into it, like a thief . . . being dragged off against his will to punishment; but he does it spontaneously and voluntarily. And this willingness or volition is something which he cannot in his own strength eliminate, restrain or alter. . . .[5]

Our slavery or disease may include actual physical dysfunction, but it goes much deeper than that. It is an infection of the human heart. Although voluntary, we are inclined to it. We want it. Our will is bent toward it. Indeed, we are powerless. Where we are powerless is in changing our inclination and desires. We cannot do it apart from God.

This enlarged perspective indicates that in sin, we are both hopelessly out of control and shrewdly calculating; victimized yet responsible. All sin is simultaneously pitiable slavery and overt rebelliousness or selfishness. This is a paradox to be sure, but one that is the very essence of all sinful habits. If you deny the out-of-control nature of all addictions, as some Christians have done, then you assume that everyone would have

FIGURE 2.1.
THE DUAL NATURE OF SIN

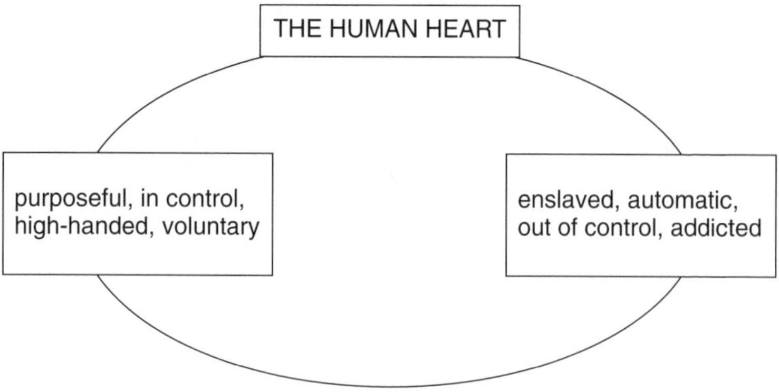

THE HUMAN HEART

purposeful, in control, high-handed, voluntary

enslaved, automatic, out of control, addicted

the power to change himself. Change would be easy. You would simply say, "Stop it. You got yourself into it, and you can get yourself out." There would never be a sense of helplessness or a desperate need for both redemption and power through Jesus. So this cannot be our position.

At the same time, there will be other problems if you ignore the in-control, purposeful nature of addictions. Victims will be quick to place blame outside themselves. They are left with no way to understand their guilt. The redemptive work of Christ is replaced by an emphasis on "healing" that is not rooted in the grace of forgiveness. If personal responsibility is ignored, addicts are ultimately helpless before their alleged disease. All they see in the future is the fear of passing it on to their children. Scripture counters these fears with "and that is what some of you *were*" (1 Cor. 6:11). Where there is sin, God always offers forgiveness and the power to cast it off.

With this biblical reframing of addictions, perhaps we should suggest a more precise definition. *Addiction is bondage to the rule of a substance, activity, or state of mind, which then becomes the center of life, defending itself from the truth so that even bad consequences don't bring repentance, and leading to further estrangement from God.* To locate it on the theological map, look under *sin*. More specifically, since sin is a broad category that includes both self-conscious disobedience and victimizing slavery, find addiction on the side that emphasizes slavery.

Now add an intersecting but less fundamental category. For a more complete picture of addictions, add a category that accounts for the many influences that make each person's addiction unique. This category includes all the contributing circumstances in our lives: ways we were sinned against by others, our economic backgrounds, parental examples, sibling examples, genetic tendencies, and a host of other possible influences. These could be summarized as nature *and* nurture. In secular thought, these influences are separated more than joined, but from a biblical perspective, they exert the same kind of pressure on us. They both function as temptations that induce our hearts to say "Yes" to reckless desires.

This is the beginning of a biblical model that truly understands the experience of addictions. Heavy drinkers and other addicts genuinely feel out of control, but they are also making choices rooted in their own self-centeredness and pride. Since this is an apparent paradox, we tend to emphasize one or the other. Theology, however, keeps us balanced. Sometimes we will stress the in-control nature of our hearts; at other times we will emphasize the powerlessness and slavery of addictive behaviors. Yet good, practical theology keeps this larger spectrum of sin in mind. It also recognizes that sin is not the only biblical doctrine relevant to addictions.

FIGURE 2.2.
**ADDICTIONS AT THE INTERSECTION OF OUR SIN AND THE
INNUMERABLE INFLUENCES ON OUR LIVES**

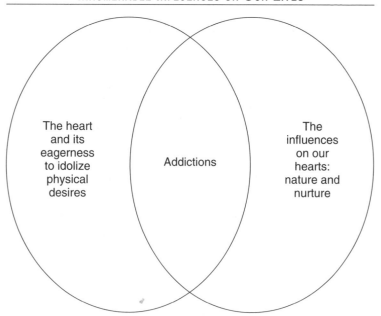

The heart and its eagerness to idolize physical desires

Addictions

The influences on our hearts: nature and nurture

Does Sin Turn into a Disease?

As Christians wrestle with Scripture and try to blend it with the AA perspective, a hybrid is emerging: addictions begin as sinful choices and end up as diseases. This seems to combine the best of both worlds, both the worldview of Scripture and the years of experience behind the disease approach. Is this a biblically legitimate way of capturing the difficulties of addictions?

The sin-morphing-into-disease approach seems to make sense. It is obvious that what happened during a person's first drunken binge is very different from what happened during his 542nd binge, which came after five rehabs and three alcohol-related divorces. Every reasonable parent is concerned when a teenage child is driven home from a party intoxicated, but we feel even more concern about the father who will get drunk again, and lose his job and a few more friends before the week is out. In other words, we intuitively act as if the beginning stages of addiction are categorically different from the later stages.

Scripture is quite capable of explaining this progression, and it uses several metaphors and principles to do so. These teachings will be examined at greater length in the next chapter, but for now the answer is fairly simple: sin is the fundamental problem, from start to finish. However, there are differences between the early and later stages of certain sins. For one, life becomes much more complicated.

- Lies and broken promises take their toll on relationships.
- The addictive substance feels more like a family member and friend, and it is hard to imagine life without it.
- The addictive behavior serves more and more purposes as it is practiced. At first, a purpose for drinking was to be accepted by one's peers. Later, alcohol was also used for comfort, release from pain, punishing a

parent or spouse, punishing oneself, and dozens of other reasons. The more purposes that are attached to the addictive behavior, the more the addiction will seem identical to life itself.

- The body gradually feels sick, is malnourished, and craves more.
- Hopelessness and guilt feel like they can only be banished by the next indulgence.
- We begin to believe our lies. What started as lying to others has turned against us. We tried to keep other people from seeing our private addictions; now we can barely see them ourselves. We once tried to persuade others that we didn't have a problem; now we have persuaded ourselves that we don't have a problem. When we are blind to our own problem, there is no reason to change.

A more precise way to think about the progression of addiction is that it begins as the sin of the naïve and develops into the sin of one who is hardened and trapped. It starts as a sin with few consequences and develops into a sin with painful consequences. At first, the consequences might be a lingering headache or a little less spending money. With prac-

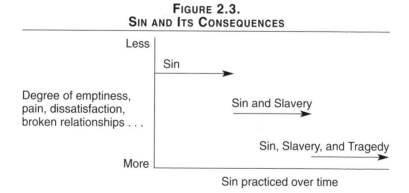

FIGURE 2.3.
SIN AND ITS CONSEQUENCES

tice, everything is spoiled: the body is sick, the soul is numb, and relationships are broken. Practiced, repeated sin results in slavery, a multitude of painful consequences, and God abandoning people to their own desires so they are left always wanting one more. Such a profile can only be described as a great tragedy.

BACK TO THE DARK AGES?

Throughout any discussion on sin, especially when we are relating it to addictions, there is often a vague sense that we ought to be apologizing. It feels as though we are causing the field to regress rather than progress. This comes from the echoes of those who once said that "every soul is worth saving; but . . . if a choice is to be made, drunkards are about the last class to be taken hold of."[6] The doctrine of sin has been used to bludgeon addicts. And then there is the very practical concern that any mention of sin will keep addicts from seeking help.

Sadly, these concerns have substance. The problem, however, is not with the doctrine of sin. Sin is a reality. The problem is that the human heart naturally says, "I am OK and you are not." It justifies and accuses. It judges itself as OK and judges others (in this case, those who struggle with alcohol and drugs) as inferior. The caste systems of India express this tendency on a grand scale, as does the racism within the United States.

The answer is not to avoid the truths of Scripture for fear that they will be misused. Systems and programs that bypass Scripture will eventually have significant problems of their own: bad theology always yields bad fruit. The answer is to allow the doctrine of sin to become an ordinary feature of our view of self and our public discourse. As Scott Peck underscored in *People of the Lie*,[7] we get into trouble when we think too highly of ourselves, or when we deceive ourselves into thinking that we have a bit more moral fiber than our neighbor. The overarching precept of the Christian religion should be humility.

This humility protects us from being harsh and judgmental. So does the admission that none of us have ever climbed out of the mire of sin with our own moral bootstraps. Another help is to remember that the diagnosis of sin is never the last word. Instead, the last word is Jesus Christ. Sin should take us right to Jesus. The way out of addictions is to talk more about Jesus, the Redeemer and Liberator, than about sin.

Are you concerned that the addict will get stuck in guilt if we talk about sin? The addict is stuck in guilt and shame already! The friend's job is to point fellow addicts to the One who forgives, liberates, loves, and empowers. As someone released from his own slavery to sin, a good friend shows an addict where to find life and hope. The biblical arithmetic is this: for every one look at your sin, take ten looks at Christ.

Doctrine must not only be practical, it must also naturally point us to Jesus Christ.

PRACTICAL THEOLOGY

Does using sin as the way to understand addictions still sound judgmental or mean-spirited? If so, blame my poor writing, not Scripture. One way that God loves his people is by sending his Spirit to "convict the world of guilt in regard to sin" (John 16:8). This is not condemnation; it is God's way of rescuing us. Sin is a path that leads to tragedy and despair. If someone saw you on such a path and did nothing, *that* would be unloving. But the Spirit of God awakens our hearts to the presence of sin in our lives, and then convinces us that he forgives sin because of Jesus Christ, and gives us peace. It is when we experience *no* conviction of sin that we should be most alarmed.

As You Face Your Own Addiction

1. If you are distracted by this discussion of disease or sin, and you feel like physical susceptibilities are getting short-changed, please understand that the goal of this chapter is not to minimize the effect of the body on addictions. Rather, it is to emphasize the role of the heart—the core of our being where our tendency toward sin is especially apparent.

Consider the illustration of Jesus healing a paralyzed man (Matt. 9:1–8). When this man was brought to Jesus to be healed, Jesus said, "Take heart, son; your sins are forgiven." Jesus was not ignoring the man's physical symptoms. Instead, he was highlighting the even deeper problem and deeper solution.

2. Is it still difficult to see the spiritual core of addictions? Here are some simple questions that might expose it: While you struggled with addiction, was it ever accompanied by the fear of the Lord? Did you ever have a keen sense of the presence and holiness of God when you struggled with addictions? Did you ever have a sense that you were spiritually growing in repentance, faith, and obedience while in your addiction?

When we have a disease, we can still be growing in the knowledge of Christ, but addictions are incompatible with spiritual growth.

3. Has your addictions program encouraged confession of sin to the Lord? If not, consider ending your day with confession of sin. Just be sure to remember that we live before the God who is quick to forgive us because of the cross of Christ (1 John 1:9). If you are in a program that encourages confession, allow God's Word to deepen and refine it. For example, talk about sin before God rather than wrongdoing. Consider the wanderings of your imaginations and not just your overt behavior.

4. Do you feel hopeless at times? Joyless? If you think that the knowledge of your sinfulness will intensify these problems, consider the example of the biblical writers. Facing their

sinfulness was hard and sometimes painful, but when confession of sin was linked to the knowledge of forgiveness of sins, hope and joy were the result.

For example, in Psalm 130, the psalmist is in the deepest depths of misery. His despair was such that he could feel death even more than life. To bring him out of the pit, the Lord brought to mind his great forgiveness (v. 3).

> If you, O LORD, kept a record of sins,
>   O Lord, who could stand?
> But with you there is forgiveness;
>   therefore you are feared.

The apostle Paul also has forgiveness of sins as the permanent foundation for his joy and hope.

> In him [Jesus] we have redemption through his blood, the forgiveness of sins, in accordance with the riches of God's grace that he lavished on us with all wisdom and understanding. (Eph. 1:7)

As you consider confession and forgiveness, be careful not to compartmentalize. You are not simply bringing health to another sector of your being, you are dealing with the essence of your very soul. Confession and forgiveness are not aids to dealing with addictions, like exercise or eating well. They are the very heart of the cure.

As You Help Someone Else

1. Notice how a pattern is emerging: addictions are part of ordinary human experience. The problems themselves are very serious, but they are common to everyone. Do you see how you are like the addict you care about? Take some time to consider your similarities rather than your differences.

2. Have you ever approached the addict in a way that was

hypocritical, judgmental, sinfully angry, or impatient? If you love someone who struggles with addictions, there is no question that you have sinned against them recently. Pursue them and ask their forgiveness.

New Ways of Seeing

The unfolding of your words gives light.

PSALM 119:130

Addictions research needs something new. Its vision has been controlled by one particular lens, and even though this lens highlights certain features of the addictive experience, it obscures as much as it reveals when it is the only way of seeing. To reduce all discussion of addictions to one image is to sacrifice helpful perspectives that bring meaning and understanding. In Scripture, multiple "models" are used to help us learn about Jesus. For example, he is king, subject, master, servant, shepherd, sheep, brother, healer, redeemer, priest, prophet, vine, light, the way, and truth. If we focus exclusively on one metaphor we will miss the breadth and depth of his identity and mission. No wonder Scripture presents four books about Jesus, each with a slightly different perspective.

In the case of addictions, the disease metaphor has been *the* controlling metaphor, and it has jealously guarded its turf. No other perspective has been invited to broaden our understanding, let alone offer a major conceptual overhaul. Of course, the disease metaphor has usefulness; otherwise it would not have controlled our thinking for so long. It highlights the way we can feel controlled by something other than our own will. What it doesn't highlight are two essential theological teachings. First, the bondage we experience is rooted in Adam. When he fell into sin, we all fell (Rom. 5:12–17). More obvious bondage becomes apparent as we practice sin, but our bondage is more than the consequences of what we do. It is who we are. It is our nature. Second, the bondage we experience is intentional. It is a *voluntary* slavery. As sinners, our preference is to give ourselves over to our desires. We choose slavery.

The exclusive reliance on one metaphor is not the only encumbrance within addiction discussions. Even more troublesome is the fact that the metaphor of addictions is gradually losing its metaphorical quality. Instead of saying that addictions are *like* a disease, in that they have many things in common with more traditional diseases, more people are simply saying that addictions *are* diseases.

The word *disease* can be used literally or metaphorically. In its literal or more technical sense, it is a diagnosable condition with a primary, physical cause. For example, diabetes is a disease caused by a deficiency of useable insulin. Doctors diagnose it by running blood tests and checking for the presence of certain physical symptoms. At present, it can be treated but not cured. As with most diseases, the patient's behavior has a significant effect on the progress of the disease: cardiac patients exercise, asthmatics use ventilators, diabetics watch their diet. But if there is a cure, it is external to the patient. The diabetic cannot heal himself.

If we describe disease this way, addictions do not fit the definition. With addictions, the "cure" *must* come from within. The addict *must* make choices to reject, defeat, and forsake his addiction, a course of action that would be insufficient to cure someone of breast cancer, epilepsy, or diabetes. Having said this, I would affirm that, at the deepest level, we all must rely on God—something outside of ourselves—for all things. But relying on God or other people does not mean that we have a physical disease. AA itself states that "alcoholism is largely a spiritual disease requiring a spiritual healing."[1] Although addicts can show some physical differences when compared to those who have not struggled with addictions, there is no reason to believe that these biological differences do anything more than either *result from* heavy use of a substance, or *influence* addictions. As an influence, these differences are similar to the effects of parenting, friends, or socioeconomic status. They can pull or incline us in certain negative directions toward chemical dependency, but they can be resisted. They are not one's unavoidable destiny, as many addicts in recovery can attest. As such, the word disease, in its most technical sense, is *not* a precise way to describe addictions.

Given that the disease metaphor is hardening into a reality, and the metaphorical use of *disease* has limitations, one task for a theology of addictions is to consider other available metaphors in Scripture. We need more of Scripture's light.

IDOLATRY

One of the most common portrayals of the human condition, and one which captures both the in-control and out-of-control experiences of addictions, is the theme of idolatry. From this perspective, the true nature of all addictions is that we have chosen to go outside the boundaries of the kingdom of God and look for blessing in the land of idols. In turning to idols, we are saying that we desire something in creation more than we desire the Creator.

This sounds like strange language to Western ears, but idolatry is perhaps the most dominant image in Scripture. It abounds in potential applications. Did you ever notice how many biblical stories can be summarized with these questions? "Whom will you worship? The Creator or the created thing, God or man, the Divine King or worthless idols?" The basic story line of the Old Testament is about people who find idolatry irresistible. Then God, ultimately through Jesus, comes to rescue his people out of their enslaving practices. Accordingly, all sin is summarized as idolatry (e.g., Deut. 4:23; Eph. 5:5).

Even the Ten Commandments, a body of teaching that almost everyone would say offers wise guidance for today, give special prominence to prohibitions against idolatry. They are the first two commandments, and they receive substantial elaboration.

> You shall have no other gods before me.
>
> You shall not make for yourself an idol in the form of anything in heaven above or on the earth beneath or in the waters below. You shall not bow down to them or worship them; for I, the LORD your God, am a jealous God, punishing the children for the sin of the fathers to the third and fourth generation of those who hate me, but showing love to a thousand generations of those who love me and keep my commandments. (Deut. 5:7–10)

Do we have idols in our society? Have you ever walked into a home and noticed the household gods or a personal talisman? Probably not. In Western culture we rarely make visible gods. To detect our idols, we must begin by realizing that Old Testament idols were concrete, physical expressions of new loyalties and commitments that had been established in the human heart. The prohibition against idolatry is ultimately about "idols of the heart" (see Ezek. 14:3).

With this in mind, notice the paternal warning at the end of 1 John: "Dear children, keep yourselves from idols" (5:21). Like a parent offering his final words of wisdom before his children depart, John clearly was concerned about idolatry. Yet his letter does not even mention observable, physical idols. Instead, in keeping with the theme of idols of the heart, it speaks of "the cravings of sinful man, the lust of his eyes, and the boasting of what he has and does" (2:16). John is concerned about the pernicious, unseen Baals that are constructed more by the heart than the hands.

In other words, Scripture permits us to broaden the definition of idolatry so that it includes anything on which we set our affections and indulge as an excessive and sinful attachment. Therefore, the idols that we can see—such as a bottle— are certainly not the whole problem. Idolatry includes anything we worship: the lust for pleasure, respect, love, power, control, or freedom from pain. Furthermore, the problem is not outside of us, located in a liquor store or on the Internet; the problem is within us. Alcohol and drugs are essentially satisfiers of deeper idols. The problem is not the idolatrous substance; it is the false worship of the heart.

The heart's instinctive plotting in this idol construction is amazing. We know that we are called to imitate God. This means that we are to live for God's glory, not our own. We are to make him famous, not ourselves. A noble calling, to be sure, but we choose to forsake it or "exchange" our calling and give glory to idols instead (Rom. 1). This is a surprising move but it is quite purposeful on our parts. You see, being created in God's image is somewhat humbling to our sinful nature. It means that we are not the ultimate original. We do not get glory for ourselves, and we are totally dependent on the One whom we imitate. To avoid this, we renounce our imitating status and turn to objects of worship that we hope will give us what we want.

The desired payoff? The purpose of all idolatry is to manipulate the idol *for our own benefit*. This means that we don't want to be ruled by idols. Instead, we want to *use* them. For example, when Elijah confronted the Baal worshippers on Mount Carmel (1 Kings 18), the prophets of Baal slashed themselves and did everything they could to manipulate Baal to do their will. Idolaters want nothing above themselves, including their idols. Their fabricated gods are intended to be mere puppet kings, means to an end.

So it is with modern idolatry as well. We don't want to be ruled by alcohol, drugs, sex, gambling, food, or anything. No, we want these substances or activities to give us what *we* want: good feelings, a better self-image, a sense of power, or whatever our heart is craving.

Idols, however, do not cooperate. Rather than mastering our idols, we become enslaved by them and begin to look like them. As idols are deaf, dumb, blind, utterly senseless, and irrational, so "those who make them will be like them, and so will all who trust in them" (Ps. 115:8). Idolaters lose their spiritual moorings; they are lost at sea. Idolaters are controlled by the lure of the sirens: "This is the way to feeling good, pleasure, belonging, and a better self-image." But they are doomed to crash on the rocks.

How can these lifeless idols exert such power? They dominate because of a powerful but quiet presence that hides behind every idol, Satan himself. As obedience to God demonstrates our allegiance to him, so when we set our affections on created objects, we demonstrate our affinity for Satan. Therefore, God's Word reminds us, "For our struggle is not against flesh and blood [or alcohol and drugs], but against the rulers, against the authorities, against the powers of this dark world and against spiritual forces of evil in the heavenly realms" (Eph. 6:12).

So far, this discussion applies to every human being. We set our affections on ourselves and choose idols that will (we hope) satisfy us, and we avoid the worship of the true God. But what about the different types of addictions? Can't we make some distinctions between a person addicted to alcohol and one addicted to work? Should we stress the unity in all addictive behavior at the expense of the obvious differences? After all, not everyone has a covert lifestyle for which they will seemingly sacrifice everything. What is the difference between idols that are satisfied by a big paycheck, respect of colleagues, or the adoring love of a spouse, and idols that are satisfied by mind-altering or physical sensations?

The answer is an important one: some idols hook our bodily passions and desires. This group of addictions includes drugs (legal and illegal), alcohol, sexual sin, and food. These idolatries can provide physical pleasure, relieve physical tension, and soothe physical desires (Fig. 3.1). Such payoffs can be difficult to resist.

Satan enters this drama because he has a special interest in exploiting the body's natural needs and desires. If something feels physically good, you can bet he will try to take advantage of it. As usual, his purpose is in direct opposition to God's. God has created us with physical needs and desires which, when kept within appropriate limits by a heart of faith, can lead to pleasure. Satan wants to overturn God's order and have physical desires rule the person. Instead of food, sex, or rest being treated as God-given pleasures, they are exalted to become ruling lusts that enslave. Pleasure then becomes fleeting or elusive. At best, it lasts only as long as the high.

When physical sensations become entrenched as a habitual satisfier in someone's life, another cycle is superimposed (Fig. 3.2). The heart becomes more than an idol factory. Along with its incessant idol production and demands for satisfaction, it also becomes a slave to the physical desires of the body.

In light of how easily our physical desires can get caught in the crossfire within our souls, it is not surprising that the apostle Paul implores us to be vigilant. "I do not fight like a man beating the air. No, I beat my body and make it my slave"

FIGURE 3.1.
THE EARLY CYCLE OF ADDICTIONS: REBELLION

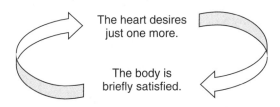

The heart desires just one more.

The body is briefly satisfied.

FIGURE 3.2.
LATER STAGES OF ADDICTIONS: BONDAGE

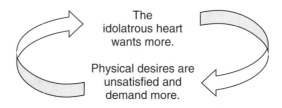

The
idolatrous heart
wants more.

Physical desires are
unsatisfied and
demand more.

(1 Cor. 9:26–27). In this, the apostle Paul reiterates that nothing short of a declaration of war will dislodge our favorite idols.

Now, make this more personal. Think of some of your idols that are expressed as bodily desires. Sex, drugs, and food are the most obvious. Consider one that seems less important, such as a craving for sweets. You know you don't need them, and you may be full from a meal, but if they are available you might experience a strong craving for them. Then you rationalize or make deals with yourself: "I will have ice cream now and skip dessert tonight," or "What difference will a handful of M & M's make? Am I under the law?" The strategy is the same as that of a substance abuser. Interestingly, as in the case of most drug or alcohol abusers, if these sweets are definitely not available, the cravings are minimal.* Have you ever tried to diet? It is one of the most difficult spiritual disciplines. How many times have you started a diet, only to give up a few days later? Feeling guilty, you try it again, then again. Such is the experience of substance abuse.

Have you ever found yourself flirting with sexual temptation through a long gaze or sexual fantasies? Have you ever found yourself captured by the allure of pornography? Have you ever

---

*The exception is when there is clearly a physical addiction to a particular drug. In these cases, the absence of the drug will make physical cravings *more* intense until the person is no longer physically addicted.

been involved in sexual immorality even though you were aware of God's call to be holy (1 Thess. 4:3)? These are additional examples of the way pleasurable physical experiences are a favorite focus of our idolatrous hearts. Instead of running from temporary physical pleasures that are ungodly, or simply enjoying (but not being dominated by) physical pleasures that are gifts from God, we quickly get tunnel vision and see nothing but "one more." Self-control over bodily desires is an exercise in faith that lasts a lifetime. "Relapses" are not uncommon.

Can you see how the biblical theme of idolatry fits hand-in-glove with modern addiction? Drugs and sex are the modern golden calves erected by addicts to find meaning, power, or pleasure apart from God. Addicts often believe they have found life, but any payoff they experience is short-lived and deceptive. They are blinded to the fact that they are having a banquet in a grave. They are truly out of control, victims of their own lust.

> For the addict dope is God. It is the supreme being, the Higher Power, in the junkie's life. He is subjugated to its will. He follows its commandments. The drug is the definition of happiness, and gives the meaning of love. Each shot of junk in his veins is a shot of divine love, and it makes the addict feel resplendent with the grace of God.[2]

Tyler started smoking marijuana when he was thirteen. Peer pressure was the stated reason. Little did he know that he had already bowed low to another idol. Although he knew God, he worshiped the gods "opinions of others" and "peers must think I'm cool." Drugs seemed to satisfy these ruling desires. Even though he didn't get high the first time he smoked (he didn't even like it), he felt accepted. He was proud that others knew he smoked, so he continued. Of course, his goal was not to worship marijuana; it was to use it for his own purposes.

Gradually, the drug began to represent the idolatry that was in his heart. His marijuana became an object of worship. He would think about it, plan how to get it, and even avoid friends in order to perform his cultic rituals. By the time he was fifteen, Tyler was in a drug rehabilitation clinic, enslaved and out of control. His idol had betrayed him.

Tyler was deceived by a rival kingdom (Table 3.1). These are the spiritual realities behind addictions. They may seem overly dramatic at first, but that is only because we don't see them very clearly with the naked eye. They only come into view as our vision is aided by Scripture and enlightened by the Holy Spirit.

Here is the truth. Using the perspective of idolatry, addicts are blinded by their own desire. They refuse to see themselves as dependent on God. God's glory and fame is not their goal. In their self-addiction or selfishness, they worship and bow down before false gods. Addicts have defected from the living God. Instead of worshipping in the temple of the Lord, they perform addictive rituals that give them more perceived power, pleasure, or identity. They see in their addiction a form of magic (Deut. 18:10–14). The promises of the idol, however, are lies. Any identity, power, or peace they bring is false and temporary. There are only two choices: putting your faith in

TABLE 3.1.
THE TWO KINGDOMS.

The triune God	Satan and idols
Light	Darkness
Truth	Lies
Worship, trust, obey, and love God	Worship, trust, obey, and love our desires
Freedom	Slavery
Life	Death
True pleasure and joy	Transient pleasure, but ultimate pain

a loving God and thus knowing freedom, or putting your faith in idols (Satan) and being enslaved. Curiously, our selfish pride prefers slavery.

Jim, I wonder if you have ever noticed that, for you, alcohol is very much like the idols of the Bible. These idols start out as helpers. The people thought that God could not be fully trusted to give them what they wanted, so they looked for blessing from other gods. In the Old Testament these false gods promised rain or fertility. Today, we are less concerned with rain and fertility, but we are very concerned about being pain-free, or about our identity and self-worth. I wonder if alcohol was a way to fill the holes in your identity. I wonder if it became a way to find "blessings" such as power or pleasure apart from God, or alongside of God.

But here is the real killer about idolatry: Idols end up having control over us. It seems that there is no getting away from the basic questions of life: Whom will you worship? Who will be king? Who will have dominion?

Are addicts self-consciously making these idolatrous decisions? In most cases, no. Remember, we are looking at what is behind the scenes. Sin by its very nature is covert. As people who want to help addicts, we need something very powerful to break the hold of idols. Pleas, tears, arguments, or threats will not penetrate. Reason is useless. We cannot simply say, "Stop doing drugs, get control of yourself, stop worshipping an idol." As a result of spiritual oppression, drug worshippers may be very intelligent, but they can be oblivious to the destruction and slavery associated with drug abuse. They need the power of God (1 Cor. 1:18), the message of Christ crucified and risen. Other therapies can offer sobriety, but only this good news is powerful enough to liberate the soul.

ADULTERY

Idolatry is an especially prominent theme in Scripture that sheds new light on the problem of addictions. Yet there are others as well. One of its natural partners, especially since idolatry is ultimately a personal relationship, is sexual lust and adultery. Adultery emphasizes the more intimate features of idolatry. The sense of being controlled and being dominated by another, the lies, and the obsession are all there. The idolatrous object, however, is a person (or functions like one).

Go to an AA meeting and listen to the language. Chances are you might think that people were having affairs. They are talking about something they loved. They once thought of nothing but that object. They felt complete when they were with it.

[My wife] said to me that I was going to have to make a choice—either cocaine or her. Before she finished the sentence, I knew what was coming, so I told her to think carefully about what she was going to say. It was clear to me that there wasn't a choice. I love my wife, but I'm not going to choose anything over cocaine. It's sick, but that's what things have come to. Nothing and nobody comes before my coke.[3]

The picture is reminiscent of the foolish young man who is being beckoned to the house of the adulteress (Prov. 7). This tale of surreptitious lust starts innocently enough. A young man is meandering down the street, but there is a certain intention to his steps. It is as if he is throwing out the banana peel so he can slip. It is dusk, and he is walking in the direction of a particular house, one where he knows there is a sexually provocative woman. When the woman sees him, she showers him with alluring words. His seduction soon follows, and what started out as a somewhat hopeful walk ended in much more than he could have imagined. Yes, there was pleasure for a moment. The young man was purposeful in his pursuit of it. But it was the pleasure of an animal eating meat from a deadly trap. Little did he know that he had walked past sexual pleasure and had a one-way ticket to the "chambers of death." His sensual banquet was, in reality, a banquet in the grave.

Equally vivid is the story of Samson (Judg. 13–16). Perhaps no other narrative portrays the irrational nature of sin so clearly. By the time Samson met his match in Delilah, he was already a veteran of foolish relationships. But with Delilah his lust defied all reason. Over and over she was exposed as a betrayer, yet Samson was intoxicated with her. Although aware of her plotting, his desire still blinded him. He was a classic example of a man who was both fully responsible and hopelessly out of control.

How can this be applied to a struggling addict? Adultery introduces more personal language for addicts. They indulge in a secret life that will eventually be exposed, either immediately or in eternity. Deception is commonplace. People are unfaithful to their spouses and enter into a relationship with their beloved. Why do they do it, especially when it could result in such pain for themselves and others? They do it because they love the pleasure and the fawning attention of the other person. They do it because they love their desires above all else. They do it because they feel like they need it. The relationship becomes their life.

But we still want to ask, "Why did you throw away everything you had for this affair?" It all seems so foolish. Yet there will be no satisfactory answer. Sin is not rational. It doesn't make sense. It doesn't look into the future. It doesn't consider consequences, especially if they are not immediate. All it knows is "I WANT—I WANT MORE."

Jim, it sounds like alcohol became your mistress. Your identity was wrapped up in your relationship with her. She gave you all sorts of good things. Whatever holes you felt in your sense of identity were filled with her. Chances are you will miss her, try to visit her, dream about her, and remember her fondly. You'll be surprised at the number of things that remind you of her. But remember: she was a betrayer. She was actually a poisonous snake, and your good times were actually a banquet in a grave. Her goal was your death.

The object of your love has been a bottle that sometimes met your desires. Our goal is to find something that is much more beautiful than she seemed. Sure, we will talk about where you went wrong, but most importantly we must talk about Jesus, the One who is to be your first love. And the only way to learn to love him is to know him from the Bible.

One more thing to remember: adultery is complex. We move toward it because of our own selfish desires, but in the end the mistress controls us. So the bottle is in one sense the enemy, but the real enemy is the selfish desires of our own heart. We will have to fight with things we see, like alcohol, and things we don't see, like our hearts' desires.

Of course, as we say this to Jim or even think it, God's Word expands this theme to include us all. In the Sermon on the Mount Jesus said, "Anyone who looks at a woman lustfully has already committed adultery with her in his heart" (Matt. 5:28). Furthermore, James 4 indicates that those of us who have been in quarrels are most likely experiencing the same root problem as Jim. We say, "I want," to our desires. The experience of addictions is not far from any of us.

FOOLISHNESS

Another theme that overlaps with idolatry and adultery is that of foolishness. For this, the entire book of Proverbs, which examines wisdom and folly, is must reading. Its aphorisms and sayings are memorable and get right to the heart of our daily struggles. The basic idea is that there are two different paths: the way of wisdom and the way of folly. Folly is characterized by thoughtless decisions to pursue a course that is briefly pleasurable but ultimately painful. According to Proverbs, our natural inclination is this particular path.

As you consider the sayings that contrast the foolish and wise person, you soon find that the fool, although wise in his own eyes, acts in ways that are patently ridiculous. Theologians occasionally talk about the "noetic effects of sin." *Noetic* means that sin affects the way we think. Put bluntly, sin makes us stupid—not intellectually, but morally.

> They [idolaters] know nothing, they understand nothing;
>> their eyes are plastered over so they cannot see,
>> and their minds closed so they cannot understand. . . .
> He feeds on ashes, a deluded heart misleads him.
> (Isa. 44:18, 20)

The fool's attention wanders, never focused on wisdom (Prov. 17:24). He ignores all consequences (Prov. 9). He is persuaded that his way is the right way, so there is no reason to listen to others (Prov. 14:12; 28:26). He thinks he will always get away with it, but he will be exposed (Prov. 15:3). He goes with his feelings, not realizing that they can mislead (Prov. 14:8). Of course, the fool feels the consequences of his behavior at times, and he might even have glimpses into how he has brought pain on others (Prov. 17:25), but consequences are no deterrent (Prov. 27:22). The destructive pattern is repeated because folly is enjoyed (Prov. 26:11).

As with idolatry, Scripture paints an unretouched picture, hoping that it will bring us back to our senses. It also promises that God will give grace to those who desire it so that they can leave their idols and take the path of wisdom. The triune God delights in giving wisdom to those who ask, and he gives it liberally.

ATTACKED BY A BEAST

So far, the evolving definition of addictions is that it is voluntary slavery, showing signs of both purposefulness and victimization. One metaphor that especially emphasizes the victimizing nature of idolatry is that of being captured by a wild beast. Both Satan and sin are like wild animals. "The devil prowls around like a roaring lion looking for someone to devour" (1 Peter 5:8). Similarly, sin crouches at the door and desires to master us (Gen. 4:7).

There is no subtlety here. No wooing, attractive women. No idol that holds out promises it can't keep. This is just plain old in-your-face, rip-you-apart warfare. Sin and Satan victimize. They enslave, and the earlier we see their intent, the more opportunity we have to be prepared.

Jim, do you ever find yourself getting spiritually lazy? Coasting? Some people might be able to get away with that—at least on the surface. But part of God's goodness to you is that you have to be consistently on alert. It's as if there is a beast just waiting for you to let down your guard. In fact, there *is* a beast just waiting for you. It could strike anywhere and at any time. It wins when we think it is gone.

At first glance, the beast is alcohol, but when we look more closely, "We have seen the enemy, and he is us." It is sin in our hearts, especially when our hearts are influenced by Satan himself.

It's time for us to get ready for a fight. Even though you don't feel able to defeat this foe right now (sometimes I don't think you even want to), sobriety is God's plan for you. If he has called you to be sober, he will give you everything you need to fight. And, it might not seem like much, but I am going to continue to fight alongside you.

DISEASE OR ILLNESS

Not surprisingly, Scripture *does* use illness as a metaphor for our spiritual condition. In fact, one of the best known passages in Scripture uses the imagery of sickness and healing.

> Your whole head is injured,
>   your whole heart afflicted.
> From the sole of your foot to the top of your head
>   there is no soundness—
> only wounds and welts
>   and open sores,
> not cleansed or bandaged
>   or soothed with oil. (Isa. 1:5–7)

> But he was pierced for our transgressions,
>   he was crushed for our iniquities;
> the punishment that brought us peace was upon him,
>   and by his wounds we are healed. (Isa. 53:5–6)

Have you (or has someone you know) been captivated by a disease model? Here is the point of contact. Scripture, indeed, emphasizes that sin has many things in common with a disease. For example, it affects our entire being, it is painful, it leads to death, and it is absolutely tragic. Yet there are also ways in which sin is not like a disease. It is something we do rather than catch, we confess it rather than treat it, the disease is in our hearts rather than our bodies, and only the forgiveness and cleansing found in the blood of the Great Physician is sufficient to bring thorough healing.

PRACTICAL THEOLOGY

This quick biblical overview only highlights a few useful biblical metaphors, but already there is a clear message. Since addictions are illustrations of idolatries that affect us all, we should expect the principles of change for addictions to be very similar to those for any other sin problem.

- Don't excuse it. That would simply encourage the self-deceptive consequences of sin.
- Confess it as sin against God.
- Look to Jesus as the One who shows grace and mercy to idolaters.
- Grow in faith by knowing God as he reveals himself in Scripture.
- Learn to delight in obedience. Search out Scripture to find ways to obey.
- Don't rely on yourself but partner with and be accountable to wise people.
- Pursue wisdom—the skill of godly living that comes out of reverence for the Lord. And pursue it aggressively. Don't just avoid sin; hate it.
- Realize that addiction, like all sin, doesn't impose itself on us unless we have been willing to entertain the seeds of it in our imaginations. Therefore, change must be deeper than overt behavioral change. We are targeting our hearts.

As You Face Your Own Addiction

1. Review these steps of change. Where are you strong? Where are you weak? Talk with someone else about these issues. Lay out your plan for growing in your areas of weakness.

2. Is Scripture sounding more practical? More lively? More relevant? God's Word speaks to addicts.

At this point in your life you have shown more discipline

than you might realize. You have read material about addictions, and you may have become regular at an addictions group. Consider one more discipline. In light of Scripture's relevance to addictions, read God's Word every day for the next thirty days. If you don't know where to begin, start with one of the Gospels, such as John, or one of the Epistles, such as Ephesians.

3. Does anything seem harsh or unloving so far? If so, the problem might be that you still have a knee-jerk response to any discussion of sin. You are still thinking of how it can be used as a club. What you are examining, however, is called the good news: the kingdom of God has come in the person of Jesus Christ, and he has liberated the captives. This is cause for celebration! It is beautiful. It is what you deeply desire. It is the path of life itself. It is the path on which God never tires of extending grace and mercy: "The LORD longs to be gracious to you; he rises to show you compassion" (Isa. 30:18).

As You Help Someone Else

1. Scripture has one answer—Jesus Christ—but it gives us many ways to get to him. What road works best for the person you are helping? Idolatry? Adultery? A beast's attack? Try each one. Each metaphor highlights particular truths.

2. Addicts must know that they are being given a gift, and those who are helping addicts must know how to give this gift in a way that reflects its cost and beauty. Beautiful gifts must be presented in the most attractive way possible. Ask the person, "Does what we talk about sound like condemnation, or does it sound like a beautiful gift?" The biblical path you are walking together is a hard one, but it should feel like life rather than death, hope rather than despair.

4 The Descent into Addiction

The woman Folly is loud;
    she is undisciplined and without knowledge.
She sits at the door of her house,
    on a seat at the highest point of the city,
calling out to those who pass by. . . .
    . . . little do they know that the dead are there,
    that her guests are in the depths of the grave.

Proverbs 9:13–15, 18

Let's put one of the biblical themes to work. We could select any one of them, but since idolatry is so prominent in Scripture, it will most likely have especially rich relevance and application. And, indeed, it does. In fact, since there are so many applications, I will focus on just one—how idolatry helps us analyze the gradual descent from naïve experimenter to addict.

It was once thought that those who were susceptible to addictions became addicts the moment they tried their desired substance. While it is true that some people seem to fall in love quickly, for most people idolatry is a slowly developing courtship.[1] Idolatry is a gradual journey that begins even before the first shot of booze, Internet hit, toke of a marijuana cigarette, or bulimic binge.

BY NATURE WE ARE ALL "DESCENDERS"

When it comes to addictions, we tend to divide humanity into two groups: those who are prone toward addictions and those who aren't. The reality, of course, is very different. All human beings have already fallen into sin. We were born in the pit. Then, without Adam's help, we made further descents on our own. We have all experienced ungodly cravings, and we all know something of voluntary slavery. The only difference is that some people have addictions that are more noticeable and have more tragic consequences. Also, some people are clinging to Jesus Christ, having been liberated from slavery and empowered to climb—and even to soar.

Therefore, there is no "us" and "them" with addictions. The descent should feel familiar to us all. Yet our familiarity with this descent should not make us think that we have no business helping others. Quite the contrary. Having known something of voluntary slavery ourselves, we are more patient with those who are ensnared. We are also more eager to partner with them and lead them to Jesus Christ, the One who liberates them and carries us out of the pit.

FIGURE 4.1.
THE DESCENT OF IDOLATRY.

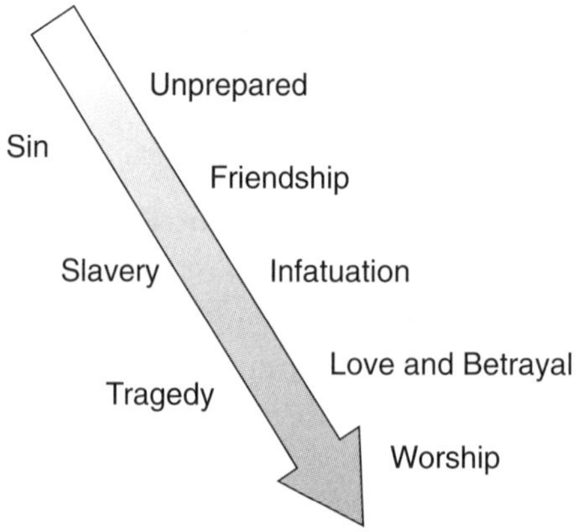

Sin

Unprepared

Friendship

Slavery

Infatuation

Love and Betrayal

Tragedy

Worship

BEING UNPREPARED OR INDIFFERENT

The actual descent begins without much fanfare. When looking into the Grand Canyon, the first step down seems insignificant. Rather than a huge, noticeable leap of rebellion, addiction is marked by small steps of spiritual casualness or indifference, and a lack of sensitivity to right and wrong. It doesn't capture our attention; spiritual indifference and apathy don't attract notice. After all, everyone coasts now and then, we think. What we are doing really isn't that bad. The trail looks smooth so we ignore the warning signs that seem to be everywhere: "Do not merely listen to the word, and so deceive yourselves. Do what it says" (James 1:22).

Ancient Israel began its descent in such a way. The Lord said, " 'Be careful, or you will be enticed to turn away and worship other gods' " (Deut. 11:16). "Do not make a covenant with them [the foreign nations] or with their gods. Do not let them live in your land, or they will cause you to sin against me, because the worship of their gods will certainly be a snare to you" (Ex. 23:32–33).

Yet the people received these commands somewhat casually, without the fear of the Lord. They were content to "merely listen." Unprepared and without vigilance, their casualness quickly led to treaties and intermarriage with surrounding nations. It culminated in a repeat of the slavery and tragedy of Egypt when God gave them what they wanted. He allowed them to be overtaken by and assimilated into the idolatrous lands of Assyria and Babylon.

In teen drug abuse, these gradual first steps are the rule. Teens rarely set out to take drugs; instead, it "just happened."

There was a group of us and somebody just happened to have some marijuana. I had never seen it before, but I knew some friends who mentioned trying it and they never had a problem with it. So I tried it. (A tenth-grade girl)

Others might be curious or want to be part of a special fraternity. They don't set out to be rebellious drug addicts. It is just a social thing to do—a simple experiment.

> I started smoking pot in ninth grade. I knew other people who smoked but I was never invited. I first smoked with a friend at his house. I didn't even know he smoked until he brought out a bag of pot and some rolling papers. . . . He rolled a joint and we smoked it. It was nice. No big deal. But I felt a little older and wiser, and part of a group. (A 25-year-old man now trying to stop smoking marijuana)

In Jim's case, his drinking started as "experimentation."

> I had my first drink—I will never forget it—while I was on summer break after my first year in college. I was nineteen (below the legal drinking age) and working for a company in the city. I would occasionally go to lunch with a woman from the office, who I see now was an alcohol abuser. She always had a couple of martinis before lunch. One lunch with her I thought, *Why not?* So I did, and I liked what alcohol did for me. But at that point I was able to stop, and that was the end of it.
>
> When I went back to college, I would drink at most two or three times a year. Maybe I would have drunk more if I'd attended another college, but where I went to school drinking wasn't important. Alcohol wasn't readily accessible, plus I didn't have much money. But I do remember one time in particular when I went on a four-day binge with some friends.

Escalating experimentation is usually against a background of small rather than large, obvious disobedience. For example, the Israelites' first steps into idolatry were surrounded by constant warnings (Deut. 13:12–16). Only quiet disobedience could get past their corporate consciences. It started with a treaty with an alleged "very distant country" that turned out to be neighboring Gibeon (Josh. 9). It continued with the failure of Manasseh to drive out the Canaanites (Judg. 1:27). The steps were small and seemingly innocuous, but within a generation, the Israelites were familiar enough with the surrounding people that they were serving their Baals (Judg. 2:1–12).

This is the way sin deceives. In order to slip past our consciences, it must begin with small steps of disobedience. Were the Israelites aware of their steps toward idolatry? Probably not. Idolatry is automatic. When the sentry of our hearts is not vigilant, idolatry is like an instinct. It happens naturally. If you had warned the Israelites at this early stage, they probably would have denied incipient idolatry. From their perspective it certainly didn't feel like outright rebellion. But it was.

Some of the ways to address addictive hearts will come in later chapters, but there are issues that arise at each stage that beg for immediate discussion.

How can I drug-proof my children? The most common fears that parents have for their children are that their daughters will become pregnant or their children will use drugs. Are there ways that we can help teens—and each other—to avoid even this first step? There are some good books that you can consider,[2] but there is no magic formula. Since the descent into addictions is a problem of worship, the most important thing you can do is "keep asking that the God of our Lord Jesus Christ, the glorious Father, may give you the Spirit of wisdom and revelation, so that you may know him better" (Eph. 1:17). Are you being surprised by the holiness of God? Are you learning more and more to worship him alone? As you are, proclaim it to those around you. Talk about the Lord more.

Also, consider what you believe God desires in the other

person. Are *you* doing those things? Are you confessing your own sin? Are you speaking honestly about your own spiritual lethargy? Are you alert to where your own imaginations are reckless and ungodly? Are you quick to seek help? Do you value the rebuke of a friend as a blessing?

Finally, are you providing an atmosphere in which others can speak openly to you, without fear of your anger, judgment, or sermons? Ask family members. Are you perceived as humble and patient by those close to you? Are you quick to anger? If so, no one is going to be eager to speak honestly with you. Do you pursue and invite others?

How can I know if I have—or someone else has—taken the first steps down? This question is not commonly asked, but it certainly is important. If we even *ask* it of ourselves, we can be fairly confident that we are on the way up rather than down. Those who ask it are appropriately suspicious of their own hearts. They know that their hearts can deceive, rationalize, and defend themselves from the truth.

The good news is that addictions don't just happen. They need a mind that has set its imaginations and affections on its own desires. So don't just look at overt behavior. Where are your affections? What gets you excited? Depressed? Afraid? Angry? Hopeless? What are these emotions saying about what you worship or what you love? These questions will begin to reveal if something other than Christ is controlling you.

"My friend seems to have taken a quick plunge into drug abuse. Is that possible?" There are exceptions to this gradual descent. Some addicts seem to make a determined, self-conscious plunge into drugs, alcohol, or sex. In these cases, be especially alert for more purposes than the ever-present "I WANT MORE." For example, a self-conscious decision to aggressively use sex, drugs, alcohol, or food might be a way to escape from a difficult home, relieve emotional pain, express anger, keep

hopelessness and depression at bay, or self-destruct. A wise friend or mentor will listen for what the idolatrous use of a substance is saying. He can then bring truth and love to bear on those primary concerns.

FRIENDSHIP

As you listen to an addict's history, you may notice a point where experience and truth part ways. It's the time when addicts themselves feel like everything is fine and under control, but they are starting to do things just because the idolatrous object tells them to. They leave good friends and spend time with those whose affections are devoted to the idolized substance. They start spending money they don't really have. They are thinking about the idol more often. Everything is fine, they think, but they don't see clearly enough to judge. Things are getting darker. It's as if you were outside at dusk, trying to see the moment it gets dark. The process is imperceptible. The eyes adjust, and suddenly it is black.

Perhaps a teenage girl is getting tired of saying "no" to drugs. *Why not give it a try?* she thinks. *Just an experiment.* After a few tokes she wonders what all the fuss is about. *It didn't do much for me,* is the common response. Yet she has just crossed over a huge barrier: she opened a door to an illegal drug which, on some level, she knows is wrong. Drugs have slipped past the moral sentry of her mind, and they can now do it again with greater ease. She may not use drugs again, but given opportunities, she has no reason to say "no," and she may learn to appreciate their perceived "blessings." Another possibility is that she has finally stumbled upon a secret that will satisfy many of her desires.

> The first few times I tried cocaine, I felt like I was much more aware of everything. When I would go outside, trees seemed to be a new shade of green, the

sun would be more intense. The more intense awareness made me feel indestructible. I felt on top of the
world, and nothing made me feel like that before. (A
high school senior)

The soon-to-be-addiction may be fun at this stage, and it
may promise even better things to come. People feel very
much in control. They might feel more alive. But they are far
down a path of foolishness and will probably need a very vivid
lesson to return (Prov. 19:25).

John came from a family that blended Christianity
with Marine-like discipline. He learned that as long as
the external appearance was OK, he could try whatever he wanted. So when he was twelve, he started
sniffing glue. Marijuana came next, alcohol and cocaine followed soon after. By age fourteen he could
no longer conceal his drug use, but every form of discipline his father could imagine was not sufficient to
cause him to stop. Then, at age sixteen, his best friend
died of an overdose. John stopped his drug use and
hasn't touched it for the last three years.

For those who continue, the temporary pleasure offered
by the budding relationship (between themselves and their
chosen substance) begins to satisfy the desires of their hearts.
For example, if these desires (or lusts) demand popularity, the
fraternity of substance abusers meets that felt need. If they want
freedom from pain, drugs deliver. Power? Cocaine satisfies.
Pleasure? It can be had whenever you want.

"I am in control" is the common refrain at this stage. Users
feel accepted, relaxed, better able to deal with (that is, avoid)
relationship problems, and mentally sharp. It is as if they have
found some secret power, all without depending on God. But
appearances deceive. Any time we are finding life, meaning,

or joy apart from our Creator, our growing alienation from him will only lead to misery.

Are there gateway drugs that ease the descent from one drug to something worse? We tend to think of some drugs as especially dangerous and others as less so. Marijuana is not that bad, heroin is horrible. Yet the gateway drugs—which are very dangerous in themselves—are cigarettes and alcohol. Since these are legal by the time we are twenty-one, we don't always consider the very serious consequences of either one.

Have you developed a friendship with cigarettes or alcohol? If you are under age, you have already descended further than you realize. If you are above the legal age, you are nurturing an appreciation for mind-altering experiences.

INFATUATION

In cases of actual sexual adultery, relationships at this next stage become more intimate. Conversations test limits. Perhaps two people might share how they are dissatisfied with certain aspects of their marriages. They might look for ways to be alone and find any excuse for touching. Even if there has been no sexual relationship yet, the man and woman are well on their way and in need only of the opportunity. Why do they do this? Because they like it. It feels good. But the relationship takes on more importance than just good feelings. It also satisfies many other idols. Now, there is belonging, feeling loved, the excitement of flirting with the forbidden, and the thrill of having a secret shared with only a few. The reasons for the adulterous relationship are now more complicated than mere personal attraction.

At this point, the secret relationship usually has a cost. It may be affecting work, finances, and marriage, but, again, reason does not reign and bad consequences are not enough. Those who are committed to more downward steps probably aren't even recognizing the bad consequences. They might notice that things are not going *that* well, but everything bad is the fault of other people. Problems at the job are blamed on a suddenly incompetent or jealous boss. Dissatisfaction with one's spouse is a result of the spouse's lack of love. Changes in friendship are attributed to people "just growing apart" or problems in the other person.

Blame is kicking into high gear.

In drug or alcohol abuse, there is a more regular use of the drug. In the early parts of this stage, drug abuse might be controlled by factors such as price and social or familial disapproval. Later, presuming availability and interest, the use escalates. Perhaps what was once a casual and social event is now a more consistent experience. From a few times a month, to two or three times a week, to whenever the drug is available.

As Jim's history unfolded, a key element was "unsupervised" opportunities. At college, in the army, and on business trips, small steps of disobedience gained momentum.

> After getting out of the army I hardly drank at all, mostly because I couldn't afford alcohol all the time. Then I was given the kiss of death. I got a job with an expense account and business trips out of town. [Jim had married after college, before he joined the Army.] On these trips, my old acquaintance with alcohol was quickly renewed. Soon there were times on the road when I would sit at the bar and skip dinner. After all, after drinking quite a bit you can't taste anything, and receipts don't distinguish between alcohol and food.
>
> I didn't see any warning signs. I wasn't a sloppy, binge-drinking drunk, so it was easier for me to overlook the drinking. But I was drinking regularly. How I got home from social events I will never know. But I was twenty-nine years old and feeling pretty indestructible.

Drinkers begin to hide alcohol. Toilet tanks are a favorite place, though Jim preferred the basement.

By the time our first child was born I was drinking before dinner. Just one. But I soon started filling it to the rim. Then I used a bigger glass. Finally, I found the biggest glass in the house and never used ice. But it was just one. I also started hiding bottles, mostly in the basement. No one could ever figure why I spent so much time there.

When an addict is caught, excuses are masterful. They are offered immediately, without hesitation. They are bold, without averted eyes or a hint of "I just got found out." Inevitably, they will somehow make friends and loved ones feel guilty.

SPOUSE: Honey, I found a bottle of Scotch hidden behind the books in your office. I . . .

ADDICT: That is the problem around here! You are snooping around like some Gestapo! Marriage is based on trust, and you are violating that trust. I put that bottle there months ago—I don't even remember why now. But it doesn't matter. I can't believe how you attack me!

While infatuated, drinkers devise occasions to drink and avoid places where they can't. Blackouts are common, which might be one of the goals. Some drinkers drink to forget, and the temporary amnesia of alcohol abuse allows just that. During a blackout, heavy drinkers may seem alert and in control, but they have little or no memory for certain events.

Those who are infatuated with sex take circuitous routes in order to pass an adult bookstore. They know that it is more public than their Internet pornography, but the risk is worth it.

A near-universal feature at this stage is promises that are

easily made and quickly broken. If a family commitment gets in the way of the growing addiction, "yes" quickly becomes "no."

What can family or friends do? It's at this point that family and friends begin to see that something is wrong. They might not have a name for it yet, but chaos seems to be everywhere. On further reflection, however, the chaos seems to be present only when the infatuated person is present.

The natural response at this point is to try to make life a little easier. Accommodate the person. Don't provoke him because it might push him over the edge. If you are a spouse and you have children, you try to create as much normal time as possible for the family. You might spend more time asking the kids about their day. You do everything you can to have some nice meals and you take the lead in conversations so they don't turn sour. You are looking to counterbalance the chaos. But be careful. This is where those familiar with the cycle of addictions talk about *enablers*. Enablers are the nicest of people, but they are not trying to really deal with the problem. They are trying to smooth it over.

Don't be pulled into attempts to cover up the problem. The Christian life is lived out in the open. If you see a problem and you don't know what to do, get help. The basic strategy for dealing with life's problems is that we first deal with them ourselves. If we are still stuck, we enlarge the circle and ask others for help. God gives us his Word and his people as our primary resources.

> Bill, I don't know what has been happening recently. I am always wrong in your eyes. You are always irritated. You spend more and more time away. And you have been drinking more than ever. I am going to get help. If you want to come, I would be glad to have you join me. But at this point, I need help.

The infatuated person can have a variety of responses to such a statement. There might be more intense anger and threats, a season during which the person seems as good as gold, or appeals that "this has been a really hard time for me right now; things will get better, I promise." But get help in any case. Talk to your pastor, a friend who understands and can offer wise counsel, or someone who has gone through a similar experience. You could even try an Al Anon meeting. Don't be isolated, and don't think you can deal with the chaos by yourself.

How should I deal with always feeling like it is my fault? When someone accuses you of something, your first response is to consider the accusation. Just listen. If we see truth in it, even if it is only a kernel, we confess it. Since Christ has taken the judgment of our sin upon himself, it should be relatively easy to confess our sins to someone else. The death of Christ on the cross frees us to be able to look seriously at our own hearts.

Yet Matthew 7:3–5 indicates that seeing our own faults does not disqualify us from confronting the other person in love. Rather, Scripture indicates that confessing our own sin is the very thing that *does* authorize us to speak to another about his own sins. It is only then that we can speak in a way that is not judgmental.

> I can see ways in which I have responded in frustration. I really am sorry and have asked you to forgive me. I will get help for that. But I can't let the discussion of our problems stop there. Would you be willing to let me speak into your life as well?

Be prepared for anything. You are facing a person who is experienced at avoiding blame and placing blame on others. Any attempt you make to address the other person's heart might end in you wondering, "What just happened?" The chaos and blame will just find a new level. But that doesn't mean that you remain silent. It only means that you will need more help to think creatively about how to live and speak.

LOVE AND BETRAYAL

The addiction is now expanding its turf. Not only is it a near-daily feature of the person's life, it also becomes a treatment for everything. Whatever the emotion, the answer is found in the addictive behavior. It can vent anger, alleviate depression, temporarily quiet the emptiness of loss or failure, celebrate a happy occasion, dilute guilt, and so on. Everything is alcohol (drug, food, sex) soluble.

If families are aware of the problem, they are preoccupied with it. The addiction dominates them. They hide car keys, drive around town looking for the drinker's car, and dilute the bottles of alcohol around the house. Yet they rarely confront the problem directly and effectively. Sometimes they won't say anything at all. In fact, many times families have no safe subjects. Everything seems to intensify the chaos or provoke anger.

At this stage, one particularly ingenious strategy for substance abusers is to create problems in the home. Sometimes they will provoke marital or familial tension for days or weeks prior to a drug binge. Although not always clearly thought out, this is a calculated attempt by the drug user to find an excuse for subsequent drug use. The self-deceiving user thinks, *There is just too much pressure on me at home. My wife never lets up. If she doesn't change, I can't handle it any more. I have no choice but to use drugs.*

Selling drugs—something drug users thought they would never do—is now common, and stealing from parents is the rule. One woman sold pieces of her jewelry each weekend in order to keep her and her friends partying. Another sold herself. Lying is now a way of life. In order to deal with their consciences, the addicts' excuses get more and more bizarre, almost comical. Every problem is always someone else's fault—they really believe that.

Perhaps even more frightening, addictive behaviors shield abusers from learning how to live. Instead of learning how to deal with conflicts in relationships or work, abusers look to their idol to offer temporary fixes. And with each use of their substance, they lose skills in living. They bypass opportunities to grow in wisdom. No wonder they seem more and more like foolish children.

In spite of the evidence that the addict's chosen idols are no longer friendly, unpleasant consequences are quickly forgotten. Users still believe the drug doesn't "have" them. They think it is even helping, or at least it makes them feel normal. They believe the drug has placed their self-image on a firm foundation. They believe that they have a *deeper* sense of reality and truth. Yet their idolatry is becoming more apparent. Even they themselves might realize that there is a greater cost, but they don't care. Perceived advantages outweigh disadvantages. Their substance abuse has artificially given them feelings that everything is still OK.

What are friends and family going through at this stage? Even if the addictive behavior is not yet exposed, families and friends will go through nearly every emotion possible. Sometimes they feel like they are going crazy: "Maybe it is my problem after all." Other times they think everything is fine. They can feel angry, afraid, controlled, threatened, betrayed, jealous, and hopeless. Life has become unpredictable for them. They are never sure what is going to happen next. Unless they are skilled at turning quickly to the Lord, learning how to cry out to him, they will obsess about ways to curb the addictive behavior.

WORSHIP

Finally, addicts become abject worshippers. "You used to offer the parts of your body in slavery to impurity and to ever-increasing wickedness" (Rom. 6:19). The downward spiral of idolatry finally comes to rest at slavery. Idols originally promised freedom. The gods could be at your disposal, doing your bidding. They held out life, camaraderie, and pleasure; but they deliver slavery, "for a man is a slave to whatever has mastered him" (2 Peter 2:19).

Adulterers become obsessed. They become paranoid if the other person has time that is unaccounted for, and they get jealous for no reason. Interestingly, they feel like they own their sexual partner but in reality they are enslaved by their desires. They are affected by their lover's every attitude, comment, or mannerism. If the adulterous relationship is broken, it can result in depression, rage, and suicide. Life is found only in the relationship.

With alcohol and drugs, this is the stage of almost daily use or dependence. Drugs or obsessive thoughts of drugs are a constant companion. This does not mean that people are always high or drunk. No, the natural course of this stage is that there are binges with periods of moderation or abstinence. But addicts always think about their substances, and they are often physically dependent during their binges, meaning that if they stop using the drugs, there are physical withdrawal symptoms.

> Like a morning cup of coffee, Paul would begin every day with a marijuana joint. Without it he was jittery and argumentative. With it he was relaxed and ready for another day of a difficult marriage and an uninteresting job.

At this stage, nothing comes before the drug. To close friends, the power of the drug is obvious. To the ones who are dependent, denial reigns. Sometimes this denial is simply outright lying, but lies always point to an even deeper *self*-deception. The addict has become a fool, without insight into the relationship between the drug and its consequences. Drug abusers still don't think they have a problem! This may sound incredible, but, again, think about your own experiences. We are often very blind to our own sin. For example, in marriage, some people say that it was years before they had any inkling of their blatant selfishness and pride. During those years, the excuses were, "People just don't understand me," or "If she [he] would just show more love. . . ."

In this most severe stage, it often seems that addicts have no guilt, even though they are worshipping an idol and hurting many loved ones in the process. Is this true? Have they succeeded in killing their conscience? In some cases, yes. Some drug abusers, adulterers, and other addicts, through a great deal of practice and hardness of heart, are morally insensitive. Their consciences have been seared. However, you will probably find that addicts feel much more guilty than you might think at first. They feel guilty for hurting others, guilty for the lies, guilty for the broken relationships, guilty for rebelling against a holy God. And, if they use drugs or alcohol, the only way they know how to deal with their guilt is (guess!) to do *more* mind-altering substances. They see no other way out.

Jim experienced medical problems before his family knew anything about his drinking. He had an alcohol-induced seizure. Sadly, only he knew the real cause, and the seizure certainly wasn't enough motivation to stop drinking. Nor were other health problems. He would get sick to his stomach after every dinner because he couldn't handle booze and food. But he would just throw up and start drinking again.

Finally, the end arrived. Jim came home early from work to an empty house. After a few drinks, he passed out while walking upstairs. When his wife returned, he was still passed out after falling down the entire flight. Thinking he had suffered another seizure, his wife immediately called the paramedics. At the hospital, the emergency room physician told her that Jim's blood alcohol level was enough to kill most people. Jim was detoxified from alcohol and immediately sent to an in-patient program. The grief of those who love addicts who have descended deeply cannot be overstated. Since addicts love their idol above all else, you have no relationship with them, and you are watching them self-destruct. You might be paralyzed by the grief if you weren't so angry or there weren't so many questions that either haunt you or demand attention.

- What did I do wrong?
- If I do anything, things will get worse, but if I do nothing I don't see how I can continue. What should I do?
- Should I be silent and submissive (1 Peter 3:1)?
- Is it biblically permissible to have the person leave the home or to leave myself?
- What should I tell the children?
- What should I tell my friends?
- If the person asks forgiveness, does that close the door on discussing what happened?
- If I told others, wouldn't he (she) feel betrayed?
- Can I divorce?
- What do I do if I feel like I am in danger?

We will consider more specifics about what to do when addictions are exposed in the next chapter.

PRACTICAL THEOLOGY

Here are some theological features of this chapter that should be underlined.

As You Face Your Own Addiction

You will be tempted to read the descent into addictions and focus on ways your battles were different, and perhaps your experience *was* significantly different from the pattern here.

But there are certain recurring themes that definitely fit: blaming others, lying, and increasing blindness or lack of insight into yourself (Fig. 4.2). All these, of course, are energized by a desire to be independent of God, as well as by inaccurate understandings you have of God. Since God is light, any time we try to live life apart from him, we will be in darkness.

As You Help Someone Else

If you are helping someone else, then get help for yourself. Don't do it alone. A wise person seeks advice (Prov. 20:18) and listens to advice (Prov. 19:20). God has distributed many gifts to his people. These gifts are given so that the church of Christ will be thoroughly served and complete (1 Cor. 12). You have been given gifts to serve others, and you have needs in which you must be served by others. The final word in the counsel you receive will be to love (1 Cor. 13). The challenge will be to determine what form that lovingkindness will take.

FIGURE 4.2.
ESSENTIAL FEATURES OF ALL ADDICTIONS

PART 2

Essential Theological Themes

Speaking the Truth in Love

Brothers, if someone is caught in a sin, you who are
spiritual should restore him gently. But watch yourself,
or you also may be tempted.

GALATIANS 6:1

Whoever turns a sinner away from the error of his way will
save him from death and cover over a multitude of sins.

JAMES 5:20

What are the chances of this happening? You answer the
phone and hear someone say,

> I simply had to call you. I have been struggling with
> alcohol dependence (pornography, overeating, pre-
> scription drug dependence, laziness). I know that it is
> hurting my family and I know that it is against God. I
> need help.

Let's just say that it is rare, at best. If it does happen, you
are witnessing a very dramatic work of God's Spirit.

Maybe someone struggling with depression will call you,
but someone struggling with an addiction probably won't. Addicts, even when they are hopeless and in great pain, still pre-

fer covering up their problem. Why? Shame, the possibility that they will have to give up their addiction, fear that they don't know how to live without it, and many other reasons. Jim's addiction wasn't discovered until he was found passed out in a pool of his own vomit. He was among those who are especially blessed to have God reveal their secret sins and through that, to gain the opportunity to examine his life in the light of God's grace.

My goal in this book is to show how the theological riches of the Bible speak practically and meaningfully to the problem of addictions. In the last chapter, we chronicled the descent into addictions to demystify its progression, and we considered a few practical questions along the way. In this chapter I will focus more on what we can do to help, especially before the person is really willing to work on the problem.

You will notice that, while the theme of idolatry is still the theological backbone, other biblical themes such as lust and legalism will also make an appearance. But keep in mind the biblical exhortation that surrounds them all: we must speak the truth with humility and love. This is hard to do under the best of circumstances. It will seem almost impossible when an addict's sins begin to be expressed toward you. It will force you to call out to the Lord for grace to change, which is exactly what he desires for us.

DETECTING ADDICTION

Even though addictions tend to become more public as lies multiply and the addiction is practiced, when it finally becomes apparent, most of us feel like fools because we didn't see it earlier.

I began to think that Doug could be using drugs when I noticed that he often had tremendous bursts of energy followed by long periods of sleep, sometimes more than fifteen hours. During those times his moods would swing from happy to sad to irritable to angry. When I noticed that some of our heirloom silver was missing, I decided to look in his room for evidence of drugs. Under his underwear I found a cigar box that contained a small plastic bag of white crystals, three razor blades, small straws and a pocket mirror. It was then that I knew he was using cocaine. (Mother of a 15-year-old cocaine user)

Before you can help someone caught in a sinful habit, you must see it. With alcohol, drugs, food, and sex, this may be the most difficult step for family and friends. Everyone has missed signs of drug and alcohol abuse, bulimic binges and purges, and dangerous obsessions. You will too. In fact, covert addictions will often be right in front of you and addicts will deny it. This is simply the nature of sin: it tries, as long as possible, to stay out of sight.

So what do we do? Should we say that love always trusts (1 Cor. 13:7) and therefore believe whatever someone says to us, knowing that it is possible that we are being deceived? Or should we be constantly suspicious of everyone? As is its custom, Scripture offers a third way that makes sense. It reminds us that we are not omniscient police. Our confidence cannot come from our own abilities to detect lies and addictions. Rather, it comes from the fact that God loves us and often exposes our sin so others can see the danger we are in and help us move toward safety. It also reminds us that people can lie, and, if someone has a history of lying, it might be wise *and* loving to maintain a certain degree of suspicion.

What should we be alert to? Since idolatry is difficult to contain, its consequences will eventually spill out into other areas. Here are some of the changes you might notice. Some are specific to alcohol or drugs; others are relevant to sex, food, and the long list of other activities or objects that can capture us. I will mention these changes only briefly because lists like this are available in almost any book on addiction. Even in secular books with a disease model, such lists are helpful in their *description* of common symptoms and behaviors.

Work. Have work habits changed? Are they late getting to the job? Are they prone to extended lunch hours? Do they bring home less money? If they are in school, is attendance down? Are grades significantly lower? Is concentration poor? You might hear comments such as "Get off my back" or "I'm sick of work, this town, everything." Problems at work and school are the number one symptom of substance abuse. Rarely can substance abuse be contained in a way that leaves work or school unscathed. Even if the problem is not related to addictions, such changes still call for more active intervention.

You would think that work- or school-related changes would be easy to detect. Yet there are always excuses for a lower grade ("The teacher hated me"), and co-workers are quick to cover for the addiction problems of their peers. If you have school concerns, check them out with teachers. If you have concerns about work, ask bosses or co-workers. Should you tell the person that you are talking to other people? When in doubt, yes. You want to set a course that values openness and honesty. If you think that this openness will unnecessarily bring more conflict, then get advice.

Relationships. Has their peer group changed? Are they more secretive? Do they spend a lot more time alone in their room? If underage, are they spending time with a group that smokes cigarettes and drinks alcohol?

Spiritual Life. Have there been any obvious changes in their spiritual life? Do they seem more hardened to the truth? Have they been caught telling lies? Do they break commitments? Have they had any recent problems with the law?

The dilemma with this category is that many loved ones are not very good at getting this kind of information. While there are some problems that are obvious, such as breaking the law and getting caught, we can be less aware of the condition of the heart. Too many of us presume that external behavior that conforms to community standards is equivalent to a growing relationship with God. Rarely do parents or friends really take time to understand the interior spiritual life of another. Have you taken the time to know what is in a person's heart? What motivates him? What she loves?

Physical Health, Emotional Changes, Cognitive Changes. Have they been losing weight? Are they more prone to colds or sinus problems? Are they unusually tired at times? Are they unusually restless at times? Do their pupils ever seem unusually large or small? Do their eyelids ever seem especially droopy? Are their eyes bloodshot after school or after seeing their friends? Do they have alcohol on their breath?

Does their thinking sometimes seem strange or illogical at times? Are there unusual mood swings? Have there been significant changes in their personality? Do they seem depressed? Have they ever mentioned suicide?

A "yes" answer to any of these questions is not proof that a person is involved with drugs or alcohol. These are clues rather than signs. It does mean, however, that a physical exam is warranted.

Underage Use of Legal Drugs. As mentioned in Chapter 4, one of the more reliable indicators of illegal drug use is underage smoking or drinking. Certainly, these are problems in themselves, arguably even larger than the abuse of illegal substances. Nicotine is perhaps the most addictive of any drug, and alcohol is one of the biggest killers in this country. But cigarettes and alcohol are also the gateway to illegal drugs. When there has been evidence of either underage drinking or cigarette smoking, the odds are that there has also been experimentation with illicit drugs. Therefore, if you know they have been involved in underage smoking or drinking, let them know that you are aware that illegal drugs are probably more accessible to them. And let them know that if they have been doing illegal drugs, you would like to give them the opportunity to speak the truth about it.

What about alcohol abuse in a person who has reached the legal drinking age? If a person's religious convictions permit drinking in moderation, the questions are a little different. Has there been public drunkenness? Drunk driving? Blackouts? Consistent morning drinking? Change in personality when drinking? Does alcohol lead to any problem at all in the person's life? Have others ever had to cover up for the person's drinking? A wise rule of thumb for drinking in moderation is that there should be no more than two drinks every twenty-four hours, and drinking should be limited to five days a week.

Drugs or Drug Paraphernalia. Have you ever found illegal drugs on a family member? If so, you will likely be told that they belong to an anonymous person who said they were herbs. The truth is that your family member is using drugs. Have you ever found papers for rolling cigarettes? Unknown substances in aluminum foil or plastic bags? Pipes? Straw-like objects (for snorting cocaine)? Small spoons? Syringes? Have you noticed a growing chemistry lab in the house? These are just some of the devices used to prepare or administer drugs.

If you feel completely naive about drug paraphernalia, you might want to look at some drug books that include illustrations, consult with your local police, or invite some experienced parents to dinner.*

Urine tests are the most reliable way to detect drug use. If

---

*If you suspect drug or alcohol use, you might consider a nontechnical screening test that focuses on the way most illegal drugs change the ap-

someone has a track record of drug abuse and lying, urine tests are probably a good idea. There are laboratories in most communities that will perform these tests for a fee, and your local community mental health center should be able to tell you where to find testing kits you can administer yourself. Drugs stay in the urine for at least twenty-four to forty-eight hours.

What if the person confesses to drug use before it was exposed?
There are rare cases when people confess to drug use (or alcohol abuse, sexual sin, bulimia) without having already been exposed. Assuming that the confession is not a manipulative ploy to stave off the discovery of something worse, you can celebrate the work of the Holy Spirit. Although there is still work to be done, speaking the truth and living publicly is evidence of God's liberating grace at work in the addict. As a general rule, whatever he or she was doing is outweighed by the beauty of truth-telling.

PREPARING TO CONFRONT

If there is evidence of addiction but no admission of it, it is time to speak with the person. At this point we encounter one of the clearest biblical principles of all: friends, parents, and counselors must search their own hearts before any confrontation. When they do confront, they should do so as one addict to another, pointing the way to freedom. This is why it is important to remember that the roots of drug abuse are

pearance of the eyes. Make a general observation of the eye. In room light, look for dilated or constricted pupils (in normal light, the black pupils usually span one-third of the diameter of the colored iris), redness, watering or glazing, swollen eyelids, droopy eyelids. Another test you can do at home (which is more accurate than a cursory eye check) is to test saliva. One kit is called the QED Saliva Alcohol Test. As the name suggests, it is specific for alcohol.

common to us all. Not all of us are addicted to an intoxicating substance, but all of us have our own private idols. This preparation leads to a "gentle tongue" (Prov. 25:15) and compassion. It keeps discussions and confrontations from being me-against-you battles, and it makes "the teaching about God our Savior attractive" (Titus 2:10). If there is going to be a battle, you want it to be between the person and God, not between the person and yourself.

> The pious fellowship permits no one to be a sinner. So everybody must conceal his sin from himself and from the fellowship. We dare not be sinners. Many Christians are unthinkably horrified when a real sinner is discovered among the righteous. So we remain alone with our sin, living in lies and hypocrisy. The fact is that we are all sinners![1]

In most cases, preparation should also include getting advice on how to confront. Talk with people who have biblical wisdom and some experience with confrontation. In most situations, it would be best to ask for advice without revealing the name of the person you must confront.

Along with prayer, personal repentance, and seeking counsel, there is another preliminary step in personal preparation. Since deceit goes hand in hand with drug abuse, you must create a context where it is as easy as possible to tell the truth. This may sound obvious, but many people, especially parents, don't always want to know the truth, and their kids know it. The truth can destroy their myth of the perfect family. It might (they think) sully their reputation in their church or community. Other parents want to know the truth, but they might respond with rage, and their kids know that too.

How do you respond to the truth—even when it is deeply distressing? Are you approachable? Can people easily tell you the truth, knowing that you will be able to handle it?

My parents listened when I told them I drank. They understood that. But when I tried to tell them about my curiosity about other drugs, they overreacted so much that I was sorry I ever mentioned it. I never said anything about it again. (An eleventh grade boy)

If you really want to lay a foundation for honesty, you must be a person who is quick to acknowledge your own sin, and who will not overreact to sin in those close to you. To keep from overreacting, you must be persuaded that the problem is ultimately before God. As the psalmist said, even though his sin had dire consequences for an entire nation, "Against you, you only, have I sinned" (Ps. 51:4). It is not our law that has been violated; it is God's. Furthermore, if someone persists in addiction, he or she is in danger of being estranged and alienated from God, under his judgment. Therefore, this is a time more for tears than anger, even if the person has lied to you and stolen whatever was there to take.

CONFRONTATION

At one time the prevailing wisdom was that friends had to wait for the addict to hit bottom before they could offer help. This strategy has changed, however. Counselors and friends have found that for many, the bottom never comes. Bad circumstances alone are rarely enough to stop the momentum of substance use. Therefore, friends have become much more active in intervening. God's Word states, "Rescue those being led away to death; hold back those staggering toward slaughter" (Prov. 24:11). When you are on a rescue mission, you try to do everything you can to help.

The basic strategy for confronting an addicted person is a familiar one. Found in Matthew 18:15–17, it is commonly called church discipline. You begin by confronting the person by yourself. If he or she does not listen, you go with one or two others. If there is still no response, the church gets involved until finally the person is, essentially, confronted by the world. Does it sound harsh? It shouldn't. It is done with humility and love. The goal is always to rescue and restore.

Even though church discipline has been one of the distinguishing features of the Christian church, it is not a popular topic these days. Most modern churches neglect church discipline. In that light, it is interesting to note that secular approaches have embraced an approach to confrontation that mirrors church discipline. It is technically called *intervention*.[2] In essence it says that we can no longer wait for people to destroy themselves and others. They must be presented with the facts about their problem. They are out of touch with reality and need others to present it to them. Furthermore, this is best done by a group of people who deeply love the substance abuser. Curiously, intervention is hailed as one of the most significant advances in drug treatment. Yet church discipline is the original and intervention the imitator.

With Our Children
The one-to-one confrontation might start like this.

> Son, you have been on my mind a lot recently. I have wanted to talk to you, but frankly, I have been scared to upset you. That, I know, is my problem. But I realize now if I were silent, I would wrong you. You say you are not doing cocaine, but I found a pipe in your room last week. Silverware has been missing from the closet. And sometimes I don't even recognize you—you are angry one minute and calm the next.

In this case, the witness did not actually see the person smoking the drug, but the presence of drug paraphernalia and bouts of anger must be confronted. Of course, the vast majority of people confronted like this will either get angry or deny the charges.

> You don't know what you are talking about. How can you accuse me? You think I would do such a thing? Somebody gave me that stuff months ago. It's no big deal.

Then what? Do you say that the person is lying? If you have good evidence, yes. But be very careful here. You are at a critical moment. Pay attention to the relationship. You are raising these issues because you love him. You are not confronting him for your benefit, but for his. Don't let the person blame and defend. Stay on track, and don't give in to your own frustration or fears. Don't play by the person's defensive and attacking rules. Don't take the insults or disrespect personally. Keep in mind that this person is most likely in danger. The fact that you have been hurt by his words and actions might not be the most important issue at this moment. Whatever disrespect you hear is ultimately disrespect toward God himself. You are witnessing a person who wants radical independence, and you know that any life other than that of faith and dependence on Christ is doomed to failure.

If you have no idea what to say, then don't say anything. Just think through the interaction, consider ways that you may have sinned, pray about how to love this person, and seek advice. You don't have to say everything the first time. If you feel spiritually prepared to continue the exchange, focus on what is clear, and focus on the relationship.

> Since you are saying that you haven't touched the silverware, I'll go to the police today and report it missing. But the silverware isn't the most important thing. Have you noticed that so many of your words are attacking, defensive, or disrespectful? I love you deeply,

but I was afraid to even raise these issues because I thought it would end in anger. I didn't want to see our relationship erode any further.

Whether or not you are using drugs, I don't know for sure, but I think you are carrying around a large world of secrets. There is only so much I can do about that. What I can do is keep trying to talk to you when it seems like you are trashing relationships. I'll also have to get help in thinking through where to go next.

If you have ever made it this far in the conversation, as either the confronter or the person being confronted, you are blessed. If you have *been* confronted like this, then someone truly loves you. If you have confronted someone like this, then you are willing to risk your relationship in order to help the other person. You have been blessed with wisdom and love. But, as you know, this is just the beginning. In this situation, and in the hours, weeks, and months ahead of you, there will be many times when you will confess your own sin, cry, call out to the Lord for more wisdom and love, and receive counsel and prayer from a small group of people who can give you wisdom and keep your conversations in confidence.

Yet right now, the number of questions is rapidly growing. What if, when you report missing items to the police, they are fairly certain that it was an inside job? Or what if they can point to one particular person in the family? Do you press charges? Since you probably have limited options, pressing charges may be your best decision. Other options include having the person make restitution, and using the event as leverage to send the person to an in-patient program.

What do you do with drug paraphernalia? Do you take it? Leave it? Report it? Most people would agree that you would at least take it, but get ready to be blamed for trespassing on private property. Tell the accused that you will seek counsel regarding what to do with what you collect.

Is there such a thing as private property for teens in our homes, especially teens or young adults who have a history of deceit and illegal behavior? There are differences of opinion here. Some parents prefer to give teens privacy because they believe it will communicate that the parents are willing to trust the teen. They hope it will help promote a better relationship. If you adopt this position, understand that it is the Constitution that talks about the right to privacy, not Scripture. God's Word certainly has clear teaching on private property and laws that punish stealing and the destruction of someone else's property, but these guidelines don't clearly apply to parent-child relationships.

Scripture seems to lean in the direction of rejecting the concept of privacy in the parent-child relationship. Although giving children space as they get older can be a way to bless them, and knocking on closed doors should be the norm, a child who has acted foolishly deserves more careful scrutiny. If this is seen as an invasion that angers the teen, then it may be saying more about the child's own heart than a lack of parental wisdom. Our lives, after all, are public. We live before the face of God. In some sense, our spiritual lives—our faith and our willingness to follow Christ in obedience—is the entire church's business.

There are still other questions. For example, what do you do with the rapid mood swings? The fluctuations from anger to serenity? Seek experienced counsel. If the accused doesn't live with you, there might not be much you can do beyond what you are already doing. You could again tell the person that you will seek counsel from your pastor, physician, local Al Anon, or other experienced friend. You will at least want to be alert to the way the person's mood swings affect you. If you respond in anger, you will have to consider your responses more carefully and give them with gentleness. If you are fearful, you will have to learn how to speak out with boldness or bring someone with you. If you lash out at everything, you will have to learn when to make a point and when not to. If you are silent, you will have to remember that God has determined to use words as his agents of change.

It might not arise at this particular moment, but if the person is living with you, this is the time to evaluate guidelines for the home. What would the person have to do to be dismissed from the home? Once again, get advice. Don't let your shame over an unruly family member outweigh your desire to act wisely and lovingly.

Your goal is to have clear rules for which infractions are indisputable and consequences are unambiguous and predictable. For example, you don't say, "Be nicer to your siblings." Instead, you might say, "Demeaning comments to anyone in the house will not be tolerated. If anyone speaks disrespectfully to another, he or she should deal with that relationship by asking forgiveness. We will meet together weekly to discuss this."

There are ambiguities even in this, and the consequences have not yet been outlined. If you are not sure what would be the wisest consequences, take time to think them through. It is likely that you have more options than you think. For example, you can stop insurance payments on a car, have the person get a job, have the person meet with a wise counselor, or have his belongings put in storage until he finds a place to stay.

Sadly, there are some situations in which it is difficult to find effective consequences. A hard-hearted child will do what he wants in spite of anything his parents do. If the child is a minor and hasn't been caught breaking the law, parents are still legally responsible for the child and it is difficult to force him out of the home. Some parents have signed over legal guardianship of unruly children until the teen is of age. Many have endured years of hardships.

The more severe consequences (such as having the child move out, transferring guardianship, or reporting the child to the police) should be reserved for especially serious infractions of certain rules. These could include drugs being found or used in the house, behavior that is having a deleterious effect on other children in the home, physical violence or threats of physical violence, and stealing. In these situations, the child is clearly saying that he is unwilling to be part of the family, and he should not receive the protection that a family normally affords.

These decisions, of course, must be made only after there is agreement among your advisors, and you have made the line clear to the child. Otherwise, the pain of putting a child out will probably cause you to waffle on this especially hard decision. It will be hard because you simply love your child and don't want to see him suffer more than he already is. You are afraid that some of the consequences of moving out might be too dangerous (e.g., he threatens suicide, or lives with other active drug users) and you can't imagine living with yourself if your decision results in serious harm. Also, you already feel guilty because you have rehearsed so many past events in which you could have responded differently. These are some of the reasons why unified counsel is so important. Such decisions are perhaps the most difficult you will ever make. Interestingly, however, many parents who have finally made the decision to put a child out because he was unwilling to abide by basic guidelines of civility have often seen the good fruit of their decision and wondered why they didn't do it sooner.

Keep in mind that you are implementing a version of church discipline. The goal is love and restoration. The method is to allow them to experience the natural consequences of their demand for independence.

With Spouses

When the addicted person is a spouse, the chaos that addiction brings is even more burdensome. With children, there is often a spouse or even an ex-spouse who can share the burden. But when the addicted person is your spouse, you feel isolated and caught in a life-threatening maelstrom.

With children, you can more easily see the child's behavior accurately and make wise decisions. With spouses, too often you feel as if *you* are the one with the problem, so you can be paralyzed by choices.

With children, it is easier not to take their behavior personally. With spouses, everything feels very personal, and it *is* more personal. The addicted spouse is making decisions *for* the addiction and *against* the spouse. In light of these added difficulties, the spouses of addicts need consistent pastoral care.

Here is one of their daily questions: How can you not be controlled by something that is so . . . controlling? Think of what it would be like to never know what the day will bring. What will your spouse be like tonight? Angry and raging? Contrite and weepy? Defensive and critical? And how do you deal with the broken promises? Sometimes he does what he says he will, other times he doesn't. If he *never* kept his word it might be easier. At least it would be predictable and you would try to contain your hopes. What is important for Christian spouses is to keep in mind the larger purpose and proper motives.

The larger purpose, of course, is the glory of God (1 Cor. 10:31). We would like to see changes in another person's life because we believe that such changes would bring glory to God.

Life is about God. It is about worshipping him, trusting him, knowing him, and loving him. The deepest problem for addicts is that they are not worshipping, trusting, knowing, or loving the true God. Instead, they are running and hiding from God or rebelling against him. If they violate moral laws, they are God's laws, not our own. With this in mind, spouses and families can remember that the deeper problem is the addict's relationship with God himself.

On a very practical level, a way to bring glory to God is to love others in the way that Christ has loved us. This is the way to be less dominated by the addicted spouse. It keeps him or her from being *our* idol. If you love someone for the glory of God, you will be less controlled by his erratic or ungodly behavior. The challenge here is that biblical love has many variations. It can take the form of covering the offense and not raising it, avoiding the offender when sin is blatant, gently holding up a spiritual mirror so the person has an opportunity for self-analysis, confronting with boldness, or calling the police. This is why spouses and families need help. Most of us don't have to be constantly on alert, always thinking of wise ways to express love. We don't always have to wonder whether love should take an active, confrontational form. Most likely, families will be called on to show love that travels the entire biblical spectrum.

When the family receives encouragement to fix their eyes on Jesus (Heb. 12:2), and they have hearts that are committed to love, there are some guidelines that are customary, especially with drugs and alcohol.

- Ask often, "What is God's calling in my life now?" God has not abandoned you. Instead, he has particular interest in those who have been sinned against, neglected, or abandoned (e.g., Jer. 23:1–8). He has a purpose in your life. You are God's ambassador. Focus, therefore, on those things which God says are your responsibilities. For example, you are not the best person to check up on how much the person is drinking. Better to have someone outside the family maintain accountability. As a rule, you don't go out of your way to search for hidden liquor. If you try to keep up with the schemes of an addict, you will always be a few steps behind.

- Do most of your analysis on your *own* heart, not your spouse's. This serves several purposes. (1) You will remember that you have been given a great gift in the forgiveness of sins. (2) You will see where you must forgive others. (3) You will be able to help the other person see his sins in ways that are not hypocritical. (4) If your self-examination is biblically guided, it will help you to see clearly. You won't feel as crazy or filled with self-doubt.

- Discern the differences between nagging and loving confrontation. (Nagging tends to be more focused on ourselves and our own frustrations.)
- Don't argue when the person has been drinking. When a foolish person is being foolish, avoid him.
- Look for ways to touch the person's conscience. This means that you won't be preachy, but you will hold up the mirror of truth in front of the addict. For example, you could share with him some of the consequences of his sin that he might not remember.

> Bill, since alcohol keeps you from seeing the consequences of your behavior, I want you to know what you did last night.

> You didn't keep your word to the children yesterday. You said you forgot. But they didn't forget.

- Don't be persuaded to keep secrets. Although you may be embarrassed to admit to others that you live with someone with such serious struggles (it can be as embarrassing as revealing that your spouse is an adulterer), you need the help of others. If the family member refuses help, at least you can seek it. Part of that help may include further steps of church discipline that some people call *intervention*.

INTERVENTIONS

You have already seen the sinful behavior and privately confronted the addict. You may have done it dozens of times.

Mike, there are some things I would like to talk with you about that are pretty hard to discuss. I want you to know that I am raising these issues because I care for you. I love you as a brother. The last few times I have been with you when you have had an opportunity to drink, you have always drunk too much. You were drinking without self-control, rude to other people, and flirtatious with women. You didn't even remember going home. Mike, I love you and I am really concerned. What you're doing is wrong. You can't put off dealing with this. What I am most concerned about is what this says about your relationship with God. It says that you are running from him or ignoring him rather than knowing him, loving him, and worshipping him. And any time we run from the Lord, our life gets worse.

If the person refuses to listen, the next step is to bring one or two others. If he or she continues to refuse help, enlarge the circle to include "the church" (Matt. 18:17), which would include someone in a position of pastoral authority.

Here are some practical suggestions for a successful intervention. Intervention typically involves a small group (five to eight people) of close friends and loved ones who have witnessed the addictive behavior or its effects. These people commit themselves to confronting the person in love. The group might consist of a pastor, spouse, son or daughter, employer, relative, and co-worker. Anyone who has observed the sin pattern and loves the person enough to be willing to risk the relationship is a possible candidate.

A person experienced in interventions is a useful though not essential consultant. Such a person might anticipate some of the rebuttals you are likely to hear. For example, heavy drinkers are amazing in their ability to provoke guilt and keep loved ones off the subject. A person experienced in working with them can suggest responses that would keep the group from getting sidetracked and remain focused on its goal. The next step is to bring the group together to plan an intervention. The agenda for the meeting is as follows:

1. Consider who would be best to participate in the intervention.

2. Have a time of personal repentance and prayer, remembering that the gap between the substance abuser and you is quite narrow.

3. Have each person explicitly describe some of the apparent signs and consequences of the addiction that he has witnessed. These should be very specific, citing dates and behaviors. Otherwise, addicts tend to counter with specific times they did not misuse substances. After each participant gets feedback from the others regarding clarity and brevity, these accounts should be written down to be read at the actual intervention.

Mom, I love you. I have always looked up to you and I couldn't have made it through college without your support. I'm here to tell you how worried I am about your drinking. You are always saying that you don't spend enough time with your grandchildren, but we have had to keep them away from you at times. When you were at our house in July, you were drunk. You either ignored the kids or were very short with them. Johnny even cried because of the way you spoke to him when he asked you to play a game. Mom, we don't trust you with the kids, and, if you continue drinking, we will have to keep them from you.

Some interventions have had more success when they included someone who was especially loved and someone who was especially respected. The one who is loved can read his or her letter last.

4. Prepare follow-up options. Before a face-to-face intervention, you should prepare follow-up options that either guide the person if he heeds counsel or bring consequences if he doesn't. For example, the consequences of refusing to seek help might include:

- cutting off all funds
- locking the door if the person doesn't come home by curfew
- having a secured password for those involved with pornography
- asking him to move out of the home
- not allowing children to drive with the person who is often high or intoxicated
- not allowing the children to be alone with the addicted person if drug or alcohol use is possible
- calling local police whenever drugs are seen or found in the home
- pursuing further stages of church discipline

If the person acknowledges his or her need for help, follow-up options depend on the particular idol that the person worships. For drugs and alcohol, it might include:

- counseling
- AA meetings or meetings with local Christian groups (Addictions Victorious is a national organization with many local groups)
- hospital detoxification
- a long-term structured program
- daily meetings with friends from church
- urine samples
- going with him when he tells his addiction buddies that he won't be seeing them any more
- handing all monies over to a trusted friend

Some follow-up options will demand research. For example, if it is possible that the person is physically dependent on a substance, you should consult someone who is knowledgeable about withdrawal symptoms.* Detoxification might not be necessary, but this is not the time to take chances. An inpatient detoxification program would probably be helpful and may be necessary. Detoxification at a safe place, monitored and away from drugs, is another option.

If a physician strongly suggests hospitalization, then you must make another decision. Should the addicted person go to a detox ward in a hospital (in which case the stay will probably be no longer than one week) or should the person be admitted to a drug rehabilitation hospital (in which case the stay might be longer)? The practice in drug rehabilitation counseling is to go with the longest program possible, but that does not mean that a longer program is either necessary or even helpful. At the risk of attacking a sacred cow, longer hospitalization may not be worth it. As a rule, in-patient programs make little or no difference in abstinence rates.

Longer hospitalization, however, may have some benefits.

- Since drug and alcohol abusers are masters of stealth, longer hospitalization is one way to have better surveillance for a few weeks.
- Some drug or alcohol users feel that it takes time to get out of the mental haze induced by their favorite substance. The longer the program, the more time there is for the mental haze to clear and the person to think normally.

---

*If the addict has gone without the substance for a few days and has had no serious physical symptoms, then hospitalization is not necessary. If the person has suffered convulsions during previous detoxification, then get medical supervision.

- Some addicts find it helpful to have the time away from bad influences, to experience the confrontations in group meetings, and to hear the horror stories of other addicts going through the program.

The disadvantage is that the vast majority of rehab programs, Christian and secular, will strictly follow the AA program.* This being the case, if you believe that an in-patient program would still be useful, you should usually assume that it will *not* be Christ-centered. This means that sobriety might be accompanied by indoctrination into a sub-biblical worldview. And if addicts have determined that AA saved their lives, they will likely resist any hint of criticism about the program. This doesn't mean that you don't use secular programs. Often there is very little else available. It just means that the hard spiritual work will take place when the addict gets out.

Since most in-patient programs have similar philosophies, you will probably evaluate them in terms of certain practical questions rather than their biblical orthodoxy.

- How long is the program?
- What is the total cost?
- What is covered by insurance, and what arrangements can be made for the balance?
- Is there a waiting list?
- What are the ages of those in the program? Do they match well with the person considering admission?

If the decision is to undergo detox outside a hospital setting, it should be preceded by medical consultation, and there must be a partner or team ready to help. The withdrawal process will take at least a long weekend. A week is best. Unless

---

*For in-patient Christian programs, you should check the Internet.

advised otherwise, drug users should quit all drugs of dependence and they should quit cold. Home detox does not always work. The addicted person may refuse any supervision and go back to the addictive substance. If it fails, you learn from the experience and try again. Whatever the case, detox should be the first step. In fact, since alcohol and drugs are mind-altering, you should probably postpone other issues until the person is drug-free.

5. Set up the intervention. When you have decided on the follow-up options and appointed a person to facilitate the intervention, decide on a time and place to meet with the addicted person. The ideal place is one where the substance user cannot ask anyone to leave, as he might if you meet in his own home or office.

Families and friends often struggle to decide if they should tell the addict about the intervention. Should they be up front, or should they prepare something more on the order of a surprise party? Openness would be consistent with your desire not to be pulled into the web of secrets and deceit, but most interventions are done without addicted people knowing in advance. If love rather than anger is clearly expressed during the intervention, addicts typically appreciate what was done after they are sober.

AND IF THE PERSON REFUSES HELP?

If addicts refuse to acknowledge their problem or are unwilling to change, the next step is to enforce the consequences and get ready to confront again. How could the group have been more persuasive? Did the person being confronted sidetrack people from their agenda? If so, then keep pursuing the person in love. The first intervention is by no means the last hope.

If addicts still refuse to deal with their sin, the "how-tos" depend, in part, on their relationship with a church. If they are members of a church, then the next stages of church discipline are applicable (Matt. 18). If they are not members of any church, then further formal steps of church discipline are impossible. But families and friends shouldn't give up. Through wisdom, creativity, prayer, and the counsel of God's people, there are many options available. One option is to learn from the last intervention and plan for the next. Remember that this is a rescue mission. If the first rescue attempt doesn't help, try again.

Some situations, however, may not be able to wait for another intervention. For example, what if a parent is intoxicated and leaves small children unattended? Some people are mandated to report any case of potential child neglect to their local child protection services. If so, they should report it. Those who aren't mandated reporters should also report such behavior, if the person has been unwilling to change or receive help and the situation is dangerous.

What if the enslaved person is physically abusive or potentially harmful? The church must physically care for those who could be harmed. Most likely, such protection would be provided through a court order or temporary housing. Such decisions are for extreme situations, but these are often extreme situations. If there is violence, have a church member accompany the violated person to initiate legal protection.

Is divorce permissible when there have been years of chaos from addiction with sporadic violence and frequent verbal expressions of rage? Conservative views of divorce consider adultery and abandonment as grounds for divorce. Many people would argue that chronic addiction is at least as fracturing and corrosive to marital trust as sexual adultery. Also, there are many addicts who will never say, "I want a divorce," but they have certainly abandoned the marriage, using it for reasons that don't include love and fidelity.

What if the addict is wrecking the family finances? If the

spouse is working, she could give all her funds to a trusted friend who could manage some of the daily finances. This, of course, is an imperfect solution because in an era of easy credit, there are always ways to find more money. All you can do is shield money in whatever way you can. In most states, the only time a spouse is not liable for her husband's debts is when there has been a legal separation or divorce.

Do decisions such as those that protect finances encourage a woman to be unsubmissive to her husband? First Peter 3 should be required reading. Submission is relevant even in times of suffering. Submission, however, has limits. We do not submit if we are told to sin. We do not submit if our actions ease the sin of others. And we do not submit if we are told to do something that will jeopardize the well-being of our children. For some women, this teaching certainly complicates an already confusing situation. Yet whatever complications it introduces, they are opportunities to pray and seek the counsel of others.

If physical safety is not an issue, and there is agreement that some of the more severe consequences are not yet appropriate, spouses and families must remember that God often calls his people to walk a very difficult path with him. If you are called to walk that path, don't become weary. Solicit prayer and counsel. Meet weekly with a few committed friends and your pastor for prayer. Pray for a wise and discerning love (Rom. 12:9–21). Pray for a love that will point the addict to Christ.

Don't overreact to the addict's irresponsibility or times of intoxication. The addict will use it to draw attention to you rather than the real problem. Also, overreactions such as extreme anger or extreme fear usually work against wisdom rather than with it. Remember that addiction is against God more than it is against you. This doesn't mean that you should be passive, although there will be times when you won't know what to do. In fact, there will be times when you *should* be angry. Just ask God to temper your anger with patience and love.

Love and wisdom are your guides. They lead neither to enabling nor condemnation. Instead, they surprise with grace, aim for the conscience, and allow the user to feel the consequences of his actions. As Proverbs 19:19 indicates, "A hot-tempered man must pay the penalty; if you rescue him, you will have to do it again."*

FOLLOW-UP: ENGAGING IN THE BATTLE

After detection and, if necessary, detoxification, the work begins. Many families, friends, and churches err at this point. Sin, slavery, and idolatry do not go away overnight. There is a Christian myth that change is an event rather than a process; that it is more like a light switch that is turned on than a battle that must be engaged. For some reason, we tend to think—wrongly—that immediate liberation from the slavery of addiction is more glamorous than the gradual process of taking a little bit of land at a time. Such expectations have implicitly encouraged addicts to tell great, though fabricated, stories of liberation instead of simply being honest about their struggles, and finding in that honesty something highly praiseworthy.

We must remember that for everyone, the Christian life is an ongoing battle. It is a daily process of mortifying the flesh. We must "encourage one another daily, as long as it is called Today, so that none of you may be hardened by sin's deceitfulness" (Heb. 3:13). To our shame, Alcoholics Anonymous has a better understanding of the need for daily exhortation than the church.

This battle must be highlighted when addiction has been

---

*"Tough love" is often recommended at this point. That should mean that we don't make it easy for the addict to continue the addicting relationship. It does *not* mean that we ignore grace, mercy, and other clear biblical guidelines.

discovered by others instead of confessed by the addict him- or herself. When an addiction is discovered, the addict's sor- row over being caught can easily be misinterpreted as repen- tance. There may be no repentance at all, just unhappiness about the consequences. In these cases, the battle has yet to be engaged.

PRACTICAL THEOLOGY

This chapter doesn't begin to cover all the possible deci- sions that those who love addicts will face. Addictions bring chaos, and chaos is unpredictable. In the providence of God, however, this chaos is used to teach us to depend on the all- wise God and the gifts and experience he has given to the church.

As You Face Your Own Addiction

1. Who are the people who have been used to change you? Do you see a theme? Most likely, they clearly loved you, they did not speak in judgment, they were able to say hard things to you, and they hung in there with you even when you were out of control. As you remember these people, thank God. They are ways he met you with his grace.

2. Do you feel judged by others? Are you using that as an excuse to withdraw from people who care for you? Any steps toward isolation and independence are steps into darkness. Don't go there. First, consider what they are saying. Are they right? Are there even kernels of truth in it? If so, be a hearer. It is one of the hallmarks of a wise person. Being rebuked is not the same thing as being hypocritically judged.

3. If you have been discovered in your addiction and your life seems miserable, be careful. Are you yearning for the days when your addiction was deliciously secret? Are you more troubled by the consequences than by the sin itself? If so, you are still enslaved by the addiction. Talk openly and honestly

about this to someone. If this seems like too big a step, go to an addictions group and talk about it there.

4. Remember: this is about your relationship with God.

As You Help Someone Else

1. It certainly would be easier to sit on the sidelines and say nothing when we suspect that someone has a problem with alcohol, drugs, or sex. Anger, too, would be easy. We'd just get our frustrations off our chest and move on. Love, however, makes life both messy and blessed.

2. If you are not a family member, try to understand how difficult the family's life has been. Try to understand the chaos. As you do, you will be more persistent in prayer, more committed to finding wisdom in Scripture, and more open to considering the more severe consequences as a way to restore the addict.

3. You are now about to see a biblical principle in action: you will feel like you are being radically changed, regardless of what the Holy Spirit does with the addicted person. You will see sin in your life. You will call out to the Lord in desperation in ways you haven't before. You will see the Lord answer prayers for love and wisdom in ways that will strengthen your faith. At some point, you will be tempted to think that helping the other person with his addiction is for *your* benefit! There is no reason to be thankful for addictions, but we certainly can be thankful that addictions cannot disrupt God's plan for good.

Respecting, Listening, and Inviting

Love is patient, love is kind.

1 CORINTHIANS 13:4

As far as we know, the addicted person is now fenced from the object of worship and willing to receive help. He has accepted help from people outside the immediate family. He carries very little cash and no credit cards. His Internet use is monitored by friends. He has given his daily schedule to others, and his time is accounted for. As you already know, there is no foolproof barrier between the addict and his idol, and most addicts have learned to lie easily while they look you in the eye. But let's say that you have reason to believe the person is not actively involved with his addiction. Now what?

AA and its various clones, such as Narcotics Anonymous and Overeaters Anonymous, are typically the staple of most plans. They are the first place many people turn to for help, which is not surprising since there is very little else available. Even if people don't go to the actual meetings, they will still be heavily influenced by AA thinking. Almost any meeting, book, or mentor will be colored by AA teaching. Watch evening TV for a few hours and the AA model of change will appear somewhere. AA so dominates our thought about addictions that it is literally impossible to have struggled with addictions and not be influenced by it. The question is, should AA meetings be part of biblical discipleship?

If addictions are truly "spiritual diseases," as AA claims, it is odd that Christians would choose to be mentored through the change process by an organization that is not Christ-centered or biblically grounded. Why would Christians want to go outside the church to deal with spiritual problems? The answers to that question, sadly, are all too obvious.

- You don't have to explain yourself to people at AA. They already understand what you have been doing and what you are going through.
- Members of AA don't tend to give thoughtless, naïve, or judgmental counsel.
- AA makes sense to people. It doesn't work in sermon-length material; it works in catchy mottoes and clear steps. It is not theology but it is certainly practical.
- AA members are compassionate but tough-minded. They will call you on evasiveness, lies, and ingrained, destructive styles of thought. They will see through some of your masks. The result is that you become more at home with honesty and authenticity.
- Talk about drugs or alcohol to clergy, and many won't know where to start. The others will send you immediately to AA.

AA has common sense and compassion, but it is not Christian. The church has theological horsepower and both the mandate and power to love, but it doesn't always apply either its theology or its practice to addictions. Some opt for a Christian version of AA, of which there are more and more. Yet these groups seem to have more in common with AA, and its strengths and weaknesses, than the church. So what are our options? Should we avoid AA or embrace it?

A Christian approach, of course, is neither blindly accepting nor reactionary. Instead, it emphasizes wisdom and discernment. If people find some help in AA or its Christian imitators, they should be discerning, examining everything through the lens of Scripture. It helps to recognize that AA has gradually changed over the years. When Bill W. started AA, he used *disease* more in a figurative sense than a literal one. Although he was not always consistent in this, he would often use the word *disease* in a way similar to the way Scripture uses it—as a metaphor for our spiritual condition. Now, however, the disease metaphor is more often used in a literal way at AA meetings, and illness language is mandatory. The result is that forgiveness of sins and the imputed righteousness of Christ are no longer absolutely central to the process of change. The gospel, the thing of "first importance" (1 Cor. 15:3), becomes secondary.

Where do Christians need to be careful and discerning if they pursue accountability and help through an AA-type program? Here are some questions to ask.

- Is sin or sickness my primary problem? Do I think of addiction as something I have or something I do?
- Do I summarize my life by asking, "What do I really desire? Christ or _____ (alcohol, pornography, shopping, and so on)?"
- Am I emphasizing both *voluntary* and *slavery?*
- Am I being defined more by my past addiction than by the blood of Christ?
- Do I stand in judgment of the church because I think it has naïve views on addiction?
- Do I come to church to educate it or because I need to worship the Lord with others? Do I need the ministry of others even as they need me?
- Am I meeting regularly with Christians of various backgrounds, or am I finding my fellowship with people who don't know Christ but know my struggle with alcohol?
- Am I keeping in mind the larger goal, which is to glorify God?

Ideally, if someone chooses to go to AA, it would be best, at least initially, to be accompanied by a discerning friend. This would provide an opportunity to debrief and examine the meeting through a biblical lens.

Of course, the ultimate goal is to have the church mature in its biblical thinking on addictions to the point where, in the decades to come, it has a reputation for compassion, understanding, and a Christ-centered model of change that works. At this point, the church isn't attractive to many Christians who struggle with addictions. Yet God promises that a maturing church will have the favor of the nations, and the nations will stream up to it. The vision is for the church to be attractive to many people who don't know Christ and struggle with addictions.

"WELCOME"

An effective church will have addicts in it. After all, the church is, in part, a hospital for sinners in different stages in their struggle with sin. The challenge of the church is to assist sinners at all these stages, which certainly is no small task! We must flush out the self-deceived, expose the dishonest, confront the rebel, offer forgiveness for the guilt-crushed, provide hope for the despairing, and support the surrendered. In addition, the church must invite in and hold the attention of those who formerly would not have dared (or desired) to look to the church for either hope or help.

Simply put, we treat others as we have been treated. As Jesus has enthusiastically and persistently welcomed us, so we welcome others.

> "Come to me, all you who are weary and burdened, and I will give you rest." (Matt. 11:28)

> "Go to the street corners and invite to the banquet anyone you find." (Matt. 22:9)

"Come, all you who are thirsty,
    come to the waters;
and you who have no money,
    come, buy and eat!
Come, buy wine and milk
    without money and without cost." (Isa. 55:1)

To date, however, the church has had difficulty in welcoming, assimilating, and speaking meaningfully to people struggling with drugs, alcohol, or anything that would be considered an addiction. Our sermons rarely explain the dynamics of our ongoing battle with sin. Our worship does not always communicate, "God is here." Parishioners too often are reluctant to share and seek counsel for their own struggle. We are prone to judge those whose sins we think are worse than our own. We don't relate easily to people who come from a different culture, and the drug culture is, indeed, a different culture. In short, our churches sometimes come across as havens for saints who have assimilated a certain church culture. Addicts or former addicts will instinctively avoid such places.

From start to finish, friends, mentors, and Christian acquaintances must be welcoming and inviting to *fellow* addicts. As Christ has welcomed us, we welcome others on Christ's behalf. We offer biblical help as one addict to another, pointing the way to freedom, talking about the magnificence of the kingdom of God, and warning about the perils of idolatry.

Perhaps you have never been controlled by alcohol or another addictive substance, but we all know what it's like to be mastered by our own desires rather than by Christ. In fact, good preparation for welcoming an addict would be to summarize your own ruling desires. What tends to compete with Jesus for your affections? What desires have a tendency to surreptitiously grow to idolatrous proportions? Think of times you quarrel or are frustrated. What about despondency that comes when a teaching you gave was not appreciated? What about when your desire to be loved by your spouse becomes a stronger desire than that of loving him or her? What about when your desires for personal reputation or comfort gradually grow until they take on the appearance of sacred shrines? Certainly, some of these—such as my desire to be loved by my spouse—are good things. The danger with all desires is not so much *what* we want but *how much* we want it.

Another way to expose idolatrous tendencies is to complete the statement, "If only I had _____, then I could be happy!" Chances are that you will name a desire that can enslave you.

To reinforce the similarities between yourself and the addicted person, remember that Scripture does not make drunkenness—the prototype for addictions—a sin that stands above all others. Instead, drunkenness is placed alongside "ordinary" sins such as jealousy, selfish ambition, and envy (Gal. 5:19–21). These more commonplace sins are familiar to us all. With this in mind, you now come to the addict as a brother or sister, not as an expert who has personally conquered all of your personal sin patterns.

> CHRISTIAN FRIEND: Since I don't think you really believe that Jesus welcomes everyone who turns to him, I want to welcome you in his name.
>
> TRISH (just three weeks out of heavy cocaine use), thinking: *Sounds a little holy roller-ish to me.*
>
> CHRISTIAN FRIEND: Honestly, have you ever really been welcomed anywhere? Where someone was glad to see you?
>
> TRISH: Maybe my drug dealer. That's about it.
>
> CHRISTIAN FRIEND: This may just seem like words right now, but when we seek Jesus, he is excited to see us (cf. Zeph. 3:17). Somehow, I want to be able to express that to you.

Everyone has his own style in welcoming. Whatever your style, it should be motivated by our Heavenly Father, who pursues and invites us to know him.

KNOW THEIR STORY

In AA, people tell their story. In church, people give testimonies. Either way, when mentoring people who were once enslaved by sin, you want to know them. Knowing and understanding a person is not a standard subject in theology books. But, like welcoming and inviting, it is a clear theme in Scripture. One reason we pursue knowing others is because we are simply interested in knowing them. Knowing is part of respecting another person, and it is fundamental to friendships. Another reason we want to know people, especially those we have opportunity to disciple, is that we want to use Scripture precisely. For example, our initial impulse might be to address a person's obvious anger. But if we listened longer, we would also hear about his fear, and realize that fear is a better entrance into his life. We might emphasize arrogance when it's actually guilt that overwhelms the person. We might focus on the lust for alcohol when the deeper lust is to be desired by the opposite sex.

Scripture says many things. The question is, What is the Spirit of God saying *now* to this particular person? In order to match Scripture with the person, we must know the stories and themes of both. Therefore, personal ministry rests on personally knowing someone. We want to know the person and the larger context of the addiction. We want to understand the momentum behind the current struggle.

Having said this, however, I should add that before you get a more extensive history of the addiction, it might be wise to ask about any issues requiring immediate attention. For example, if Jim's wife is leaving him tonight, then Jim is not going to want to spend time talking about the history of his drinking.

CHRISTIAN FRIEND: Before asking more about how alcohol entered your personal story, I was wondering if there are any immediate issues that we should talk about. For example, I know there are problems at home as a result of what you did. We both know that it will take time to rebuild trust with your wife and kids. But is there anything that needs immediate attention? Are there urgent problems in your job that we should discuss now?

JIM: Things at home are a little rocky, a little tense, but Mary is going to hang in there with me. She has definitely been through a lot.

If the person is married, someone should be meeting with the spouse (and the spouse can then meet with the children). Marital problems usually get worse soon after the addict begins walking a path of change. While friends are delighted that the addict is seeking help and avoiding his once-cherished idol, the family is beginning to think of all the broken promises and lies that have gradually crushed relationships. Their lives were once dominated by fear and survival; now they have a chance to reflect on what happened to them. They remember the chaos and never want to go through it again. They think that the addict should radically and quickly change. They feel like they have paid their dues long enough.

If you are trying to help a teenage drug user, you should also consider the family. Drug abuse in teens is a good cue for parents to say, "Lord, search us." Parents do not bear the blame for their children's sins, but they may have contributed to them. Addictive behavior can actually be a teen's way to deal with family problems apart from the truth of Christ. It can be an escape, or even an attempt to unify quarreling parents. For once they have something on which they can agree—their child has a big drug problem—and parents will often unite to fight that problem. As prominent and as deserving of attention as these family issues may be, we must never minimize the drug problem itself. It is not merely a symptom of family turmoil. The drug abuse itself needs attention. Therefore, friends, pastors, and mentors must encourage parents to take wise initiatives. Parents must confront the child and set limits, they must not overreact, and they must receive encouragement and guidance along the way. With teens, written contracts can be helpful because they clarify expectations and consequences. They also restrain parents from making rash, angry decisions. If possible, parents and child should work on a contract together. Let the teen know that you as a parent are working on it. Encourage him to contribute what he thinks would be helpful. The child does not control the process, but the contract is for his benefit. Allowing him to participate shows respect.

The contract should focus on areas that can actually be monitored. For example, you don't write, "You will not get high on the way to school" unless you are driving the person there. Instead, you could write, "You will not brings drugs into this house. We will do random searches as a way to help you with this. If we find drugs, we will _____." If you make a rule about something that you can't monitor, you are creating opportunities for more lies and deception.

In setting up the contract, it would be wise to be alert to community norms. (Consider contacting a school guidance counselor or local rehab center for suggestions.) This does not mean that we simply do whatever the world does. But many people in our communities have been thinking practically about addictions for decades, and some of their guidelines can keep us from being too restrictive or too lenient. When the contract is settled, sign it and use it. Since it might need subsequent refining, schedule times when it can be reevaluated.

Let's get back to Jim. If urgent circumstances haven't required an extensive detour, you can begin to fill in the blanks about the immediate problem and then hear his larger story.

Jim, there is usually a momentum to all addictions. When did you notice that alcohol use was gathering momentum in your life? Could you tell the story—the long story rather than the short one?

As we saw earlier, Jim's drinking began while he was in college. He had a summer job where one of the workers favored a few martinis for lunch, and Jim joined in. Yet it wasn't love at first sight. When he got back to college, he drank only a couple of times a year.

His drinking escalated during a mandatory time in the Army and then all but disappeared when he was discharged, largely because he didn't want to spend the money. Then, alcohol began its relentless work when he landed a job that required traveling and gave him an expense account. For the next twenty years, he consumed more alcohol from one year to the next until he was thought to be dead after a serious seizure and fall.

Hearing a story like this is only the first step in knowing a person. There is much more to understand. But already you can help Jim understand and interpret his own story.

CHRISTIAN FRIEND: Jim, is this the larger picture of your drinking? I certainly don't understand as well as I hope to, but I think I have a general outline. There have been a number of powerful influences in your life: your family tended to avoid problems rather than work on them; your time in the military gave you the opportunity and even the encouragement to drink; and there are some areas in your life where you feel like a failure. I'm sure these are just a few of the inducements to drink. But another thought struck me as you were talking. In many ways your history follows the history of Israel.

JIM: Come again?

CHRISTIAN FRIEND: Tell me if this fits. We want Scripture to be as relevant as possible. We want it to describe and explain what happened to you.

The Bible asks the question, Who will be king? The one true God or worthless idols? Curiously, the answer wasn't very straightforward for the Israelites (just like it isn't straightforward for any of us). They started moving toward idols very gradually by rubbing shoulders with foreigners. They found they weren't so bad so they moved closer. Then they began to see that their gods made some promises that were very appealing: rain and fertility in particular. Maybe, they thought, they could worship both God and idols, and in so doing get what they wanted. But the promises by the other gods were false promises. Gradually, these foreign gods demanded and received worship, and the children of Israel started walking in the dark.

Let me put it this way. The story of the Bible is entitled, "Whom Will You Worship?" The story of our lives has the same title. And ultimately, the idols we worship are shaped by our own desires.

This is a very rudimentary sketch, but it teaches people to see their lives in light of biblical traditions and themes. It ties them in to the history of the church. Too often, addicts don't find anything in Scripture that relates to their situation. While they have underlined nearly every page of AA's Big Book, Scripture seems silent. To remedy this perception, we want to embed the addict's individual story in the larger story of Scripture. We want Scripture, on every page, to speak in a lively and meaningful way about both Jesus and ourselves.

What Comes at a Person

As a person's story develops, there are two perspectives that Scripture brings. First, the story will reveal some of the influences, circumstances, or things that come *at* us. This list includes parents, employers, friends, physical abilities or disabilities, academic strengths and weaknesses, and many others. These influences do not cause us to sin, but they can act as temptations to sin that make us more vulnerable. They can be sources of pain for which the sufferer does not yet have biblical answers.

Jim's influences were unremarkable. His parents loved him, there was no heavy drinking in the home, and he had seemed to avoid many of the difficulties we typically encounter through life. Other addicts have very different stories. They may have been victimized by alcohol abusers while they were growing up. They may have experienced physical violence and capricious punishment. They may have witnessed endless parental fights that eventually culminated in divorce.

Some people who have had painful experiences turn to alcohol or drugs as a way to say "Nothing matters," or "Just give me a few moments when I can forget." In such cases, idolatry is still the ultimate cause of the addiction, but Scripture also speaks with great compassion to those who have been victimized and sinned against by others.

Is it possible to speak to both idolatry and pain? Can we simultaneously say "You are responsible" and "You have been victimized"? This apparent paradox is difficult to maintain, but it is similar to the discussion about the sovereignty of God and human responsibility: both are necessary. If we ignore either one, unbalanced doctrine will eventually yield bad fruit in a person's life. Emphasize responsibility to the exclusion of victimization and you are leading the person to a harsh, stoic God, who is not really the Holy One revealed in Scripture. Emphasize victimization to the exclusion of purposeful idolatry and the person never has the opportunity to deal with the deepest of all his problems.

Often, people who have both sinned and been sinned against react with anger. If the angry person is provoked by a real injustice, it would be wrong for a friend or counselor to ignore that fact. Take time to listen as they speak of injustice. Often, this simple act will help them admit what they intuitively know: that injustice does not excuse their own sinful anger. When in doubt, begin with suffering when you are trying to help a person. Notice the way Ezekiel 34 speaks to idolatrous people who have been led astray by leaders. It begins with God speaking against the perpetrators on behalf of the victimized sheep. The Lord then goes to great lengths to say that, since the appointed leaders betrayed the flock, he himself will now shepherd them. In the context of Ezekiel, God is certainly not overlooking the idolatries of the people. Clearly, compassion and rebuke are not mutually exclusive.

What Comes Out of a Person

The second perspective that Scripture brings to our history is the perspective of our own hearts, or what comes *out* of us. This perspective is one of the unique and defining features of a Christian approach. To paraphrase John Calvin, the heart is an idol factory. In our hearts we are always actively worshipping, trusting, desiring, following, loving, or serving something or somebody. When Scripture speaks of the heart, it typically is emphasizing that we live before God, in all things and at all times. We respond to him either by trusting in him or trusting in our self-serving idols.

These spiritual allegiances of the heart are sometimes hidden, but like the quality of fruit on a tree, the heart will eventually reveal itself in word and deed (Luke 6:43–45). Any violation of God's law is an expression of the heart, as is faith and obedience. Our emotions are also, more often than not, animated by the orientation of our hearts. When our worship is true, we experience joy, peace, love, and hope, even in difficult situations. When our worship is false, and the things we desire are unattainable or impotent, we can be grieved, bitter, depressed, angry, or fearful. Our emotions usually *mean* something, and it is wise to ask, "What are my emotions saying?" "What are they pointing to?"

In less religious language, here are some questions that can reveal the heart:

What do you truly want?

What is your purpose in life?

What or whom do you really love?

When do you get most sad and depressed?

When do you get hopeless? (The person is not getting what she desires.)

What do you get most excited about? What brings you the greatest pleasure?

What is your dream?

How would you like to be remembered?

What do you especially want to avoid?

With addicts, the idolatrous purposes of their drinking or drugs multiply as they invest more time in their addiction. If we had asked Jim what his purpose was in taking his first drink, he would have found the gravity of the question somewhat odd. "I had a drink because the person I worked with offered me one. Why are you looking for some deep, dark purpose?" However, as his story unfolded, it became clear that more and more desires in his life became attached to the bottle.

Drinking was a way to express anger and rebellion toward his parents or anyone else who bothered him. He would "drink at" other people. Drinking was a way to say, "I deserve what I want."

In other words, Jim's drinking typically expressed an aggressive, angry heart. His life was littered with justifications for his anger, holding on to every perceived wrong committed against him, arrogantly judging those he deemed less intelligent than himself, and determining to do what he wanted without the interference of others. Drinking, therefore, was both a problem in itself and a symptom of other problems of the heart. If a change in external behavior—not taking the first drink—were the only goal, other causes of his drinking would go untouched.

Most substance abuse programs agree: the drinking itself is a real problem, but it is also a symptom of other problems. Christian programs depart from others by defining these problems as primarily against God. As Scripture indicates, even though our lives can hurt others, it is ultimately against God himself that we have sinned (Ps. 51).

This means that "turning our will over to God as we understand him" is, at best, sterile and superficial. A more biblical perspective is that we have been committed to turning away from God. We have sought autonomy and personal freedom. We have said, "No one can tell me how to live my life." The problem is not so much that our independent path is no longer working for us, so we need help. The problem is that we are rebels who must lay down our arms, beg forgiveness from the One on whom we declared war, and accept his conditions of surrender.

This is where a Christ-centered approach gets especially good. The conditions of our surrender cost us nothing. We don't have to pay for the damage we have done against God. We don't have to go to prison. We don't have to ask forgiveness for the rest of our lives. All we must do is trust that, whatever the cost, the true God has already paid it. The result is that we are not only forgiven, but our God also accepts us as family members rather than slaves. He says that we belong to him and no other.

This is not to say that the causes of all drinking are purely aggressive—either against God or other people. Some want to decrease the pain of a broken relationship or soothe the blows to self-esteem when rejected by an employer or lover.

Yet these folks have much in common with Jim. At root, they still have constructed lifestyles that center on their own pain, comfort, significance, or security. As AA wisely observes, they too have a fundamental allegiance to their own independence. The various purposes of the heart don't emerge immediately. Although some of its autonomous purposes may be apparent to other people fairly quickly, it takes time to see these Godward purposes more clearly, especially when we have spent much of our lives avoiding these issues. This means that, once again, addicts are human. Like everyone else, they can see the purposes of other people but they are blind to themselves. We are all in need of the insights of wise people and the enlightenment of the Spirit of God.

CONSIDER THEIR CONVERSION

At some point in a person's story there might come the thought, *Is this person really converted?* If there has been no deepening sense of sin, little or no evidence of the fruits of the Spirit, and a lifestyle where there was clear bondage to sin, it could be that the person never truly put her faith in Jesus Christ. This does not mean that addicts must know the date they accepted Christ as their Savior. It means that *now* is the time for them to honestly consider the allegiances of their hearts.

It takes some wisdom to know when and how to talk about a person's conversion. When in doubt, raise the issue sooner rather than later.

> CHRISTIAN FRIEND: Jim, tell me. In light of the story you are telling, do you think you were ever truly converted?
>
> JIM: I hadn't really thought of that question. I had assumed that I was.
>
> CHRISTIAN FRIEND: Can you understand why I am asking the question?

How would someone like Jim examine his soul? Richard Baxter, a wise Puritan preacher, gave this exhortation to new converts. The language is a bit archaic, but the questions are thoroughly relevant to our hearts today.

> Are you heartily willing to take God for your portions and had you rather live with Him in Glory, in His favor and fullness of love, with a soul perfectly cleansed from all sin, and never more to offend Him, rejoicing with His saints in His everlasting praises, than to enjoy the delights of the flesh on earth in a way of sin and without the favor of God? Are you willing to take Jesus Christ as He is offered in the Gospel, that is to be your only Savior and Lord, and to give you pardon by his blood shed and to sanctify you by His Work and Spirit and to govern you by His laws? Note that to be willing to be ruled by His laws in general and utterly unwilling when it comes to particulars is no true willingness or subjection. You must know that His laws reach both to heart and outward actions, that they command a Holy, Spiritual, Heavenly life, that they command things so cross and unpleasing to the flesh that the flesh will be ever murmuring and striving against obedience. . . .[1]

No one should be paralyzed by these questions. They can be used to examine our allegiances and spur us either to seek Christ more wholeheartedly or to admit honestly, "I have not put my faith in Christ or been willing to follow him as Lord." If the person professes faith, ask if she has been baptized. If not, this is the time to follow Christ's command and be baptized, signifying union with Christ. But regardless of the person's spiritual condition and the clarity of her profession of faith, she will need to hear more of the beauty, love, and holiness of God.

Scripture speaks of the radical change that we experience when we have been given new life in Christ. If there has been no obvious change, then there is a more important issue than sobriety. Scripture is clear: "Neither the sexually immoral nor idolaters. . . nor drunkards nor slanderers nor swindlers will inherit the kingdom of God" (1 Cor. 6:9–10). To avoid this fundamental concern of the human heart would certainly be unloving.

SECURE A COMMITMENT

You may or may not see the need to speak about conversion. But as the addict's story and purposes gradually unfold, it is valuable to secure his or her verbal commitment to work on the addiction and its roots. To use a phrase from C. S. Lewis, Jim's problem should function as "God's megaphone." God has gotten his attention and it is time to "listen. . . to a father's instruction; pay attention and gain understanding" (Prov. 4:1). After all, the stakes are high. Not only are some of Jim's relationships in jeopardy, but there are severe warnings in Scripture about his previously covert life. Presently, God has shown him great favor by treating him like a son and allowing the actions of his heart to be seen by himself and others. Now is the time to respond to God's grace. As the writer of Hebrews says, we must encourage one another "Today, so that none of you may be hardened by sin's deceitfulness" (Heb. 3:13).

Change, however, is frightening to many people. Although they may now realize that their addictive lifestyles were filled with bad consequences, they were at least familiar ones. Also, the addicts had a strategy to help them get through the week. Their idols helped when they were depressed or lonely, when they wanted to distance themselves from others, when they felt like a failure, or even when they wanted to celebrate. To give up something so central is not easy. In fact, if the addict thinks that he will never use his addictive substance again, he may be terrified and think it is impossible. This is why addiction programs focus on one day at a time.

In light of the nature of the problem and the urgency (as well as hope) in Scripture, consider asking the person to have a time of commitment, and to renew such a commitment every day. This is not to say that he must have a private altar call. Usually, addicts are *too* willing to respond to an altar call. They tend to do it instead of doing the hard work of fighting the daily battle. What you are trying to do is to verbalize God's vision. This is his plan, and, by grace, you want to follow him.

Addicts tend to be more schooled by secular perspectives than Scripture, so whenever possible, use specific Scripture as the basis for the commitment. For example, together with the person seeking help, find a passage that brings insight and hope.

[Christ] died for all, that those who live should no longer live for themselves but for him who died for them and was raised again. (2 Cor. 5:15)

You turned to God from idols to serve the living and true God, and to wait for his Son from heaven, whom he has raised from the dead—Jesus, who rescues us from the coming wrath. (1 Thess. 1:9–10)

The grace of God that brings salvation has appeared to all men. It teaches us to say "No" to ungodliness and worldly passions, and to live self-controlled, upright and godly lives in this present age, while we wait for the blessed hope—the glorious appearing of our great God and Savior, Jesus Christ, who gave himself for us to redeem us from all wickedness and to purify for himself a people that are his very own, eager to do what is good. (Titus 2:11–14)

His divine power has given us everything we need for life and godliness through our knowledge of him who called us by his own glory and goodness. (2 Peter 1:3)

These are just a few of the passages that ground us in the grace of Christ. Say them aloud often. But don't say them as if they were a magical mantra that will bring change if spoken enough. Instead, whenever addicts speak truth, they must learn to say it with faith. They must learn to say "Amen" to the truth.

BUILD WALLS OF PROTECTION

Another part of knowing people is to be aware of the walls that need to be erected against the object of their lusts.

Proverbs 25:28 succinctly demonstrates the need for these walls. "Like a city whose walls are broken down is a man who lacks self-control." The addict is like a defenseless city. Marauders go in and out at will and the inhabitants seem defenseless to respond. The task is to gradually build the walls so that there is ongoing protection.

As you help addicts erect these barriers, your goal will be more than simple sobriety. Your purpose is to lead them away from slavery to their addictive desires to freedom as they worship and obey the Lord of Lords. But early on, you will be content with very small (and sometimes mechanical) steps. With this in mind, an important step is to keep a distance between the addict and the addictive substance.

Listen, my son and be wise,
    and keep your heart on the right path.
Do not join those who drink too much wine
    or gorge themselves on meat,
for drunkards and gluttons become poor,
    and drowsiness clothes them in rags.
(Prov. 23:19–20)

Do they have the abused substance in their home? Do they keep a bottle hidden "just in case"? Is the adult bookstore on the way to work? Do they maintain contact with their drug-abusing friends? In adulterous relationships, someone might keep a key, some letters, or a picture. Drug abusers might retain their drug paraphernalia (such as pipes). In the back of their minds, they cannot conceive of life without the addictive substance, so they keep a memento—just in case.

This is where you want to help them to declare holy war on the idols of their hearts and the associated substance.

> When the LORD your God brings you into the land . . . Make no treaty with them [foreign idolaters], and show them no mercy. . . . Break down their altars, smash their sacred stones, cut down their Asherah poles, and burn their idols in the fire. (Deut. 7:1–5)

Any souvenirs are a potential snare.

In Jim's case, he was drinking everywhere, for any occasion. Especially potent snares, however, were business trips.

CHRISTIAN FRIEND: You mentioned that your business trips have always been times when you indulged yourself. No one really knew if you were buying food or alcohol. Do you have any business trips coming up soon?

JIM: Not for about three weeks.

CHRISTIAN FRIEND: Do you think that it could be dangerous?

JIM: Yes, no question about it. I am already afraid of it.

CHRISTIAN FRIEND: Jim, do you see the Spirit in that? You know more about your vulnerabilities. How about this? Let's come up with a plan that would provide some sort of wall of protection for you.

GIVE HOPE

If people are willing to follow Christ, there is immense hope: hope in God's forgiving grace, hope in God's love that is faithful even when we are not, and hope that God can give power so that we are no longer mastered by the addiction. Since resisting the cravings of the addiction is probably the foremost concern, perhaps the clearest passage on hope is 1 Corinthians 10:13–14.

> No temptation has seized you except what is common to man. And God is faithful; he will not let you be tempted beyond what you can bear. But when you are tempted, he will also provide a way out so that you can stand up under it. Therefore, my dear friends, flee from idolatry.

It might be worthwhile to read and discuss this passage together since it is one of the classic texts promising change in the face of idolatrous temptations. Temptations will definitely come, and they will most likely come soon. But it is an experience that is common to all Christians and is shared even by Ancient Israel. Furthermore, the temptation is resistible. God promises grace to flee from it.

The context of this passage is the idolatrous leanings of the Hebrews. Their struggle gives us a window into the human heart. They teach us that we have a natural tendency to set our hearts on ourselves, seeking short-term pleasure and security rather than the glory of God. Ultimately, this selfish pleasure-seeking is testing God, and it will eventually lead to our downfall.

To avoid this destruction, God promises that when external temptations come, he will give us a way of escape. In other words, there is no situation in which we are *compelled* to sin. We are promised the strength to run from temptation, whether it be from our imaginations, our physical desires, or a friend who just scored some dope.

What are some of these ways of escape? You could brainstorm on some possibilities.

- Remember that false worship has horrible consequences.
- Avoid old drinking or drugging buddies.
- Call a good friend for help.
- Run from temptation.

The passage climaxes with the summary, "So whether you eat or drink or whatever you do, do it all for the glory of God" (1 Cor. 10:31).

PRACTICAL THEOLOGY

This chapter marks the beginning of a holy war against our sinful desires. Be careful. The first few steps will set a course. Be honest. Assume that there is a struggle raging beneath the surface.

As You Face Your Own Addiction

1. Please, be honest with those who are partnering with you. You are more than able to tell your story in a way that will make you look pretty good—but it would be a lie. This is not about pleasing people. This is about life and death. This is about you coming out of darkness and into the light.

Perhaps the best way to express your faith right now is to tell someone that you are dying to get high. Such honesty and lack of concern for your own reputation would be a clear indication of the work of the Spirit.

2. Do you feel horrible? You blew it before God and people who love you. But be careful. This is not a time to feel unworthy of God's attention. The reality is that everyone is

unworthy of God's attention. The reality is also that we stand before God on the basis of Christ's record, not our own. When you put your faith in Jesus rather than yourself, you are given his righteousness and he takes your sin. If you feel like you have to do something to be OK before God, you don't understand the gospel. In fact, you are actually prideful. You think that there is something you can do to pay God back. Your work, however, is to believe. God has unlimited patience with his people. He never tires of inviting us back to himself. His love and acceptance are beyond what we will ever understand.

3. Choose one of the Scripture passages mentioned in this chapter that is especially suited to you right now. Meditate on it. Pray it. Teach it to someone else.

As You Help Someone Else

1. Are you willing to persevere? The person you are walking with doesn't need a consultant. He needs a brother who will stick with him, who will speak honestly, love, listen, rebuke, and pursue.

2. If you are the only person involved, begin to include others. You do not have all the gifts within yourself, and you won't always be available. Who else is the addict willing to bring into the circle?

3. Begin looking for some passages of Scripture that fit especially well. Rather than overloading the person with lots of Scripture, it is usually more helpful to meditate on one particular passage. You are looking for a bullet, not a shotgun.

7 | Knowing the Lord

> His divine power has given us everything we need
> for life and godliness through our knowledge of him who
> called us by his own glory and goodness.
>
> *2 PETER 1:3*

If the root problem of addictions is false worship, the answer is knowing the Lord, the One who deserves our worship. This is true theology, the study of God himself.

In the history of AA, you get the sense that this was the original intent. If alcoholics were to change, they had to worship something other than the bottle. For example, Step 7 of The Twelve Steps is "Humbly ask Him to remove our shortcomings." Yet the original wording of this step, which was changed right before the publication of the Big Book, read, *"On our knees* humbly ask Him to remove our shortcomings." In other words, there was at least the acknowledgment that the God who delivered us was a personal God, not an abstraction that could accommodate non-Christians and agnostics.

But AA could never quite get to the personal, triune God of Scripture. Since they did not acknowledge that intoxication and addiction were personal sin *against* the Holy God, there was ultimately no need to make our relationship with him central to change. As a result, AA deleted any reference suggesting that God must be the personal God, and they inserted the well-known "God as we understood him." It is easy to criticize AA on this most basic issue, but Scripture, as we would expect, first points the finger at us. When we examine ourselves, we find that the church can come perilously close to imitating AA's casualness in teaching about the Holy One. We too are in danger of using Scripture as a practical "how to" manual, relying on useful principles rather than focusing on the crux of the gospel message. The heart of Scripture is the true God's revelation of himself, leading us to obey him, depend on him, and live in reciprocal fellowship with him.

> I keep asking that the God of our Lord Jesus Christ, the glorious Father, may give you the Spirit of wisdom and revelation, so that you may know him better. (Eph. 1:17)

> All you have made will praise you, O LORD;
>   your saints will extol you.
> They will tell of the glory of your kingdom
>   and speak of your might,
> so that all men may know of your mighty acts.
> (Ps. 145:10–12)

> [The] knowledge of the Holy One is understanding. (Prov. 9:10)

> I want to know Christ and the power of his resurrection. (Phil. 3:10)

Here is where a biblical approach to addiction must radically depart from all other recovery strategies. A biblical approach to change focuses on someone other than ourselves. Change starts, proceeds, and ends with Jesus. We look to Jesus and away from ourselves.

This might sound strange, but you don't have to turn to the true God to stop your addiction! I'm sure you've met people who kicked addictions without turning to Christ in repentance and faith. You could probably find strategies that are not Christ-centered that would nevertheless keep you away from alcohol for the rest of your life. But God wants more. He wants us to know him, serve him, fear him, and love him. Somehow, God must be bigger than our own desires—so big that we worship him alone.

Here again is the basic idea: take ten looks to the true God for every one at ourselves. This biblical rhythm must become second nature. For some addicts, even those with orthodox beliefs, the first of these ten looks will be the first ever—it will be the turning away from sin and turning toward Christ that accompanies conversion. For others, it will not be the first time. Their hearts have turned away from the living God, and now they must turn again and fix their eyes and thoughts back on Jesus (Heb. 3:1; 12:2).

WARNING: JESUS HAS BEEN DOMESTICATED

The name of Jesus is well known in the United States. Polls are always telling us that most of us believe that Jesus actually existed. Name recognition, however, is different from every knee bowing before him. "Holy" and "Lord" are conveniently absent from many discussions. We avoid the fact that Jesus was the preacher who spoke more about hell than any other. In most conversations he is more a magical pussycat than the divine Aslan who, as C. S. Lewis wrote, "is not safe, but he is good." The most obvious way we can be handicapped in this discussion is to be tempted to domesticate Jesus. "Like an ethereal Martha Stewart, Jesus seems ready to make your home His home."[1]

To keep Jesus safe and inviting, some people conveniently attribute to Jesus all things nice and to the Father all wrath and displeasure. Or, at least, Jesus loves but the Father is angry. Either way—domesticating the triune God or only Jesus—our understanding of God's self-revelation will be truncated at best, and it will be natural to limit his jurisdiction to an ever-shrinking spiritual realm rather than to proclaim him Lord of all.

Consider the discussion on unconditional love. We are accustomed to teaching that God's love toward us is unconditional, but "unconditional" flattens and domesticates God's character. It suggests a benevolent, smiling therapist whose facial expression rarely changes, regardless of what you say. Or it suggests the mother who—and I actually saw this—watched her son push and mock another child and then said, "That probably wasn't a very nice thing to do" as they left for a water ice. Stern words? Discipline that hurts? Never. It could damage his self-confidence. And what about his ADD, and the teacher that didn't like him in school, and the rejection he experienced by the older boy in the neighborhood, and . . . ?

Little did this mother realize that her practical theology was showing. Her Jesus was unconditional love, which translated into unconditional approval. She was making an effort to imitate her version of him. In her practical theology, Jesus wasn't seeking to change us; he was just trying to be nice. Therefore, her job was to offer warm affection to her son, not rebuke. And what about the other boy? Her lack of compassion for him suggests that she believes Jesus to be her family's personal guardian and lover: "Jesus loves me and my son." What happens to others is not her concern.

Jesus, however, can be angered and grieved by stubborn hearts (Mark 3:5). He severely rebuked his own disciples (Mark 8:33). The mind and emotions of God are *his* mind and emotions. His responses toward those who were both for him and against him were rich and lively. They cannot be contained by the word *unconditional,* especially when the word suggests that there is never any disapproval of a person's behavior. If there were no disapproval of our behavior, there would have been no cross.

Unconditional love or *unconditional approval*, therefore, does more than flatten and domesticate God's love. It also misrepresents it. God's love has an immense condition. It is bought at an astoundingly great price. The condition for his love was his own death and resurrection. The reason Jesus persuasively forgives Peter and invites him to care for the flock was because Peter was "in him [Christ] before the creation of the world" (Eph. 1:4). By faith, Peter was in Christ, intimately associated with his death and resurrection in such a way that he had received their benefits. Suddenly, the love of Jesus is not domesticated.

So does that mean that Jesus' love is not unconditional? If we say that Jesus' love is unconditional, we flatten and misrepresent the character of his love. If we say that Jesus' love is *not* unconditional, it seems like we are veering off into a fear-based response to God. That is, we have to measure up to his conditions before he loves us. But God's love is a deeper love. It extends to us when we are thoroughly undeserving of his grace and mercy. It extended to us even when we were his enemies. It is a sophisticated love whose definition is summarized by Christ's death on the cross.

> Perhaps we could call it "contraconditional" love. Contrary to the conditions normally required to know God's blessing, he has blessed me because his *Son* fulfilled the conditions. Contrary to my due, he loves me. And now I can begin to change, not to earn love, but *because* of love.[2]

God's love for us must never be reduced to the abstract and ambiguous "unconditional love." Rather, "This is love: not that we loved God, but that he loved us and sent his Son as an atoning sacrifice for our sins" (1 John 4:10). The love of Jesus is a very concrete love; it is always tied to the gospel itself, his cross and his resurrection. It is one thing to know that someone smiles on us; it is another to know that behind that smile was the greatest sacrifice that could possibly have been offered. One smile makes you feel temporarily warmed; the other leads you to gratitude and worship.

HOLY LOVE, HOLY JUSTICE

One way to see Jesus more clearly is to couple his love with the word *holy*. The character of Jesus Christ is often summarized as love. With this there can be no disagreement. "Be imitators of God, therefore, as dearly loved children and live a life of love, just as Christ loved us and gave himself up for us as a fragrant offering and sacrifice to God" (Eph. 5:1–2). But the word *holy* tells us that this love is nothing ordinary.

Holy is sometimes defined as "set apart," "uncontaminated," or "separate from." For example, the Sabbath was holy. It was set apart from the other days of the week (Ex. 20:8). The Holy Place in the temple was separate from the rest of the temple (Ex. 26:33). The people of Israel were to distinguish between the holy and the common (Lev. 10:10). They were to avoid the unclean and they were not to touch those things that were holy (Num. 4:15). The law of Moses was all about holiness. As such, there were partitions, walls, curtains, and prohibitions to stay away. God and the things that belonged to him were different. They were not ordinary and they were not treated as though they were.

All these holiness laws were intended to show us something about the character of God. They show us that *God is God, and there is no one like him.* He created the earth *by himself* (Isa. 44:24). He alone is morally pure. There are no other gods like him (Isa. 40:25), and we ourselves are not like him.

Holy Love

The book of Hosea illustrates this categorical difference between God and ourselves. Hosea contains the parallel stories of Hosea and his wife Gomer and God and his betrothed people. The story first follows Gomer's incorrigible adultery and Hosea's extraordinary love for her. It is even more extraordinary given the Old Testament context. Today, although some couples stay together after adultery, divorce is common. In Old Testament times, when a wife was a known adulteress, divorce was almost mandatory. Reconciliation would have been immensely shameful for the husband and his family, so divorce or death were the options. Undoubtedly, Hosea too would have divorced his wife, except that he was commanded by the Lord to be a replica of God's love.

By Hosea 11, the focus is on God and his relationship with his people. The text recounts God's redeeming love and the people's determination to keep turning to other gods. We are waiting for God to say, "Enough is enough." Even God himself can't be expected to remain faithful in such circumstances. Yet God does remain faithful with a holy love.

"How can I give you up, Ephraim?
How can I hand you over, Israel?
How can I treat you like Admah?
How can I make you like Zeboiim?
My heart is changed within me;
all my compassion is aroused.
I will not carry out my fierce anger,
nor will I turn and devastate Ephraim.
For I am God, and not man—
the Holy One among you.
I will not come in wrath." (Hos. 11:8–9)

In other words, God's love is not like our own. For that matter, neither is his power, justice, beauty, anger, or sorrow.

Instead, they are holy. Although the word *love* is used with both God and people, there is a great gap between God's love and our own.

All this seems self-evident. Of course God is not like us. He is the Creator; we are his creatures. He is divine; we are human. He is perfect; we are sinful. But the sheer number of Old Testament holiness laws (as in Leviticus) suggests that God's holiness is too quickly forgotten. God embedded reminders of his character in what his people ate, how they dressed, where they went, how they planted their fields, how they cut their hair, and when and with whom they had sex. In other words, the Hebrews needed hourly reminders of the character of God. Apparently, we can never have enough reminders of God's extraordinary character. We can never meditate on it too much.

What does this have to do with addictions? Addicts have already proven to themselves that there are things in this world that are more attractive to them than God himself, whether it is comfort, power, pleasure, or reputation. Whatever they have worshipped, however, cannot compare to the God who has revealed himself as the One who always says, "I love you," before we say it to him. More pointedly, although we know God, we are like Gomer, who went her own way. We pursued our own desires and the destruction that accompanied them. Meanwhile, God pursued us and literally bought us back from the slave market to be his. As a result, now we live for him who died for us, rather than for ourselves (2 Cor. 5:15).

HOLY MEANS "JESUS IS NOT ORDINARY"

The book of Hebrews continues with the theme of holiness. The difference is that Jesus Christ himself has become the tangible summary of God's holiness. The writer is trying to arouse the new Christians from their Old Testament slumber. With the church slipping back into old ways of thinking, the writer relentlessly proclaims the supremacy of Christ. He doesn't use the word *holy* throughout the book. However, the idea of "greater than," "better than," or "superior to" is the continual theme. The writer doesn't even begin with the usual formalities. Instead, he plunges right into his point: Whatever you compare him to, Jesus is superior.

- He is greater than the prophets (1:2).
- He is heir of all things (1:2).
- He made the universe (1:2).
- He is the radiance of God's glory—not a mere reflection like ourselves (1:3).
- He sustains all things (1:3).
- He provided purification of sins (1:3).
- He sat at the right hand of God, where he is actively ruling (1:3).

And this is just his introduction! With such a persuasive appeal, it becomes almost natural to fix our thoughts on Jesus (3:1), but the writer has just begun. He continues by reminding us that Jesus was greater than Moses and greater than the high priest. In fact, he was so much greater that the high priests paid him their tithes.

This high priestly work is the center of Hebrews (chaps. 7–10). The writer is asking, "Do you think that the work of Christ was somehow ordinary?" "Do you think his priesthood was like the daily, ho-hum sacrifices of animals and firstfruits on the altar?" "Do you think it was just a nice gesture that makes a few refinements in our lives?" No. The sacrifice of Christ was the holy sacrifice. Jesus made a *better* covenant (7:22; 8:6). He is a *permanent* priest (7:24). He is able to save *completely* (7:25). He *always* intercedes for his people; his sacrifice was *holy, blameless, and pure* (7:26). It was *once for all;* he offered *himself*

(9:14), and he sat down as a way to say, "It is finished" (8:1). This is the perfect sacrifice that takes away sin, and there is even more to come for those who wait for his return (9:28). How can we ever doubt that we have been brought near to God and fully forgiven?

This is the thing of first importance: The holiness of God demonstrated in the death and resurrection of Christ. Nothing can compare to it. It must be the final answer to everything. Somehow, the psychological distress and problems in living that plague us all must find their resolution in this gospel.

HOLINESS FORGOTTEN

In what way is God's holiness forgotten today? A few illustrations come immediately to mind.

Over the last thirty years, one of the remarkable changes within the Christian community has been the fact that we not only acknowledge anger with God, we tacitly approve it. Throughout history, people have wrestled with God's hand in our suffering, and some people would harbor anger against him because they deemed him unfair or unjust (Jonah, for example). Rarely, however, would such anger be voiced. When it was, there was always a sense that lightning could strike momentarily. Yet now, under the banner of openness and "God can take it," it is acceptable to be angry with God.

What has happened? We are a generation that is more interested in "how to" than "for whom and to whom." Also, we have emphasized our relationship with God in a way that can't carry the weight of God's holiness. Of course, we could equally err by emphasizing God's transcendence and differentness. The reality is that, in the person of Christ, God has come close to his people and become like them. Yet this in itself is holy. No other god would ever stoop so low as to be intimately associated with unclean humans and even become the servant. But our humanizing of God usually means that we also minimize his holiness. We treat him like as would treat any other person, as if he were a brother who makes us angry but then it blows over. After all, if another person brought hardship into our lives, we might be angry with him or her. Therefore, if God brings suffering, we might be angry with him for meting out such harsh treatment.

But God is God. He is the king, and we are his servants (Rom. 6:22). We are his, and he has the right to bring whatever he wants into our lives. And who are we to stand in judgment of God's justice? Isn't that saying that *we* are the epitome of justice rather than saying that God's justice is holy, higher than our own? Who are we to critique God's love, especially when we are witnesses of the cross? God's love is a holy love. We cannot compare it to the love of a person. Instead, it is greater than anything we can imagine. If we don't see it in our immediate circumstances, it is because we are equating love with getting what we want. God's love, however, always has a larger view. It is more sophisticated—deeper and more multifaceted—than we know.

The corrective is to keep the cross and resurrection in view. The cross displays holy love. The cross also indicates that sin is not something to be trifled with. It called down the wrath of God, and demanded a payment that we could never make ourselves. Only the cross can speak simultaneously about holy justice and holy love.

CHRIST: THE CENTER OF HISTORY

Jesus then is the center. He is the embodiment of holy love and holy justice. He is the holy lover. And he wants us to know it. He is the dinner guest who talks about himself. He wants all eyes on him. In someone whose life was characterized by humility and love for others, this may seem strange. A person of humility takes the lesser seat and exalts others. Jesus did these things, but because he is the exalted One who alone deserves all glory, he also called attention to himself. It was God's plan to glorify himself through the Son. To focus our attention on anything else would be to want less than the very best. Moreover, it would be idolatrous, since it would be centered on something created rather than the Creator-Redeemer.[3]

So Jesus taught people about himself.

"I am the bread of life." (John 6:35)

"I am the gate; whoever enters through me will be saved." (John 10:9)

"I am the way and the truth and the life. No one comes to the Father except through me." (John 14:6)

"I am the vine . . . apart from me you can do nothing." (John 15:5)

After his death and resurrection, Jesus became even more obviously self-referential. He made it clear that all of history had been pointing to him. While walking with the Emmaus disciples, the risen Lord taught that all of Scripture was about him (Luke 24:27–32). In fact, not only did David, Moses, Abraham, Isaac, and many others prefigure the coming of Jesus, they also looked for him. They greeted the promises of the Messiah from afar. The reason Jesus was not immediately recognized as Messiah was because, even with all Scripture pointing to him, no one could have anticipated something as absolutely glorious as the gospel of Jesus. They were looking for a military general; what they got was the kingdom of heaven.

The Apostle Paul's Exaltation of Christ

All Scripture, of course, exalts Jesus Christ. Some Scripture does it very openly. For example, the apostle Paul's letter to the Ephesians doesn't seem to be devoted to any particular problem in the church, so it is an opportunity for him to run with his passions. And his passion, of course, is Christ. He begins with praise because of Christ (1:3). He says that we have every spiritual blessing lavished on us in Christ (1:3). We have been chosen, predestined, and adopted through Christ (1:4–5). We have forgiveness of sins in Christ (1:7), and Christ is the rallying point of all human history (1:10). Before he finishes his short letter, he will have written the name of Jesus Christ over sixty times.

Paul is the consummate counselor. He speaks with great affection for his people, and speaks lively doctrine consistently coupled with application. He knows their weakness, sins, and vulnerabilities, so he gives warnings, and he prays all the time. In fact, he prays throughout the letter, exhorting his readers to pray ceaselessly, and asking them to pray for him.

As we seek to help people with addictions, one characteristic of Paul's thought deserves special emphasis: the way he weaves Christ and Christian living together. Paul's mind was shaped by Scripture, so this book has an Old Testament feel to it, only better. In the beginning, it imitates the Psalms in its recitation of Christ's glory and its offering of praise. In Ephesians, Paul is absolutely effusive in recounting the glories of God in Christ. Since he knows that he has witnessed what the Old Testament kings and prophets only hoped for, Paul has even more reason to begin everything with praise and remembrance of who God is and what he has done.*

After an extended time of praise, the apostle finally, almost reluctantly, continues. He recounts how we had been dead in our sins, but now, because of God's great love for us, we have

---

*As a conceptual help, Ridderbos observes that Paul's letters begin with the indicative, indicating what God has done, and then move to the imperative, telling us how to live in light of the cross. See Herman N. Ridderbos, *Paul: An Outline of His Theology* (Grand Rapids: Eerdmans, 1975).

been raised with Christ and deluged with blessings. He reminds us that we had been separated from Christ and his people, but in his death Jesus abolished the divisions to unite a motley group of Jews and Gentiles into one people. When Paul gets to chapter 4, he begins to specify how to have this oneness, and how to build up the other members of the body.

At this point he shows us that all theology is practical or applied theology. The heights of praise and our union in Christ lead us into small steps of obedience. Paul finds doctrine and life impossible to separate. One without the other is inconceivable, like the body without the spirit. This explains why the principles for living are always tied to Christ.

> Live a life worthy of the calling [*in Christ*] that you have received. (Eph. 4:1)

> Be completely humble and gentle; be patient, bearing with one another in love. Make every effort to keep the *unity of the Spirit* through the bond of peace. There is one body and one Spirit . . . *one Lord.* (4:2–5)

> Speak truthfully. . . . Do not let the sun go down while you are still angry, and do not give the devil a foothold [in the corporate body that is united *in Christ*]. (4:25–27)

> Do not let any unwholesome talk come out of your mouths. . . . And *do not grieve the Holy Spirit of God.* (4:29, 30)

> Be kind and compassionate to one another, forgiving each other, *just as in Christ God forgave you.* (4:32)

> Wives, submit to your husbands *as to the Lord.* (5:22)

> Husbands, love your wives, *just as Christ* loved the church. (5:25)

Children, obey your parents *in the Lord.* (6:1)

Slaves, obey your earthly masters with respect . . . *just as you would obey Christ.* (6:5)

Given the connection between who Jesus is and how we should live, the Puritan John Owen wrote, "Holiness is nothing but the implanting, writing and realizing of the gospel in our souls."[4]

When principles or steps wander from Christ himself, they become self-serving guidelines. They make our marriages, families, friendships, and work go better, but the goal is our own betterment more than the glory of God. Yes, it is a good thing to align yourself with God's way of living. There is a certain wisdom in it even when it is divorced from the fear of the Lord and the knowledge of Christ. But for God's people, the motive should self-consciously be for Christ.

"Be good" and "Do right" are fine messages, but when they stand alone they have more in common with the Boy Scouts' Handbook than Scripture. Remember that in the Bible, "This is who God is and what he has done" always precedes "This is what you must do." Action follows our knowledge of God and trust in him. It is as if God has said to us, "Now that you have seen who I am, you will want to love me in return. This is how you can love me." And then God teaches us how to love him.

PRACTICAL THEOLOGY

Now, what do we do with this when we are trying to fight an addiction or help someone else fight?

As You Face Your Own Addiction

1. A long-term heavy drinker had come to Christ and been sober for about eight months. But he was starting to think that knowing Christ didn't matter. When he compared his strug-

gles to the struggles of those who followed AA *without* putting their faith in Christ, he saw very little practical difference. He still struggled with a desire for alcohol; so did they. He still had problems in his marriage and family; so did they. In fact, he knew of other recovering drunks who seemed to be doing much better than he was. Being a Christian didn't work, it seemed to him. Why take a path that only seemed to make life a little harder? You had all the same problems but a few more laws and a lot more guilt.

His concerns make sense at first. Scripture makes no guarantee that life will be immediately easier when we say, "Jesus is Lord." On the contrary, suffering is never far from the Christian life and "taking up our cross" is a way of life. But after you have really considered Jesus Christ, the question changes. It is not, "What works?" It is, "Whom do I worship?"

"What works?" reveals our theology, our view of God. Doesn't this question suggest that we think God is a celestial genie who makes everything better? But when we really know God, we worship and love him when our lives are comfortable and when they are difficult. And doesn't "What works?" focus on ourselves rather than God? It sounds like a person trying Jesus as one tries acupuncture—for what he hoped to get. What's missing is an awareness of desperate spiritual need and the knowledge that Jesus is the reigning King. We sound like fair weather friends who stick close in the summer to use a friend's pool, but then wander off in the fall to use another friend's full-court basketball court.

It is natural and appropriate to want relief from difficult emotions, circumstances, and cravings. But when we make deals with the Lord such as, "If I will be good and pray, then you change my circumstances," we should repent of our lust for relief. We didn't want Jesus; we wanted comfort and personal satisfaction.

This struggling man must first know Christ. He must know that there is no other source of living water, forgiveness, and life itself. He must learn what it means to walk in humility with his God. He also must learn something of God's ways. Although God could certainly change us immediately and give us instantly pure hearts, God has determined that change and growth will come gradually. It will come as we learn to trust him and do battle with our sin. This is called progressive sanctification.

Why doesn't God change us instantly? Why doesn't he remove the afflictions in our lives? It is enough for us to know that God is God and simply trust him. But notice one practical advantage of this daily battle. It teaches us to cry out to him and rely on him instead of ourselves—or our addictive substance. Faith and trust are qualities God prizes. Without daily struggles there would be no compelling reason to call out to him and say, "I need you," which is a definition of faith.

2. A father of three struggled with daily heroin abuse but is now really "working the program." After an in-patient rehab where he detoxed and had a chance to consider his life without the intrusion of mind-altering drugs, he came home and attended secular and Christian meetings. Between church and AA, his dangerous times were accounted for. But he says that it is the mornings, before everyone in the house was awake, that were his most important times. When the sun is coming up, he could be found walking in the woods or reading Scripture on the porch. Either way, he was seeking God, meditating on his greatness and sacrificial love, talking to him, confessing sin, and rejoicing that he was forgiven. This is the real reason why he is sober.

3. You believe lies about God. Guaranteed. You think he can't see all things; you think he doesn't care; you think that he reluctantly forgives; you think that he is far away; you think that he loves many people but not you. Don't assume that you know him. Read the Gospels. In Jesus you will find God's fullest revelation of himself. Pray that God would teach you more and more about himself. Pray Ephesians 1:17–19 and

3:16–21. Read some good books on the character of God—always have one book that you are working through. Here are a few to get you started.

Knowing God by J. I. Packer
Desiring God by John Piper
Books by Max Lucado

4. Ask a Christian friend or your pastor, "What is your favorite book about God?"

As You Help Someone Else

Helpers need the same thing as those who need help. Since what we have—the risen Lord—has led to unceasing praise in the heavens, we want to communicate that there is nothing ordinary about him. We want to know Jesus in such a way that we are led to trust and worship him. We want to talk about Jesus in such a way that people are surprised and awed. We must know Jesus as much more than a helper. He is the source of our very life.

When you meet with addicts who want to change—or even those who don't—look for ways to draw attention to Jesus more than anything else.

1. Suggest, "Next time we get together, let's begin by discussing what we are learning about Jesus. If we aren't learning anything, maybe we could read Scripture together and simply pray that we would know him."

2. Ask the simple question, "What does your present struggle have to do with Jesus Christ?" You may not always have the answer to that question, but you know it is the right question.

3. Look for Christ in Scripture. Tell at least one person how you saw Jesus in the Word.

I am amazed to read about how unclean people wanted to touch Jesus and he them (Luke 7:11–15, 36–50;

8:40–48). When you remember that the Old Testament said that unclean objects would make you unclean, this is really amazing.

4. Be changed by the Sunday sermon. Take notes, meditate on it, and ask the pastor for help if you have problems connecting the sermon to your life. Then pass on what you've learned.

Our attitude when we minister to others is this: What Christ has done is so big it affects everything.

5. Pray that you would know Jesus. If we can be confident of anything, it is that God is not stingy in giving us the knowledge of himself. This is what we need, and this is what brings him glory. We are simply called to ask and receive.

Everyone knows that if we ask, it will be given us (Matt. 7:7; Luke 11:9). But we have all had the experience of asking for something and not getting it. As a result, there are times when we pray with less confidence, boldness, and persistence. But Scripture is adamant: If we ask, we get! The question is, For what should we ask?

The passage in Luke 11 answers this for us.

"If you then, though you are evil, know how to give good gifts to your children, how much more will your Father in heaven *give the Holy Spirit* to those who ask him!" (v.13)

Ask for the Spirit of Christ and you will get it. If we are not seeing the Spirit of Christ being poured out, it is usually because we haven't asked.

Fearing the Lord

Taste and see that the Lord is good;
blessed is the man who takes refuge in him.
Fear the LORD, you his saints,
for those who fear him lack nothing.

PSALM 34:8-9

As we grow in knowing the Lord, we do something. We respond. We can't *help* but respond. If you've just watched your favorite team win a championship, you shout. You honk your horn. You tell others. (You *don't* drink.) If you have just had someone say, "Yes, I would love to marry you," you call your friends. You dance around in joy. If we respond to these events, how much more should we expect to respond when we discover that the Creator of the universe is the Lover of our souls?

Scripture is full of teaching on how we are to respond to Jesus, who is "the radiance of God's glory and the exact representation of his being" (Heb. 1:3). We are told to trust him, obey him, magnify his name, worship him, love him, imitate him, and follow him. Most of these probably sound familiar to you. One response that might not sound as familiar—and you might prefer to keep it that way—is that we are told to fear him.

The fear of the Lord is actually essential to our response to Jesus. Without it, we will persist on a foolish path that leads away from God toward death and grief. The book of Proverbs, which is dedicated to teaching God's people how to live well, says that the fear of the Lord is the beginning of all true knowledge (Prov. 9:10). A life erected on any other foundation will not stand.

Typically, the first reaction to an exhortation to fear the Lord is that, at best, it is a primitive, Old Testament way of scaring people into obedience. In fact, even Scripture itself counsels us not to be motivated by the fear of God but the love of God (1 John 4:8). Why revert to such heavy-handed tactics?

The basic idea behind the fear of the Lord, however, is much broader than our modern understanding of fear. While the holiness of God will leave many knees knocking when Jesus comes again, a mature fear of the Lord is more akin to awe, devotion, and worship. It is a response that says, "Your glory is irresistible." "In your presence, nothing else matters. You are all that I desire." Furthermore, it is a response that is active. It does something. It is not simply a passive devotion; it follows Christ in obedience. *It searches out his will and can't wait to do it.*

Stop for a moment: "It searches out his will and can't wait to do it." Here is the ultimate protection against addictions. How often have you prayed for such a heart? Perhaps we pray, "Lord, take away my craving." But we don't pray that we would be captive to Christ, wanting his desires above all else. Our independent spirit shuns subservience. In other words, what the fear of the Lord is selling, we don't always want. As C. S. Lewis observes,

> We are half-hearted creatures, fooling about with drink and sex and ambition when infinite joy is offered to us, like an ignorant child who wants to go on making mud pies in a slum because he cannot imagine what is meant by the offer of a holiday at the sea. We are far too easily pleased.[1]

We were created to know the fear of the Lord. It should feel natural and right to us. It should feel as pleasant to us as being deeply loved. But first, our imaginations must be stirred. Since we no longer remember what it is like to have a holiday by the sea, the Lord is willing to woo us into desiring the fear of the Lord. He asks us to consider how wonderful life with it would be.

The fear of the LORD adds length to life. (Prov. 10:27)

He who fears the LORD has a secure fortress,
    and for his children it will be a refuge. (Prov. 14:26)

The fear of the LORD is a fountain of life,
    turning a man from the snares of death. (Prov. 14:27)

The fear of the LORD teaches a man wisdom.
    (Prov. 15:33)

Through the fear of the LORD a man avoids evil.
    (Prov. 16:6)

The fear of the LORD leads to life:
    Then one rests content, untouched by trouble.
    (Prov. 19:23)

Fear the LORD, you his saints,
    for those who fear him lack nothing. (Ps. 34:9)

Imagine having drug cravings subdued by the joy of knowing and obeying Christ. Imagine having temptations lose their allure because there is more pleasure in walking humbly with our God. Imagine waking up and strategizing how to please the God who loves you rather than where you will get your next drink. This would be freedom. Sound impossible? It isn't.

FATHERS, NOT TYRANTS,
TEACH THE FEAR OF THE LORD

With these great blessings in mind, it is obvious that the fear of the Lord should *not* be thought of as a response to a tyrannical ruler. Instead, it is our response to a loving and generous father who wants to give his children the best of gifts. In biblical times, the father had two fundamental concerns. One was that his children learn to honor and respect him, upholding the family name. The other was that the children be blessed so that the family line could continue for generations to come. The fear of the Lord is best understood in this context. It is the way we honor our Heavenly Father, and the means through which our Father blesses us.

For example, notice how these elements are present in one of the most significant episodes in all of Scripture. When the Israelites were liberated from Egypt, the God of Heaven was reminding them that they were his own possession, his children. Then, while they were leaving Egypt, the Father's instruction in the fear of the Lord began immediately. In Exodus 14, God told the departing Israelites to double back. He actually commanded them to go back in the direction from which they came! To make matters worse, they were to camp with their backs to the sea. Why?

For their first lesson in the fear of the Lord. They were not ready for their journey. They had gone for many years without having a clear, corporate knowledge of God, and their faith was weak. They were not prepared to revere and love their God and Father. As proof of this, when they saw mighty Pharaoh and his army, the Hebrews immediately stated that their slavery was preferable to following the God of Moses (vv. 10–12), a response that should sound vaguely familiar to anyone who has tasted of the true God but preferred his idolatrous substances.

> They [the Israelites] were terrified and cried out to the
> LORD. They said to Moses, "Was it because there were
> no graves in Egypt that you brought us to the desert
> to die? What have you done to us by bringing us out
> of Egypt? Didn't we say to you in Egypt, 'Leave us
> alone; let us serve the Egyptians'? It would have been
> better for us to serve the Egyptians than to die in the
> desert!"

Indeed, addicts are not alone. The Israelites wanted to go back to Egypt; so do we. We take a few tentative steps away from the land we knew well and then, at the first sign of rejection, failure, stress, or hardship, we can't think of anything but returning. Maybe our addiction was bondage, but it was familiar. We knew the terrain, and what to do when we were there. We didn't have to step out in faith to try something new. We forget that all those things were true because we were hopeless.

A return to slavery looks foolish when we see it in others. We want to yell out and remind them that there was nothing back in Egypt but misery. But the moment it feels like *we* are in the wilderness, our vision of the Lord is blurred and our old idolatry suddenly looks appealing again.

We can be thankful that we have a God of "unlimited patience" (1 Tim. 1:16). In the Israelites' case, they needed another opportunity to simply watch God in action. "Stand firm and you will see the deliverance the LORD will bring you today. The Egyptians you see today you will never see again. The LORD will fight for you; you need only to be still" (Ex. 14:13–14). God was giving them front row seats for a display of power that would be forever etched in their minds.

The first wonder was that God parted the Red Sea and the people crossed the previously impassable channel on dry ground. The second wonder was that God brought confusion on the Egyptian army when they tried to follow. The third

wonder was that the entire army of Pharaoh—who was considered a god—was defeated. There was not one survivor.

The desired result was accomplished. The people were
amazed. They "feared the LORD and put their trust in him"
(14:31).

Can you imagine? We have many hardships in life, and each
one can become an occasion for temptation. What are some
of the hardships that leave you more vulnerable to addictions?
Now imagine a God who is bigger than these hardships. His
basic command is, "Stand firm and watch." Your work is simple: "Believe in the one he [God the Father] has sent" (John
6:29). To do this you must learn to maintain a vision of Christ,
seeing him as the Holy One who rules and the Holy One who
loves. As the Hebrews had festivals to remember the mighty
acts of God, so we must have festivals of remembrance every
day. The story of the exodus from Egypt can be one of the stories we remember.

Following the lesson at the Red Sea, the people traveled
to Horeb or Mt. Sinai. With a display that overwhelmed the
senses, the Lord assembled all the people for one purpose:
"so that they may learn to revere [fear] me as long as they live
in the land and may teach . . . their children" (Deut. 4:10). This
display of God's holiness was so overwhelming that the Israelites pleaded with Moses to be a mediator on their behalf.
While they felt blessed to be liberated and adopted by the only
true God, the people were also terrified to come close to him.
They had already seen his power, even to the point of taking
the firstborn of Egypt, and they knew that they were no more
deserving of living in his presence than the Egyptians. They
understood that a mediator was necessary, and their Father
was pleased by their request. He gave them a mediator in
Moses (Deut. 5:23–29).

Likewise, our knowledge of the Lord must be such that
we know that a mediator is absolutely essential. We, too,
should be tempted to run and hide when we find ourselves

in the throne room of the King. Knowing the holiness of the Father should compel us to seek a mediator, and be even *more* in awe that the Father has supplied one before we asked. Jesus Christ is the better Moses, whose mediation between the Father and ourselves is so complete that we can now go up to the mountain. In fact, the Father now comes down from his mountain throne and abides with us, promising that he will never leave.

Continue to imagine. Isn't it true that addicts run away from God? We run because we want to serve ourselves and our own desires. We run because we are afraid to face the Holy One. Imagine what it would be like to know God so well that you ran *toward* him. Imagine him being so holy that you couldn't resist trusting, loving, and obeying him. Imagine if you saw him as he truly is—your only hope, satisfaction, and joy. Imagine knowing God in such a way that the happiness you found in idols seems like mud pies in comparison. It is possible.

FORGIVENESS AND FEAR

One of the problems with the perspective that addictions are a disease is that it leaves no room for this kind of fear of the Lord. A god who helps us to be strong in the face of illness is not the same as the God whose holiness reveals our sin, who shows us our desperate need for a mediator, restores our relationship with him, and empowers us to live as holy children.

Holiness is key. Without the knowledge of our Father's holiness and our response of reverence, everything about God becomes ordinary. God's works are viewed as just a little better than the actions of good people. For example, when we think about how God forgives us, we are thankful but we are not awed. The psalmist, on the other hand, had a keen sense of what really happened when he was forgiven. Psalm 130 says, "If you, O LORD, kept a record of sins, O Lord, who could stand? But with you there is forgiveness; therefore you are feared" (vv. 3–4).

How can forgiveness provoke fear? By leading us to realize that we have not committed a few unfortunate acts of unkindness toward other people. Instead, we have been rebels who have gone out of our way to avoid submitting to God. We have gone our own way, against God and for our own desires.

If someone did that to us, and if everything that rebel had was a gift we had personally given, we would not extend forgiveness easily. If we were feeling especially benevolent, we *might* offer forgiveness—but only after the rebel paid a huge, life-long penalty; only after the rebel suffered. But God is holy; he is not like human beings. His forgiveness is unprecedented, unexplainable, and unnatural. It is complete, and demands nothing of us except that we become his children and carry on the family name. In light of this, his forgiveness provokes us to a reverential fear.

Do you see how the fear of the Lord is a good thing? It is not the same as being afraid. It is a natural response to the true knowledge of God.

You would think that this kind of holy forgiveness would leave us jumping up and down with joy. But that is not always the case.

> CHRISTIAN FRIEND: Do you really believe that you are forgiven?
>
> ADDICT: I believe God forgives me, but I just can't forgive myself. I really feel bad about what happened.

Here is some of the best news that anyone could ever hear, and reactions are mixed. Some people are indifferent to the fact that Jesus forgives. Others say that they can't believe it. They can believe that other people are forgiven, but they can't believe God forgives them. So you say it again.

Jesus forgives. Turn to him; he delights in forgiving. It makes him famous when people understand that he forgives in ways no one could have guessed.

When reactions continue to be less than enthusiastic, you try again, then again. At some point, however, you realize that more teaching or better illustrations are not the answer. What is not always evident at first is that when we talk about forgiveness of sin, we have entered into the very heart of spiritual warfare.

If someone who has turned to Christ is either unmoved by the forgiveness of sins or is not convinced of it, you need to make this the issue. Not only does forgiveness teach us that God is holy and to be feared, it is also the foundation for all spiritual growth (and sobriety). Consider this: Is it possible to grow in faith when we believe that we are not forgiven? When we are guilty, we don't want to trust God: we want to run from him. How can you have a relationship with someone you think is angry with you?

Because an understanding of God's forgiving grace is so crucial to growth and change, you may find that this will be a fierce battleground. The fear of the Lord does not come naturally. It is here that Satan may want dominion, because if one-time addicts fail to grasp complete forgiveness, they can easily fall into despair and look to drugs as a temporary savior. As 2 Peter 1:9 indicates, "But if anyone does not have them [the fruits of godliness], he is nearsighted and blind, *and has forgotten that he has been cleansed from his past sins.*"

There can be a number of reasons for a lack of assurance about forgiving grace.[2]

1. Perhaps the person has never really professed faith in Christ. He may know the facts, and be able to say that the facts are true, but he has never trusted fully in Christ's righteousness. As John Murray said, "Faith is knowledge passing into conviction, and it is conviction passing into confidence."[3]

Knowledge of forgiveness must be grounded in a personal trust in Christ.

2. Perhaps the person thinks he is a good person who occasionally does bad things. And as a good person, given enough time, he can pay God back for his own sins. In other words, he doesn't see the seriousness of his sin. If his sin is truly a crime against God, only God can pardon through the blood of Jesus.

3. Perhaps the person just can't believe that she could be so loved. If this is the case, consider the amazing story of Hosea and Gomer. As we have seen, this is perhaps the most dramatic illustration of the gospel in Scripture. God reveals himself as One who is profoundly moved by his love for his people. He is not a distant God who stoically observes his people, but one who desires to turn away from his wrath and pour out his love on those he has called to himself.

If she still just can't believe, the treatment is to confess this as sin. This may sound as if you are hitting her when she is down, but consider what is really being said. She is guilty of the sin of unbelief. This is the same as calling God a liar. God says, "If we confess our sins, he [God] is faithful and just and will forgive us our sins and purify us from all unrighteousness" (1 John 1:9). She is saying, "Lord, I don't believe you." She must repent and say, "Amen, I believe."

4. Perhaps the person is mad at himself for repeating the same sin over and over again. This is actually a veiled form of pride that assumes he is capable of doing good in his own power. He is minimizing his spiritual inability apart from God's grace. To counter this, he should praise God for the ever-present advocacy of Jesus, and set out on a biblical course for change.

5. Perhaps the person is establishing his own standards for righteousness. He has passed God's requirements because of Christ, but he has not passed his own. This has a very religious sound to it, but it is essentially saying, "I am above God. Violation of *my* standards is the worst possible crime." This is

when someone might say, "I believe that God forgives me but I can't forgive myself." Here again is a person who feels bad, yet the way out is confession of sin. He is saying that *he* is the judge. Or at least he is saying that there are two courtrooms, God's and his own. All sin, however, is against God. He alone is the judge, and his judgment is final.

6. Perhaps the person is saying that he regrets the consequences of his behavior *for himself.* His world is against him, and he wishes it were not. In this case, he should see that there is a difference between consequences and forgiveness. In the divine courtroom, if we turn to Christ we are forgiven, and the joy of forgiveness before the divine judge can outweigh the pain of the social, vocational, or physical consequences of the addiction. This is probably part of Jim's struggle.

> CHRISTIAN FRIEND: Jim, could you explain what you mean when you say you "feel really bad about what's happened"?
>
> JIM: Well, it's just that my family has gone through a lot, and I sometimes feel like I have to face that every day. Plus, I know that my wife doesn't really trust me anymore.
>
> CHRISTIAN FRIEND: You're right, it certainly has been difficult for you. In fact, it might look like sobriety has meant facing all sorts of problems you didn't have to face before. Apart from faith, it might seem easier to go back to alcohol.
>
> JIM: I have thought of that. I feel like I have had this black cloud over me ever since I have been sober.
>
> CHRISTIAN FRIEND: I wonder if we are witnessing the spiritual battle. Can you hear it at all? Satan saying that God is not good? Or Satan saying that you are not really forgiven? What you are talking about is critical, and we better keep working with it.

7. Perhaps the person is spiritually inexperienced. He needs to practice looking away from himself and looking to Jesus. He needs to practice that ten-to-one rhythm.

8.Perhaps the person doesn't really believe that God is satisfied by what Christ did on the cross. Scripture, however, is clear (Rom. 5:9; Eph. 1:7; 1 John 1:7; Rev. 1:5). The evidence of God's satisfaction is the resurrection of Jesus from the dead. Jesus' bodily resurrection was the Father's signal that the penalty for sin had been fully paid; nothing remained to be done. Now the risen Lord is our constant advocate before the Father (Heb. 7:25).

9. There are times, however, when individuals seem immune to biblical exhortation and encouragement. In such cases it is possible that they do not *want* to believe they are forgiven! They may know there is forgiveness in Jesus, but they prefer guilt. Why? Because guilt has more of a pay-off than we might think. For example, the religious-sounding "I'm too bad to be forgiven" might be a veiled attempt to leave the door open for future drug use. The thinking goes this way: If they are not forgiven, then God has abandoned them, and if God has abandoned them, they might as well continue with their addiction.

There are other variations as well. For example, if we believe we are not fully forgiven, we can remain angry with others: "If I haven't been treated with grace, then I don't have to forgive others." And if they "have a right" to be angry with others, they can also justify punishing others by drinking at them.

Another deceptive possibility is, "My sins are so bad I should punish myself. What's the best way to do that? By continuing my addiction."

These ploys may sound religious on the outside, but they are actually signs of unbelief, pride, and lust. They are unbelief in that they expose our tendency to believe what we feel rather than what God says. In essence we are calling God a liar: "God says I am forgiven as I turn to Christ in faith, but I don't believe it's true." They are pride in that they expose our belief that we can do something that will help God deal with our sins. We believe that we can do something to pay for our unrighteousness. Also, they are lust in that they typically are veiled excuses to indulge old, addictive appetites.

Regardless of the underlying motives, whenever people put their faith in Christ yet struggle with believing that they are forgiven, it is a serious issue. It must remain on the agenda until it is resolved with faith.

LEARNING THE FEAR OF THE LORD

The fear of the Lord does not suddenly appear. Even though it is a gift from the Father, it is typically learned through the normal means God has established for his people.

Remembering. One way we learn the fear of the Lord is simply by remembering. We remember what God says about himself and about us. One of the recurring sins of God's people is that we forget. Even though we have Scripture available to us every day, and we have reminders in our corporate worship and the Lord's Supper, we quickly forget who God is and what he has done. We forget that the King and Father, the One who is over all the nations, has called us out of bondage to be his children who honor his name.

Forgetting isn't just the result of a faulty memory. Sometimes our forgetting is more intentional. We forget because we have been looking somewhere else. When addicts turn away from the Lord and gaze at the object of their desire, God becomes a distant memory. Since one common belief is that God is going to keep us from something good, we try to distract ourselves from remembering him. Like an adulterer who tries to forget the forsaken spouse because such memories interfere with the adultery, so addicts try to suppress the truth about God.

The most prominent means of remembering are not flashy, but they are true, God-given means. The means are reading and meditating on Scripture, and meeting with believers who can point us to the glories of Christ as we seek to do the same with them.

Confessing. Remembering comes easier when we are aware that our deepest problem is our struggle with sin. Consider praying the Lord's Prayer every day (Matt. 6:9–13). In this concise summary of prayer, we are taught the basics of human life.

- God is our Father.
- We want his name to be exalted and revered in our lives and in the world.
- We want his rule to extend deeply in our hearts and broadly throughout the world.
- We ask for daily provisions.
- We confess our sins, and acknowledge that we have forgiven those who sinned against us.
- We pray that God would deliver us from Satan's strategies.

DEFINITIONS OF THE FEAR OF THE LORD

There is no one definition of the fear of the Lord, but certain elements should appear in any definition or description.

The fear of the Lord is a son or daughter's response to the divine father's holiness. A biblical understanding of the fear of the Lord must be rooted in our growing knowledge that God is holy. This means that his attributes cannot be understood by comparing them to praiseworthy characteristics of even the best of people. His love, power, beauty, judgment, compassion, anger, and mercy are all holy. They are different from the dim reflections of these attributes that we see in one another.

The fear of the Lord is our total response to God. It goes further than an intellectual understanding. A biblical fear of the Lord is a response of our entire beings. When God teaches us to fear him, he usually does it in a way that is utterly astonishing. The cross of Christ is the climax of this teaching. It is not just about a good teacher who is falsely accused. It is a cosmic event that liberated the living and the dead, that was the final word about God's love and justice, and that began the eternal reign of Jesus Christ. Such an event does not simply interest us; it *moves* us. For that reason, there is an emotional dimension to the fear of the Lord.

The fear of the Lord expresses itself in responsive, reverential, and joyful action. Here is a reliable principle of human conduct: Whatever wins our affections will control our lives. You love your spouse; it will be expressed in the way you feel and the way you live. Your love your work; you will put in extra hours even if it means a sacrifice of time with your family—and sometimes of your health. You love pornography; you will find time and money to indulge your desires.

Addicts are moved into action by their beloved. The only way out of such a relationship is to be moved even more by someone who is much more beautiful and is our legitimate lover. Any other obedience will not last.

For example, the prophet Isaiah was given a ministry in which his love for personal safety would be tested. People wanted to kill him. To prepare him for such a test, the Lord gave Isaiah a vision of himself that would be far superior to comfort, safety, or acceptance. He gave Isaiah a gaze at his glory. He taught Isaiah the fear of the Lord. With this vision—this remembrance—Isaiah quickly said, "Send me" (Isa. 6:8), even though his mission would be a costly one. In other words, the fear of the Lord moved him. It caused him to do something. As we see throughout the book of Proverbs, the fear of the Lord animates every action of our lives, whether it is doing dishes, greeting someone warmly, or saying "no" to once loved sins. The fear of the Lord, then, is reverence that obeys.

Such a definition—reverence that obeys—is accurate, but it doesn't quite force us to consider the majesty of God. Instead, it draws our attention more to our own obedience. A fuller way to define the fear of the Lord is this:

> The fear of the Lord is knowing that I live *coram deo*, before the face of God. It is knowing that the Holy God sees every aspect of my life.[4] The result is that we live knowing that we are seen. We live publicly, and follow Christ in joyful and reverential obedience.

This fuller definition adds a significant feature to the fear of the Lord: God sees. The One who sits on the throne sees us. Our heavenly Father always has us under his watchful eye. When we have a tolerance for sin in our lives, it is due in part to our belief that we can keep some aspects of our lives secret. Isn't this the way addictions begin? We think that God is like an idol who takes naps while we secretly pursue our lusts. We think that he is like other people who only see us when we come into their presence.

There is no exception: All addictions have this lie at their very core. After all, how many people would freely indulge their addictions if they knew they lived in the presence of the Holy One? We don't even pursue our addictions in front of our boss!

The practical theology of all addictions says that God is present sometimes and absent at others. We typically indulge our sin without pangs of conscience when we believe that no one sees. How do we know this? Notice what happens if someone actually catches us. We are embarrassed; we have a sudden sense of our guilt. What we tried to keep in the dark is now exposed in the light. The reality, of course, is that we are never in private. "You have set our iniquities before you, our secret sins in the light of your presence" (Ps. 90:8). All our lives are lived out in the courts of the Lord. We are always seen and in the presence of the Holy One.

This may not seem like a very attractive truth at first. We would prefer to think that we are off in our own little corner, sinning quietly and privately. In such situations, the fear of the Lord is *not* immediately appealing. It has more in common with dread and raw fear than it does with wonder and devotion. Yet that is the blessing of the fear of the Lord. One of the great gifts God gives his people is a heart that is more and more like his own. His all-seeing gaze brings our hearts out in the open so they can be changed. The tragedy would be if our divine Father left us to ourselves, thinking that we were somehow getting away with our private indulgences. In other words, if you have been exposed, consider yourself loved. Know that God is inviting you to learn the fear of the Lord.

The fact that God sees every aspect of our lives may, at first, leave us afraid and eager to hide from God rather than in awe, wanting to embrace him. But the fear of the Lord makes us aware both of God's holy purity and hatred of sin and his holy patience and forgiveness. When we remember both, we have no reason to run in fear, especially since there is no place to run beyond the gaze of God. Instead, as we look at the Lord, we see that he invites, cleanses, and empowers us to grow in holiness.

The presence of God—to have his eyes looking on you—is a great blessing in Scripture.

> The LORD bless you
> and keep you;
> the LORD make his face shine upon you
> and be gracious to you;
> the LORD turn his face toward you
> and give you peace. (Num. 6:24–26)

PRACTICAL THEOLOGY

This material is the crux of change. There is nothing more important. When you wake up in the morning, begin by meditating on the cross of Christ until you are thankful and humbled. Plead for the knowledge of God, and plead with boldness. Use Scripture in your prayer. Ask other people to tell you how they are learning more about Jesus Christ and the gospel. Meditate on it until you are undone.

As You Face Your Own Addiction

1. Can you imagine what it would be like to really believe that you lived before God—that your life was public? It would protect you. It would bless you.

Study Psalm 139. The psalmist has learned that God's presence is his greatest blessing. The good fruit of this knowledge is that he says, "Search me, O God," instead of hiding from him.

> Where can I go from your Spirit?
>   Where can I flee from your presence?
> If I go up to the heavens, you are there;
>   if I make my bed in the depths, you are there. . . .
> If I say, "Surely the darkness will hide me
>   and the light become night around me,"
> even the darkness will not be dark to you;
>   the night will shine like the day,
>   for darkness is as light to you." (vv. 7–8, 11–12)

2. You probably feel more guilty than you think. Guilt before God is not a popular topic today. Since it is not something we often think about, it is increasingly hard to recognize. It can often masquerade as anxiety, depression, defensiveness, and shame. How does your guilt express itself?

3. Go through the list of reasons why you don't always feel

forgiven. Which ones reveal your own heart? Since we now know that God's anger has already been poured out on Jesus, how can we think that he will do anything but forgive us if we turn to him? For him to do anything less would be for him to say that the cross wasn't enough. So don't be afraid to confess sin. Don't be afraid to say, "Lord, search me."

4. Here is the most difficult part: the fear of the Lord doesn't come instantly. It is just like wisdom. It comes as we ask for it and seek it. Ask someone to pray that you would grow in the fear of the Lord. Ask her to write it on her calendar every week for the next year.

5. Pick up a good devotional companion to the Bible.

As You Help Someone Else

1. As you get to know a person who has struggled with addictions, there are so many possible issues to discuss. Don't overwhelm the person. AA says for good reason, "Keep it simple." Try to focus on one important theme, and wrap it in the fear of the Lord.

2. Does the person you are helping have an interest in learning the fear of the Lord? If not, why? This is the time when people should be converted. If our talk about knowing, loving, and fearing the Lord seems foreign to someone, invite her to Christ.

3. Are *you* growing in the fear of the Lord? You too need to ask for prayer, from the person you are helping and from others.

4. Here is a good barometer for measuring the significance of the fear of the Lord in your relationship. Are you praying together? Do you desperately want the things that God wants to give you?

9 | Turning from Lies

> You boast, "We have entered into a covenant with death,
>   with the grave we have made an agreement.
> When an overwhelming scourge sweeps by,
>   it cannot touch us,
> for we have made a lie our refuge
>   and falsehood our hiding place."
>
> *ISAIAH 28:15*

The fear of the Lord exposes us. We thought we could hide from other people. We thought we could even hide from God himself. The light of Christ, however, reminds us that our lives are much more public than we once thought.

Part of the deceptiveness of sin is that it persuades us that what we are doing is OK—until, of course, we get caught in the act. If someone is sneaking around, hitting pornographic sites on the internet, he may have some awareness that it is wrong, but he has more awareness that it is delicious. It is only when a friend or spouse shows up unexpectedly that this person feels the weight of his actions. In a similar way, the light of Christ exposes the ugliness of our lives that is hidden when the lights are out.

The bad news in this is that the light exposes our guilt and shame. The good news is that the fear of the Lord exposes us without *leaving* us shamed, forever guilty, and powerless to change. Rather, it exposes us in order to cover our shame, cleanse the guilty conscience, give grace to change, and restore fellowship with God and others. With this in mind, we are now ready to consider the darkest and most distressing feature of addictions: the lies and deception. Addictions are so intimately joined to lies and deception that you will probably never find one without the other. Coverups, white lies, blameshifting, or outright manipulative lies—chances are that the addict has developed skill in them all. If you have struggled with addictions, you have lied, and if you have lived with an addict, you have been deceived. You wonder if you can ever trust the person again.

OPENING OUR EYES TO DECEPTION

Even though deception is universal in addictions, it hasn't received the attention it should. Perhaps this is because lies are considered so much a part of the human fabric that the goal is damage control more than truth telling. Perhaps the nature of deception simply resists being brought into the light for careful inspection. Whatever the reason, a quick survey of Scripture indicates that we can never over-emphasize the dangers of lies and the blessing of truthfulness.

God Is Truth

God's Word speaks clearly and frequently about truth and lies. It is one of the best known features of God's law. If children know anything about the Bible, they know that it says, "Do not lie" (Lev. 19:11). What children don't always know, however, is *why* God commands us not to lie. It is not just that lies corrupt the social order. Although that is true, the reason goes deeper than that. The commands of God are very personal. They reveal God himself. We are commanded not to lie because *he* doesn't lie. Speaking the truth (Ex. 20:16; Zech. 8:16; Col. 3:9) imitates God's character. Falsehood violates it.

God *is* truth (Ps. 31:5; John 1:9; 14:6; 17:3; 1 John 1:5; 5:6,

5:20). It is impossible for him to lie (Titus 1:2; Heb. 6:18). Jesus repeatedly says, "I tell you the truth," and he has given us the Spirit of truth (John 14:17). Look at the references to truth in a concordance and you will find that it is one of the most frequently used words in Scripture. Truth is a cornerstone in the kingdom of God.

Think for a moment about the alternative. What if God lied at just one point? Even if it were just a small deception, everyone who puts his trust in Christ would be without hope. If he is not absolutely faithful and true, our faith is foolishness. Truth is essential in the way God relates to us.

This is why we speak the truth. Since God is truth, we—his offspring—are called to imitate him and be truth tellers. It is one way that God's people are recognized. Lies and deception are wrong because they are against God's very nature.

Satan Is the Liar

Since God is truth, and since Satan is against God at all points, it is not surprising that the kingdom of Satan consists of lies. John 8:44 says, "He [Satan] was a murderer from the beginning, not holding to the truth, for there is no truth in him. When he lies, he speaks his native language, for he is a liar and the father of lies."

Satan's deceptive character was apparent from the start. At the very first appearance of the "crafty" deceiver in Genesis 3:1–5, Satan was already the consummate liar. Notice how far he goes in his falsehoods. Amazingly, he suggests that God is a liar!

God said, " 'You are free to eat from any tree in the garden; but you must not eat from the tree of the knowledge of good and evil, for when you eat of it you will surely die' " (Gen. 2:16–17). Satan, however, in direct opposition to God said, " 'You will not surely die. . . . For God knows that when you eat of it your eyes will be opened, and you will be like God, knowing good and evil' " (Gen. 3:4–5).

In this case, Satan's lie certainly does not seem subtle. It seems like such a blatant whopper that you would expect Adam and Eve to double over in laughter. The Serpent was telling a joke, they should have surmised. The only other option would have been to be filled with righteous indignation, and rebuke or even kill the snake. Yet the lie must have resonated with their budding human pride, because they took it to heart.

This is a frightening illustration of our humanness. We are prone to believing the egregious lies of Satan. Maybe we can spot a lie being put over on someone else, but we can be blinded when it comes to ourselves. Without question, we are people who must plead for mercy and grace so that we will not be ensnared by lies.

These are the battle lines. God speaks the truth. He calls us to believe him and follow him by speaking the truth ourselves. Satan speaks lies. He wants us to doubt the goodness of God, and he bids us to follow him in speaking and believing lies. This kingdom conflict is behind all deception.

The apostle Paul is especially alert to the seriousness of lies. In his letter to the Ephesians he wrote, "Each of you must put off falsehood and speak truthfully to his neighbor" (Eph. 4:25). At first, this seems like an ordinary exhortation included in a longer list of warnings. But the apostle is alert to the larger spiritual dynamics behind all deception. He is not just giving a list of dos and don'ts. He is revealing the difference between light and darkness (4:18), giving footholds to Satan (4:27), and being an imitator of God (5:8–10). He is teaching us that there are two kingdoms that are in conflict (6:10–18), and he is training us to be strong and stand firm in the midst of spiritual battle. Speaking truth instead of lies is not simply being nice. It is a declaration of allegiance. Truth is a shibboleth—a telltale mark—revealing that you belong to the kingdom of God. This does not mean that a person who lies cannot be a Christian. It simply means that lying is very dangerous and must be combated with repentance.

Jesus himself issues the same warning about lies. In Matthew 5:37 he says, "Simply let your 'Yes' be 'Yes,' and your 'No,' 'No.' " In other words, don't weasel out of the truth by crossing your fingers or manipulating language to avoid the truth. Say what you mean and do what you say. These certainly are words that can reveal us.

Do we miss, however, the chilling comment that follows? "Anything beyond this comes from the evil one." In this succinct yet powerful statement, Jesus opens our eyes to the profound spiritual realities behind truth and lies. What we thought was a relatively innocent white lie was much more than that. It was an indication of who had mastered us at that moment.

It is important to realize that Jesus was pinpointing a fairly common practice. If someone said, "I swear by heaven that I will be there tomorrow morning," it meant that the person might or might not be there. It was a socially acceptable practice that allowed someone to say something nice but not follow through. But Jesus had a pattern of revealing the spiritual allegiances behind the seemingly minor sins that everyone commits. In this particular situation, he revealed the gravity of the action.

Addicts are like every believer in that they must look closely at the ways they have imitated Satan rather than the true God. Lies offer a temporary sense of power over others and protection for ourselves, so addicts must be helped to see that lies begin with the deception of others, move on to self-deception, proceed into darkness where nothing is clear any longer, and end in death.

What are some of the categories to look at with the addict?

- hiding
- sneaking
- blaming
- manipulating
- avoiding

- being silent as a way of avoiding
- changing the subject
- rationalizing
- giving your word but not doing it

These are just some of the ways that lying can be present in someone's life. One way to get at this subterranean world is to stick with these questions: "How do your private life and imaginations differ from your public one?" "What do you do in private that you would never want to be known in public?" These questions can show you how the fear of the Lord—knowing that God sees everything at all times—is God's way of freeing people ensnared by deceit.

But, of course, deception still insists on staying in the darkness. This is especially true when lying has become so much a part of someone's lifestyle that it is his normal language. Often addicts don't even recognize lies, in any form. They tell lies when the truth would be just as easy to tell and completely harmless.

FRIEND: Will I see you on Sunday?

ADDICT: No, I have to work this Sunday. We have a major job that has to get out by Monday.

Yet this person has never worked on Sunday. He hasn't even been asked. He is actually going to visit his mother, who lives in another state. Why didn't he just say that? No one would have criticized him for visiting his mother. Why would he lie?

Ultimately, there is no reason why. Lies make life more miserable, sooner as well as later. There is no rational reason for them. Sometimes liars themselves are amazed at how ridiculous their lies are, but that isn't enough to make them stop. They persist in lies because lies are part of the bondage of addictions—a very personal bondage to a harsh master who promises pleasure but delivers misery.

So when you ask difficult questions, you might want to ask the person to pause before answering. Every difficult question will place him at the crossroads between two opposing kingdoms. You want him to reflect on what he plans to say so he can practice truth telling. In fact, there might be times when you encourage him to ask, "Could I answer that later?" This may help him avoid instinctive lying.

If you are a friend, pastor, or counselor for someone who has struggled with addictions, one of the critical moments in your relationship is when you are lied to—and it is likely that you *will* be lied to. Addicts may not lie about events from years ago, but the closer your questions get to the present, the more personally threatening the truth might be. This creates more temptations to lie. To make it worse, if addicts do lie to you, they are digging themselves deeper into a hole. Now they have a problem in their relationship with you as well as a problem with addictions.

There are a number of ways to approach the problem. Here are some examples.

1. Talk about the lies that you are tempted to believe about God, others, and yourself, which in turn inspire other lies. Simply ask, "Why do we lie?"
2. Always keep in view the way Jesus makes promises and keeps them.
3. Be direct.

CHRISTIAN FRIEND: Here is a potential problem I have been thinking about. If I ask you about what really happened and what is happening now, it's going to be easy for you to lie about it, or at least to try to cover things up. You have lied to almost everyone who has been close to you at some point or another, and I am concerned that our relationship might get awkward if you lie to me at some point.

The problem is that it is going to be really hard for you to admit you have misled me, and then more lies will get heaped on the first ones. Once deception creeps in, it becomes more and more natural. Any ideas on how I can help create a situation where it is easy to speak openly and honestly?

ADDICT: Hmm, I'm not sure, but I know what you are saying.

CHRISTIAN FRIEND: Well, I'll ask you again. For now, I want you to know that I want to be especially aware of being open and honest. I want to practice it myself. The Scripture we've looked at has already shown me ways that I need to take my own words more seriously.

The goal for those who come alongside an addict is not to be a priest-confessor. The goal is to encourage the addict to keep walking in the light and to be alert to the deceptive ways we can be waylaid by Satan's influence.

Since it is so easy to become numb and desensitized to the "lesser" lies like avoiding and not taking our word seriously, we need consistent reminders from Scripture about the seriousness of this sin. If you need help getting started, you could begin by reviewing some of the Bible's negative examples. For example, Jacob's lies were anticipated by his name, which can mean "he deceives." His deception reached its zenith in the way he betrayed his own father and brother (Gen. 27). His lies were followed by those of his sons, who told him that Joseph was killed by a wild animal (Gen. 37:31–35). The lust of Potiphar's wife led to a malicious lie that resulted in Joseph's imprisonment (Gen. 39:13–18). Judas's betrayal of Jesus is perhaps the most blatantly Satanic of lies (Luke 22:3, 48; John 13:27). In Acts 5:1–5, the connection between human lies and Satanic allegiance is especially apparent. "Ananias, how is it that Satan has so filled your heart that you have lied to the Holy Spirit and have kept for yourself some of the money you received for the land?" (v. 3).

In all these biblical examples, lies betrayed a lack of trust in God and a heart committed to its own desires. Unbelief and "I WANT" were the echoes behind these lies, just as they are the echoes behind our own. Unbelief says, "I don't believe what God says. I don't believe he is good." "I WANT" says, "My desires—my comfort, safety, or identity—are what must be served."

The Lie of Blaming Others

One particular deception that deserves discussion is blaming. If the addict is married, chances are that his or her spouse will feel guilty. Why? Because addicts typically are experts at twisting any accusation so that others feel responsible. It is always someone else's fault. It's a variation of the modern theme, "The best defense is a good offense."

The problem, however, is anything but modern. Remember that this is the first consequence of sin: you cover yourself and blame whoever is closest. In Genesis 3:11–13, after Adam and Eve tried to cover themselves, they were instinctive (and instant) blamers. "Have you eaten from the tree that I commanded you not to eat from?" asks the Lord.

> The man said, "The woman you put here with me—she gave me some fruit from the tree, and I ate it."
> Then the LORD God said to the woman, "What is this you have done?"
> The woman said, "The serpent deceived me, and I ate."

The truth was too revealing and potentially damaging, so Adam and Eve tried deception as a way to escape the gaze of God. The only true answer to God's question was, "Yes, I ate from the tree," but their self-interest led them to cover themselves and blame others. The pattern continues to this day.

Certainly this is a pitiful, sinful response, but there is one more part of this covering/blaming dynamic that deserves mention. In one sense, Adam and Eve had the facts right. Adam did get the fruit from Eve and the serpent did tempt Eve. Perhaps if these things hadn't happened, the fiasco would have turned out differently. Although Adam and Eve's real motive was covering themselves, not accuracy, no doubt they felt justified by their excuses in much the same way that addicts feel justified in blaming those closest to them for their problems.

Addicts can quickly say or think, "If she hadn't _____, I wouldn't have gone for that drink." This means that addicts may need a great deal of practice in accepting responsibility for their addictive behavior. Remember that although other people may influence the course of a sinful addiction, they can never ultimately cause it. Addiction always proceeds from the heart. At most, other people may squeeze us so that we see what is really inside.

If you are trying to help addicts, challenge them to become experts in what Scripture says about truth and falsehood. Acknowledge that lying might be much more difficult to put off than the addiction itself, and never cease to remind them that there is grace and forgiveness for deceivers.

One thing we have to keep in mind as we talk about truthfulness is that Christ does not receive us on the basis of how well we tell the truth. God forgives us because of what Jesus did. This means that there is unlimited grace from God. In other words, after the one-hundredth lie, God does not say, "Enough, no more forgiveness." Since Jesus lives as our defense attorney (Heb. 7), grace is never exhausted. But the fact that Jesus died to forgive sins also means that he died to break the pattern of lies. By God's grace we are headed to a place where we don't have to keep confessing the same thing.

Speaking the Truth to Yourself

Sin is guerrilla warfare that is covert and deadly. Just when you think you are in control, it seeks to devour you. Just when you think you might be getting away with something, it has successfully deceived you.

In Proverbs 1 we observe men who are murderous. They see themselves as strong and in control. The reality, however, is that they "lie in wait for their own blood; they waylay only themselves" (v. 18). In the same way, deception is more than lying to others. It is also believing a lie. It is self-deception.

> There is another kind of deception that I think is even deeper than deceiving other people: it is that we deceive ourselves. Not only do we *tell* lies, we end up *believing* lies. For example, have you ever tried to lie to yourself in order to get a drink? Maybe you've said, "I'm not like all the others. It's true that they are out of control, but not me." It's one of the old standards: "I'm unique— not susceptible to the problems I see in other people."

Consider making a list with the addict of some of the ways we deceive ourselves.

- "One drink isn't going to hurt."
- "I am hopeless anyway. Why bother trying to stop?"
- "If I do it only once, it will prove that I have self-control."
- "Maybe I'll just hang out with the guys and not drink anything at all."
- "If she wouldn't treat me that way, then I wouldn't have to drink."
- "I just need a little something to relax me."

Then proceed to discuss the biggest deceptions of all.

The #1 Deception: God Is Not Good
We all have different strategies that we use to deceive ourselves, but there is one deception that we all experience. It is

perhaps the deepest of all. Deep in our hearts we question God's goodness. We think he is holding out on us. We think that he is a cosmic killjoy who wants stoic obedience. We seem to believe that he will never let us have a cookie from the cookie jar, but he likes to put the cookie jar right in front of our faces to tempt us. One of the deepest deceptions is the lie that there is something good out there and it is better than what God gives.

Look at how Scripture alerts us to this. We've been talking about Genesis 3. We have seen the lies of Satan, which suggest that God is really the liar. Satan tells Eve that God is holding out on her. The tree, the Serpent suggests, is really a good thing that will give you life. God, on the other hand, just wants to keep you under his thumb, away from good things that you will really enjoy.

Satan's lie is "God is not good." Coupled with that is "Sin is good." He suggests to us that there are greater pleasures outside the kingdom of God. But somehow, even though we know Genesis 3, and we know that Satan is coming with his deceptive tactics, we still believe the lie.

This kind of deception is often apparent among teens. Many teens who grow up in a good church will believe that Christ died for sins and rose from the dead, but they will also believe that being a Christian somehow keeps them from fun. Feeling a bit like prisoners in Alcatraz who heard the parties across the San Francisco Bay, they often view the gospel and God's law as walls that keep pleasure outside. Of course, such thinking can be found in other age groups as well, just in a more veiled form. The issues addicts struggle with are universal.

What is odd about this deception is that we can be very familiar with the enemy's strategy and still be taken by surprise. The problem goes back to what was said in chapter 1: our stated, "official" theology is sometimes contrary to our practical, functional theology. Most Christians are not going to actually say, "God is not really good; he is holding out on me." Instead, these doubts and conflicting beliefs hide in our hearts undercover, only apparent when we notice what we actually do rather than what we say.

The fact that we are not always aware of this deception is not cause for despair. It is cause for vigilance, expressed in a commitment to "encourage one another daily . . . so that none of you may be hardened by sin's deceitfulness" (Heb. 3:13). God has determined that we will not walk the path of spiritual growth alone, but in the company of others, where daily we can give and receive help.

The #2 Deception: I Am Good
(But I Occasionally Do Bad Things)

The first grand deception is about God. The second is about us. At a very deep level, we believe that God is not as good as he says, and we think we are better than we actually are. Instead of believing that we are sinners who sin, we tend to think of ourselves as good people who occasionally do bad things.

Nowhere is this more prevalent than in the literature on addictions. Secular (and most Christian) literature seems to work hard to say that addicts are not responsible for the cause of their problems. Addicts are responsible to change, but they are not responsible for getting where they are in the first place.

The real cause, many suggest, is some combination of genetics, dysfunctional parents, and self-esteem problems. With this in mind, some addicts feel that they have a right to be mad at God or others because the source of the problem is external. We've seen that this is the main reason why Jim was angry with God. He saw himself as a pretty decent guy who had been dealt a bad hand of cards. Now he was expected to do something with them, and he was not able to do it.

The Bible permits us to say that a brew of genetics, family

problems, and unclear identity can have a profound influence on an addict, but the ultimate cause of sinful behavior is always the human heart. To its credit, AA's "Big Book," entitled *Alcoholics Anonymous,* would agree.

> Selfishness—self-centeredness! That, we think, is the root of our troubles. . . . So our troubles, we think, are basically of our own making. They arise out of ourselves, and the alcoholic is an extreme example of self-will run riot, though he usually doesn't think so. (p. 62)

We are addicts because we are selfish. We all have a bad case of sinful cravings. Perhaps the most relevant Scripture would be James 1:14–15. "Each one is tempted when, by his own evil desire, he is dragged away and enticed. Then, after desire has conceived, it gives birth to sin; and sin, when it is full-grown, gives birth to death." Our addictions begin with our selfish desires.

Why is this a big deal? Why is it important to talk about responsibility for both cause and cure? First, because it is true. We are sinners, even when we are not obviously sinning. Until Christ returns, sin is part of our fabric (1 John 1:9). Second, because any other perspective would essentially nullify or limit the cross of Christ, the ultimate resting point for all Christian counseling. It is impossible to get to the good news of the cross from a starting point that limits moral responsibility. If we are born good and have been ruined by a dysfunctional environment or a biological abnormality, then any help we receive is intended only to heal. The goal is to restore an addict to his or her original good state. Jesus is there only to help us when we trip or to make us feel better about ourselves.

This, however, is not the gospel. The gospel is that Christ died for sinners and then rose from the dead. It is good news to people who sin and are sinners. It is good news for desperate people, not nice people who occasionally do wrong things. And its goal is a completely new person, not a person who has been cleaned up a bit.

CHRISTIAN FRIEND: This deception stuff goes deeper than telling lies to other people. What scares me about the whole realm of deception is that deceiving others goes hand in hand with deceiving yourself. First, we tend to believe Satan's lies about God's goodness. Then, we tend to believe our own lies about ourselves: we think we are basically OK. Behind most of my conflicts with other people is my own personal motto that says, "I am OK, but that person isn't."

Isn't this the same in the world of addictions? Have you noticed that some addicts feel condemned but they also feel like they are OK? Their problems come from outside themselves. As a result, it isn't surprising that those people think of God as an aid, a useful crutch and nothing more when they are moving toward self-control and sobriety. We have to keep remembering the truth about ourselves.

The truth is that Christ came to save rebels, people who are against him. And addiction is against God. It is believing a lie—that God is holding out on us—and saying that we live for our desires.

This may sound harsh, but it probably rings true, and it is the road to freedom. The Bible never lets us pass the buck for any of our thoughts or behavior (James 1:14–15). Passing the buck would make God's forgiveness less attractive.

ADDICT: I know what you are saying is right, but sometimes I think I feel bad enough about myself already.

CHRISTIAN FRIEND: I think I know what you mean. Let's try to think of another way to say it, because there must be both truth and beauty in the gospel. How about this: Every good thing comes from God, everything else comes from us. All the good things that are happening in your life right now—your growing in Christ and sobriety—are evidence that God is working in you. If we think of it any other way, it opens the door to live independently of God. All good things come from God.

ADDICT: So we can't really take pride in what we do?

CHRISTIAN FRIEND: I guess not. But we can take great pride in what Jesus has done for us, and we can be amazed that he loves us and forgives us.

The #3 Deception: Idols Are Harmless

The first grand deception is about God, the second is about ourselves, and the third is about the idol we worshiped. People do drugs because they like them; more accurately, they love them. The same is true for any addiction. As part of repentance, you want to help addicts to see their idolatrous relationship accurately and to learn to hate it.

Ex-drug users often remember their drugs fondly. This is especially true when they are having a difficult time in a relationship or at work. In the past, drugs would have provided relief. To prepare for these inevitable times, friends and counselors can encourage people to retain biblical perspectives on their sin. The book of Proverbs is especially useful. Some accurate pictures are "a net in full view of all the birds" (1:17); a "house [that] leads down to death" (2:18); "a double-edged sword" (5:4); "an ox going to the slaughter" (7:22); "a bird darting into a snare" (7:23); or "bites like a snake" (23:32). Then, instead of seeing a line of cocaine, they can see a harlot, an idol, or a snake. Instead of seeing themselves as an important person in a secret fraternity when they do drugs, they can see themselves as a person out of control, a city without walls (25:28), and a slave to a false god. Encourage them to be vivid in their faith.

Very quickly, those who have struggled with drugs will hear voices (i.e., Satan or the flesh) whispering in their ear, panhandling for another high. The voices have no end to their creativity. They may suggest that doing drugs "in moderation," without getting intoxicated, will demonstrate that they really have control. They say, "God has given you self-control: now prove it." Or they might say, "You are on the brink; you will soon be out of control. Drunkenness is inevitable, so you may as well do it now and get it over with."

Ex-addicts must remember (or learn) that sin is full of self-deception. It engages in guerrilla warfare. It is a myth that sin consists only of behaviors that are easy to detect. In fact, evil masquerades as light. Substance abusers, like all of us, must learn to be alert to the deceptive nature of the world, the flesh, and the devil. As an Aran Islander said, "A man who is not afraid of the sea will soon be drowned, for he will be going out on a day he shouldn't. But we do be afraid of the sea, and we do only be drowned now and again."

CHRISTIAN FRIEND: While we are talking about ways we are self-deceived, we should probably talk about one more prominent deception. Sometimes the bottle is going to look attractive. Our task is to make it look ugly and learn to hate it. Any suggestions?

ADDICT: I can start by remembering what it did to me. Or what I did to myself. I think of that every day when I am with my family. I wish it had never happened.

CHRISTIAN FRIEND: Maybe we should try to develop a picture that would help. How about borrowing one from Proverbs 9, a banquet in a grave?

SPEAKING THE TRUTH TO GOD

When our deception is exposed, we confess it. By so doing, we are speaking the truth to God. We are saying, "God, you have searched me and known me. You know all my thoughts and actions. I now agree with you that my heart has been against you. I care about my own desires more than yours." This is an essential, daily feature of walking in the light.

I have been thinking that we should probably be spending more time praying together and less time analyzing. Let's get back to the Lord's Prayer again. Confession is speaking the truth.

Initially, it is wise for confession to be in the presence of another person. Biblically, this is not necessary, but it can be another step of walking in the light. Dietrich Bonhoeffer arrived at similar conclusions.

A man who confesses his sins in the presence of a brother knows that he is no longer alone with himself; he experiences the presence of God in the reality of the other person. As long as I am by myself in the confession of my sins, everything remains in the dark, but in the presence of a brother, the sin has to be brought into the light.[1]

Most of us have had sins that we would easily confess to God, yet would be ashamed to confess to another brother or sister. Does this make sense? After all, God is the Holy One. To be exposed in his presence should be much more difficult than being exposed before sinners like ourselves. People who truly confess to God are less concerned that others learn their secret.

If we easily confess to God something that shames us to confess to a friend, we are thinking too highly of the opinions of people and not highly enough about the holiness of God.

PRACTICAL THEOLOGY

Scripture again brings penetrating insight to the topic of truth and lies. It doesn't merely say, "Don't lie." It reveals the spiritual drama played out in all kinds of deception. It then gives us the reasons and power to speak the truth.

As You Face Your Own Addiction

1. Do you want to stop the downward spiral of deceit? Like addiction itself, there is a payoff to it. Lies have gotten you in trouble, but you think they have also gotten you *out* of trouble. Do you want to be a truth teller? If you do, you have reason to be filled with hope. The Spirit of God is on the move in your heart. He will give you the grace to continue what he has started. God raises the dead; he can certainly give you the power to believe and speak the truth.

2. Lies are foolish. When you really look at them, they seem childish. They seemed brilliant and even true to you, but they are bizarre. Keep looking at them until they seem ridiculous.

3. Lies are dangerous. There is no such thing as an innocuous or innocent lie. There is no such thing as a white lie. All lies and deception are flirting with Satan himself. They should scare us. Consider a recent lie. Examine it until you can see how it came out of a heart that was in spiritual bondage.

4. Lies are malicious. They don't *seem* to be against anyone. They aren't intended to hurt. But they are against people and they do hurt. They wreck relationships. This chapter tries to paint an accurate picture of lies. The goal is not to make you feel bad. The goal is to see the truth and be blessed by it.

5. Ask a person who is further along in the battle to give you insight into the deceptive ways of the human heart. "How did you start to see the lies you believed?" "How do you stay on guard now?"

6. Pay particular attention to the lies you believe about God. What lies do you believe about God that give you permission

to tell lies? Lies, deception, and self-deception can usually be traced back to the unbelief and lies we harbor in our heart about God.

As You Help Someone Else

1. Do you create a context that invites and values truth? Do you react with obvious displeasure when the person you are helping speaks honestly? Sometimes people who have struggled with addictions will test you. They will give you small bits of truth to see how you respond.

2. Deception can come in many forms. For example, even the choice of particular words can reveal the lies we believe.

> I used to say that, because of drinking, I lost my job, my money, and my family. But that isn't true. The truth is that I gave them away. I threw them away.

When you hear words that sound like blame-shifting, point them out.

3. Are *you* willing to speak honestly about your own struggles? Is it easy for you to confess something to the Lord, but almost impossible to confess it in the presence of another? Don't ask someone to do something that you are not doing yourself.

4. Keep the fear of the Lord in view. It reminds us that we live publicly. It is our protection from lies.

10

Saying "No"

For God did not give us a spirit of timidity,
but a spirit of power, of love and of self-discipline.

2 TIMOTHY 1:7

The fruit of the Spirit is . . . self-control.

GALATIANS 5:22–23

Solomon, I think, was an American at heart: "I denied my-self nothing my eyes desired; I refused my heart no pleasure" (Eccl. 2:10). He tried what many Americans would try if they had the money and the time: unbridled hedonism. If there is a continuum from the legalistic, restrained, and ascetic to the licentious, reckless, and hedonistic, our society lives on the end that favors the self-indulgent. When our desires speak, we listen. We all need to ask for the gift of self-control and to practice the skill of self-control.

Problems with alcohol and drugs, sex and food have been common since biblical times. By all outward appearances, they are problems begging for a response of self-control. Yet even though it appears to be the perfect antidote, self-control is not always part of the addictions discussion. Addicts feel like they have tried self-control—probably hundreds of times. In fact, they have tried it so many times that many addicts are convinced that their vain attempts at self-control are the problem, not the solution. The consensus? "I have to *give up* control to a higher power."

In defense of AA, when attendees are taught to give up control, this doesn't mean that addicts sit passively and wait for some higher power to act on their behalf. The fundamental problem with AA is that it assumes that any god will do. The problem is not so much AA's view of self-control (even though faulty assumptions about God will corrupt the entire system). In some ways, there are teachings about self-control within the church that are more problematic than AA's.

Among evangelical Christians, "Let go and let God" is still a motto we live by. Our sense is that if change feels like self-effort and hard work, then it is probably legalistic and not animated by the Holy Spirit. Is this true? Shouldn't it feel somewhat effortless when the Spirit changes us? Self-control sounds like self-effort, and self-effort sounds antagonistic to the gospel itself.

This confusion suggests that now is a good time to revisit the biblical teaching on self-control.

WHAT'S THE PROBLEM?

Whatever you call it—greed, lust, obsessions, cravings, being out of control—addicts are owned by their desires and reckless indulgence. AA calls it "self-will run riot," which is a very apt description. Of the Seven Deadly Sins, three—avarice, gluttony, and lust—are devoted to excesses. In fact, sin itself can be summarized as "I WANT" or "I WANT MORE." It is a reckless consumer.

Study any country in the world and you will find lust or unchecked desire embedded in its basic institutions. In first world countries it fuels capitalistic economies. One reason capitalism works is that it understands the greediness of the human heart. In communist countries, the greediness of the middle class has been a dominant concern. But a new ideology and political structure haven't erased greed. They have just made it more apparent in the ruling class. In third world countries you find the same greediness in bribes, corruption, and theft, especially among those who have the power to get more.

Such greed is partner to idolatry. Idolatry is an expression of a heart that wants more. It says that God is not enough, so it looks for satisfaction elsewhere. Recklessness is often at the heart of idolatry, and it is not surprising that runaway desires are consistently part of false worship. For example, when the Hebrews chose idols, the result was "the people were running wild and . . . Aaron had let them get out of control and so become a laughingstock to their enemies" (Ex. 32:25).

The issue of idolatry is especially prominent in the Old Testament and less so in the New Testament. This does not mean, however, that idolatry was less of a problem in more modern times. What happened is that the Old Testament theme of idolatry passed the baton to the New Testament themes of lust, cravings, and sinful desire. This is in keeping with the New Testament's emphasis on the hidden commitments of the heart over the external object of our affections. As Scripture unfolds, it gradually looks more at our wants and desires and less at the actual idols themselves.* Scripture mocks idols as being ultimately powerless, so it loses interest in the external object. Instead, it consistently warns us to be alert to the lustful instincts of our hearts.

Notice some of the sins that are listed in the New Testament: debauchery, hatred, discord, jealousy, fits of rage, selfish ambition, envy, drunkenness, orgies (Gal. 5:19–21). These are sins of unchecked desires. They say, "I want everything, and I

---

*In this sense, the New Testament is committed to developing the tenth commandment, which is the prohibition against coveting.

want it now." Or, more simply, they say, "That was good. Let's
do it again."

Sin Is Pleasurable

A basic though neglected fact about sin is that it is enjoyable to the undisciplined heart, at least initially. We sin because
we are inclined to sin. We sin because we like to sin. This, of
course, is self-evident. Why else would we compulsively do
things that can be so destructive to ourselves and others? But
you don't hear many people making the simple admission,
"The problem is that I enjoy it." Have you ever heard a personal story where someone said that he sinned because he liked
it? Rarely. In sexual sin, men often try to persuade their spouses
that they didn't like their sin at all. The truth, however, is that
no matter how tragic the consequences of the sin, there is some
pleasure in it.

A wise first step for an addict would be to simply acknowledge the truth. "My motto was 'That was good. I think
I'll do it again.'" Sin was (and perhaps still is) enjoyable. You
liked it. You *loved* it. Of course, things could get rocky at times,
so there was a down side to the relationship. And there may
have been times when you said you weren't going back to it.
But it is too easy to forget the bad things and remember only
the good.

What benefit is there in admitting to the pleasure that accompanies lust? First of all, it would be honest. If we had gone
on and on about how we hated our addiction, there may have
been a kernel of truth there, but primarily it is a deception
and a way to avoid shame. Who wants to come right out and
admit that they loved drugs more than their spouse or children? There are limits to what most people are willing to acknowledge. Our true affections are not quickly made
public—either to ourselves or to others. We prefer to deceive
ourselves into thinking that what we did was all just a mistake
and a trap rather than a passionate relationship that we pur-

sued. This is one of the reasons why AA introductions are "I'm Bill. I'm an alcoholic." It is a way to stay honest.

A second reason to acknowledge the pleasure we took in addiction is that it keeps us doing battle. If we think we are dead to old passions, there is no reason to do battle with them. But if we remember that the old passions are still alive and kicking, we are alert and watchful.

This awareness is especially important when someone is *caught* in his addiction. These men and women swear that they will never do it again, and they sincerely believe they won't. They feel miserable. They are feeling the consequences of a covert lifestyle and the fractured relationships that accompany it. But such feelings should never be misinterpreted to mean that desires have died. They have more in common with people who feel bloated after the Thanksgiving meal. They feel like they will never eat again. But at breakfast the next morning, they no longer remember the physical pain and they are ready for more.

Sin's Pleasures Are Temporary

What reckless indulgence never reveals is that its pleasures are transient at best. There are some wise people who make hard choices because they know that sin's pleasures are only temporary (Heb. 11:25). There are others who have surrendered themselves to pleasure and eventually realized that such pursuits are ultimately vain (Eccl. 2). Too many of us, however, have accepted the lie of "Just one more, and then I will be satisfied." The reality is that "one more" *may* temporarily satisfy, but "one more" also feeds the desire for "one more" after that.

This phenomenon is captured in one of Scripture's most frightening passages. "They have given themselves over to sensuality so as to indulge in every kind of impurity, *with a continual lust for more*" (Eph. 4:19). With each indulgence, we paradoxically feel less and less satisfied, yet we are persuaded that the object of our desire is the only thing that can fill us.

Cravings revisited. Such biblical insight brings new perspectives to the discussion about cravings, physical dependence, and addictions. Over the last few decades it has been assumed in addictions research that cravings are straightforward chemical events. That is, drugs and alcohol are chemically constituted in such a way that, when habitually used, they create a profound physical dependence that defies resistance. Yet there has always been evidence that didn't easily fit the theory. For example, some people stop drugs cold turkey, yet don't experience serious withdrawal and physical cravings. Vietnam veterans, who were addicted to heroin in Vietnam but immediately stopped using when they boarded the plane home, are the most frequently cited illustration.[1] If drugs or alcohol automatically and universally produced a physical dependence, no one would be spared. Everyone would undergo withdrawal. Of course, it could be argued that the veterans who stopped when they came home simply did not have a biological propensity to addiction (an argument that can neither be proven nor disproven), but most people in the addiction field acknowledge that human addictions are complex. Like human sexual responses, they are biological but they are not *merely* biological. They can't be reduced to biology. They are biology plus something else.

It is also worth noting that cravings and dependence are not unique to addictive substances. Instead, *anything* that we enjoy, especially if the pleasure is experienced physically, is something we desire to repeat. For example, gambling and pornography do not introduce certain chemicals into the body, but their allure can be experienced in our bodies just as powerfully as crack cocaine. The orgasm, which no one would classify as physically addictive, may be the most craved human experience of all. It is probably what stands behind the power of pornography and the gamut of sexual sin. What is happening cannot be reduced to physiology. People are experiencing the siren call of sin's "one more."

Consider the following proposition: cravings are *spiritual* problems. Yes, they are also physical—everything we do and experience is physical. But there is a deeper explanation than biology. Cravings are not unique to certain types of drugs. Rather, they are the things we really want. Anything we want enough is a desire we will feel. We can "taste" victory. We are "dying" for a cup of coffee or the last piece of strawberry shortcake.

There are exceptions to this proposition. There are times when these feelings might come out of the blue, without any conscious desire, because the object we crave is linked to something else. For example, someone may have stopped drinking, but if drinking and cigarettes were part of a package, smoking may stir a desire for alcohol. In these cases, the sudden desire may not be pointing to something that is presently a real desire. This would more accurately be described as one of the sad consequences of addictive behavior: there are many memories of it, even though they are memories the person now finds more disturbing than tempting.

There may be other ways this proposition should be nuanced and refined as well. But let's focus on the rule more than the exception. Don't our cravings typically reveal what or who controls us? Do you have a hunger for God or a hunger for your own pleasures? Research will find that there are many different chemical events in the body that accompany these lusts and desires, but reliable observations can easily be explained by this perspective. Just because something is found on a cellular level doesn't mean that it is caused by those cells. We must keep in mind the unity between the human spirit and the body. Our spiritual beings are not ghosts that reside in small cubicles in our bodies. Instead, we are embodied spirits. All things spiritual are expressed physically. If we hate God—a spiritual commitment—it will be expressed in the neurons of our brains and our actual words and deeds. If we crave something, it is expressed physically. If we opt for self-control, it will be expressed physically.

Satan Appeals to Our Desires

Sin itself is the fundamental human craving that, when fed, leads to further craving and tolerance. It cries, "Give! Give!" but it never says, "Enough!" (Prov. 30:15–16). As if these were not enough, Satan comes alongside these ungodly passions and tempts us to give ourselves to them. Notice how he waited in the desert until Jesus was weak, tired, and hungry (Matt. 4:1–11). Of course, Satan underestimated Jesus. He did not understand how a sinless person lived out a human existence. He had never encountered any human being who consistently sought the glory of the Father over self-indulgence, but his strategy of attacking perceived areas of weakness is certainly apparent.

Satan waits for times when he thinks we are more vulnerable. He is the tempter. He pinpoints those things we enjoy and tells us to make them our lives. That is, if they are good in moderate amounts, they must be *very* good when we have even more. Satan appeals to our sinful desires just as he did in the Garden, and suggests that they are good rather than evil. He might even suggest that we *need* the thing desired, and how could it be right to be kept from something we need?

The especially frightening thing about Satan is that he is an expert on sin. He knows its every move. He knows what our sinful hearts crave and what they abhor. As a result, Satan can tempt us with things that seem uniquely attractive. Let's say you were spending your Saturday afternoon preparing for the next day's Sunday school class. A good friend calls and asks you to go shopping at a run-down thrift store. It might be very easy for you to say that you appreciate the invitation, but you are very busy with something more important. However, what if that same friend came by and tempted you with something you actually enjoyed? It would be much harder to stay home and continue your preparation.

Satan knows sin. It is his area of expertise. He has well-tested strategies to persuade us that sin is really not that bad and God is really not that good. Ever the opportunist, he comes rushing in whenever the imaginations of our minds set themselves on the created thing rather than the Creator.

WHAT IS SELF-CONTROL?

In this context, self-control begins to emerge as a great blessing rather than a legalistic burden. It stands against the lies of our own hearts (as well as those of Satan) and keeps us on the level path that leads to life. There are a number of ways it can be described, defined, and qualified.

Self-Control Means Living Within Boundaries

Human beings resist boundaries. Ever since sin entered the world, we have considered boundaries to be violations of our personal freedoms—curses rather than blessings. Scripture, however, reveals that it is our *lack* of personal boundaries that enslaves us.

> Like a city whose walls are broken down is a man who lacks self-control. (Prov. 25:28)

In biblical times, a city without walls was unthinkable. It would be the height of folly because it invited destruction. Any band of robbers, any neighboring country, could attack the city at will, guaranteeing suffering for the entire community. Only strong walls could bring a peaceful night's sleep. Similarly, undisciplined addicts are like defenseless cities with marauders going in and out. The only wise alternative is to rebuild the walls that protect us from our favorite idols with all haste and diligence.

This rebuilding involves many specific, practical steps. It means eating in public if we struggle with food. It means having passwords for internet accounts that must be opened by someone else; throwing out old reminders of the past idolatrous relationship; and never walking by a bar alone. Yet these walls are only the first line of defense. The most important walls are not those that keep someone from the local bar, however strong and valuable these walls may be. The most important walls are the ones that guard our own souls. "Above all else, guard your heart, for it is the wellspring of life" (Prov. 4:23).

Bars can be dangerous, and our own physical constitution may make us more vulnerable, but it is the sinful desires "which war against your soul" (1 Peter 2:11) that are the real enemy. The enemy is within. Self-control is a gift of the Spirit that helps us to fight against sinful lusts.

Self-Control Means Thinking Before Acting

Another description of self-control is simply this: THINK. Sin is like noise that makes it hard to think and hear. There are, of course, some messages that get through, such as doubts about the goodness of God, or thoughts like "God will forgive me. He knows how much of a struggle this is." What doesn't get through is wisdom.

Proverbs and James are two books especially devoted to teaching wisdom. Thoughtfulness is a key theme in them both. Not just any kind of thoughtfulness, of course. We could think about something for quite awhile and our thinking could be very wrong. The thoughtfulness Scripture commends is a thoughtfulness about God's thoughts. As the philosopher and theologian Cornelius Van Til often said, Christian thought is thinking God's thoughts after him.

This thoughtfulness is not so much an aspect of wisdom as it is a synonym for wisdom. Wisdom is living a biblically informed life. It is remembering the fear of the Lord and God's instruction before we proceed (Prov. 4). It is thinking before we act. It is considering the consequences of our actions in contrast to giving "no thought to the way of life" (Prov. 5:6). It is remembering what the Lord hates and choosing to hate those things too (Prov. 6:16–19; 8:13). It is learning from the lessons of the past. It is meditating on the good instruction we have received (Prov. 16:20) and being suspicious of our ability to justify our own plans and desires.

Notice how we are tempted to act rashly when we are arrogant, prideful, struggling with cravings, or even riddled with fear. Any time we feel something strongly we feel compelled to act immediately. Wisdom, however, is willing to count to ten—or a thousand—before acting on impulse. It seeks out counsel and submits to it. The wise, thoughtful person loves to have wise people tell her what to do, and the wise, thoughtful person loves to have God do the same.

Self-Control Is Not Emotional Flatness or Indifference

At first glance, self-control might be summarized, "The man who fears God will avoid all extremes" (Eccl. 7:18). This is sound advice, but it can be easily misinterpreted. Moderation can be perceived as a kind of stoicism in which we "rise above" our passions and do not allow ourselves to feel them. This, however, is not what Scripture commands.

Jonathan Edwards's *Treatise Concerning Religious Affections* took special interest in this topic. He distinguished between two types of affections, suggesting that one overwhelms or obsesses a person, whereas the other is an informed response of the whole person, marked by self-control. As believers, our passions should fit the latter description, as active responses to the glories of God.

Scripture, too, makes distinctions among our passions. It talks about passions and desires as either good or evil. It commands us to put to death ungodly desires and teaches us to nurture true spiritual passion. Our relationship to God in Christ should be characterized by holy, intense affections; our response to our own sin should be hatred and tears; our love for others should be such that we are moved by both their pleasure and pain. Scripture does not oppose strong desire; instead, it both approves of it and commands it. The problem is in what we are passionate about and why. Do our passions express a heart that seeks the glory of Christ? Are we passionate about the things for which Jesus is passionate? Or do our passions express our desire to serve ourselves and our own glory? It is likely that when we repent over our addictions, we should include repentance for not being passionate about Christ and the things he loves.

Self-Control Is Not Self-Dependence

Another clarification about self-control is that it is not the same as self-dependence, in which we rely on personal will power to control ourselves. Instead, self-control is a gift of the Holy Spirit, given through faith in Jesus Christ. It is a side effect of the fear of the Lord.

Self-dependence is focused on ourselves. When it is a means to improve ourselves and overcome our addictions, the purpose might actually be to *avoid* Jesus. This kind of self-effort characterizes people who attempt to master themselves so that they don't need God or their peers. In the same way that their ungodly indulgence was ultimately self-serving, their Christless self-reformation is a self-focused pursuit. We could argue that sober self-centered people are better off than drunk self-centered persons, and in a certain sense that would be true. Some addictions have dreadful social consequences, and abstinence and sobriety keep a person's reckless indulgence from hurting too many others. However, there is a deeper sense in which self-dependent individuals are no better off. In fact, they may be even worse off.

When people seek to bring order to their internal lives apart from faith in Christ, Scripture suggests that the evil chased out will be replaced by a greater one (Matt. 12:43–45). In other words, Scripture indicates that we are not ultimately our own masters. If we try to drive out one master, other masters will rush in to take its place: exercise instead of food, a slavish devotion to work instead of adultery. AA talks about "dry drunks," individuals who have reformed themselves in the sense that they are sober, but who are still mastered by the demons that drove them to drink. The only master who is not harsh and enslaving is Christ himself. In fact, even though we are his servants, the actual experience of this servitude is so joyful and blessed that it is called liberation.

HOW DO I GET SELF-CONTROL?

Against this background, self-control is a strategic countermeasure to the insatiable cravings of sin. It is a great blessing to those who find it. Because the lack of self-control is such an extensive problem, almost synonymous with humanness, it is not surprising to find plenty of biblical references to it.

A wise man keeps himself under control. (Prov. 29:11)

But the fruit of the Spirit is love, joy, peace, patience, kindness, goodness, faithfulness, gentleness and self-control. (Gal. 5:22–23)

Each of you should learn to control his own body in a way that is holy and honorable, not in passionate lust like the heathen. (1 Thess. 4:4–5)

Prepare your minds for action; be self-controlled; set your hope fully on the grace to be given you when Jesus Christ is revealed. (1 Peter 1:13)

Be self-controlled and alert. Your enemy the devil prowls around like a roaring lion looking for someone to devour. (1 Peter 5:8)

Make every effort to add to your faith goodness; and to goodness, knowledge; and to knowledge, self-control. (2 Peter 1:5–6)

The problem is that these passages don't sound very sophisticated or penetrating. In fact, they don't sound much different than a parent saying, "Stop it!" Notice, for example, that the apostle Paul tells Titus that we should just say "no" to ungodly lusts (Titus 2:12). But "Just Say No" is a campaign that was declared ineffective years ago. So how exactly do we get self-control?

Consider more closely Paul's instruction to Titus. It was written to Titus while he was strengthening the Christian church in Crete, a culture that bears many similarities to our own. Cretan society was an addictive society. It was notorious in the Roman world for the self-indulgence of its citizenry. Unlike the abstemious, ascetic tendencies of some cultures, Crete specialized in Western-style lust.

What do you teach when recklessness is in the air? Paul mapped out a pastoral strategy that targeted four different groups: older men, older women, younger men, and younger women. His central teaching was self-control.

To the older men Paul said, "Teach the older men to be temperate, worthy of respect, self-controlled, and sound in faith, in love and in endurance" (2:2). Unlike the extensive discipleship packages available today, Paul told Titus to fix the older men's attention on just a few things. Of this list, there are two words—temperate and self-controlled—that refer to a mind that isn't dulled by indulgence, whether the indulgence is in laziness or alcohol.

To the older women he said, "Teach the older women to be reverent in the way they live, not to be slanderers or addicted to much wine, but to teach what is good" (2:3). Again, self-control—this time with alcohol mentioned explicitly—is a central element. The good teaching that these older women were to provide was directed especially toward the younger women. Not surprisingly, its substance included self-control. The older women were to teach the younger women "to love their husbands and children, to be self-controlled and pure, to be busy at home, to be kind, and to be subject to their husbands" (2:4–5). The fourth group, the younger men, was given the most succinct direction. "Encourage the young men to be self-controlled" (2:6). Period. Apparently, this would be more than enough. If the young men could learn self-control over the coming decades, then they might be ready for more teaching. So, regardless of age, self-control is an essential task. Its importance to a life well lived is so obvious that Plato and Aristotle list it among their four virtues, along with justice, wisdom, and courage.[2] It is emphasized throughout the wisdom literature of the Old Testament, and it is a critical teaching in Titus's pastoral ministry. The basic idea is that we must cultivate the skill of living a thoughtful, careful life in which we do what is right despite our desires. It is tested when we are alone or we feel unsatisfied. What do we do when no one is looking? What do we do when cravings feel so strong that they hurt? Who or what will rule you then? Your desires or your God? Self-control is the skill of saying "no" to sinful desires, even when it hurts.

Do I Want Self-Control?

Scripture couldn't be any clearer. An essential feature of sin is that it loathes boundaries, preferring instead to follow its own desires. The consequence of pursuing these desires is that we are unsatisfied, deluded, and enslaved by our ungodly passions. In this context, self-control emerges as a blessing from the benevolent, triune God. Now the question is, Do you really want self-control?

Consider the question carefully. Think about it. The easy answer is, "Yes, of course. Look at what addiction has done to me." But the real answer is usually much more complex.

- You want self-control, but you want it only in pill form, without having to break a sweat.

- You want it because you are *supposed* to want it. You are not thinking yet.
- You want it, but not at the cost of saying "no" forever to something you love.
- You want it—sometimes.
- You want it—tomorrow.
- You want it, but you are waiting for God to remove your cravings first.
- You want it simply because it will make life a little easier or save you some money. In other words, you want the misery of addiction to be gone, but you don't want the grace of God and the will of God to replace it.

If you find that your answer is not as clear as you expected, go back to the basics. Do you remember that sin deceives us, so you cannot trust your own thinking? Do you know that God is good, and his gifts are intended to bless? Do you realize (especially considering how often Scripture speaks of self-control) that it is *possible* to get it? Do you understand that God actually *wants* to give it to us? Do you remember the tragedy that has been associated with your sin? Or, as C. S. Lewis asks, do you prefer playing in mud puddles when God offers you a holiday at the beach?

Now envision the crown (1 Cor. 9:25). Much as we offer candy as an inducement to the child who does not appreciate the blessings of obedience, so the Lord tells us about the lasting crowns he gives to those who pursue obedience to Christ. Yet a crown, of course, is not the ultimate prize. It is only a hint of something much better. The real prize is Christ himself. Seeing this increases our self-control, encouraging us to do things that are important, true, and good rather than things that feel urgent but are ungodly.

There are a number of ways that self-control can be waylaid. Not wanting it is one of them.

Remember the Grace of God

In the Titus passage, the apostle Paul first explained how the teaching on self-control should be offered to every age group. He then moved on to exhort us to "say 'No' to ungodliness and worldly passions" (Titus 2:12). But this simple exhortation must be embedded in the larger context of Paul's teaching to be understood accurately.

> For the grace of God that brings salvation has appeared to all men. It teaches us to say "No" to ungodliness and worldly passions, and to live self-controlled, upright and godly lives in this present age, while we wait for the blessed hope—the glorious appearing of our great God and Savior Jesus Christ, who gave himself for us to redeem us from all wickedness and to purify for himself a people that are his very own, eager to do what is good. (Titus 2:11–14)

This passage changes everything. It takes a simple command—saying "no"—and surrounds it with Jesus Christ.

Scripture never expects us to hear God's commands *to* us in isolation from the serious contemplation of God's work *for* us in Christ. Paul begins all his letters with "grace to you" and ends them with "grace be with you." Self-control is possible because of the grace given us in Jesus Christ. It is this ever-present grace that teaches us to say "no."

The "grace of God" is a phrase packed with meaning for the apostle Paul. It refers to the love and benevolence that characterize God's dealings with us. What's more, the grace of God is something very specific, practical, and concrete. The grace of God is what God has done and what he is presently doing. He has sent Jesus to liberate us from the harsh bondage to our own desires. By faith, he has set us free so that we can live for him rather than ourselves (2 Cor. 5:15). Having made us alive in Christ, the Father now gives us a spirit of self-discipline (2 Tim. 1:7) by way of the Spirit (Gal. 5:22–23). This Spirit is liberally given to those who call on the Father in the name of the Son.

This means that we are well fitted for the task of putting to death ungodly passions. On the one hand, we have our residual sinful cravings; on the other we have the Spirit who raised Jesus Christ from the dead. Although our cravings go deep, they are no match for the Spirit of the Living God. This, of course, does not mean that the battle is over and we can "let go and let God." Rather, it means that we are now empowered to engage in the battle. Just as the Israelites were given the Promised Land as a gift, yet they had to take it by force, one town at a time, so we are promised the gift of self-control and are also called to lay claim to it one day at a time.

Meditate on the Coming of Jesus Christ

The grace of God takes self-control out of the realm of hopeless self-reformation into the realm of great confidence that we can be transformed people. Yet Paul gives us even more. He precedes his exhortation to "say 'No' " with a reminder of the grace of God given to us, and he follows it by asking us to contemplate the grace that is to come.

This pattern of coupling self-control and the coming of Christ is standard in Scripture. For example, 1 Peter 1:13 says, "Prepare your minds for action; be self-controlled; set your hope fully on the grace to be given you when Jesus Christ is revealed." When Scripture calls us to vigilance in our battle with sin, it often directs our attention to our future hope.

What are the benefits of meditating on the return of Christ? There are several. First, it reminds us that there is a deadline. The battle with sin is hard, but it will someday be over. If there were no end in sight to our battle with sin, we could easily fatigue and give up. But when we know that the deadline is approaching, we become much more vigilant. Like virgins waiting for the bridegroom or a student who must complete an assignment by a certain date, deadlines make us willing to forego sleep to do what has been asked of us. They bring an urgency to the present, taking away the popular self-talk, "After just one more _____, then I will stop."

A second benefit to meditating on future realities is that eternity reveals the things that are important. When we are preoccupied with the present, our less-than-attentive consciences are more likely to permit "one more." But when we consider our thoughts and actions in the light of the return of Christ, the self-serving nature of our desires becomes more apparent.

This dynamic operates even when we think another human being might see us in our secret addictions. For example, someone might easily justify a trip to a crack house (lover's house, bar, web site, and so on) because it is "just a short visit": "I'm just dropping in to say Hi." But such thinking is exposed for what it is when that person considers what he would do if his spouse were to suddenly appear. If the potential presence/arrival of another person can reveal the ungodliness in our behavior, how much more the coming of Christ himself?

A third benefit of meditating on the grace to come is that it reveals our true destiny. This can be a very powerful inducement. Our destiny is that we will be perfect—creatures who do not know all things, but are sinless. Consider that. Don't we often excuse our addictions by thinking, *This is just humanness—I can't help it?* True humanness, however, is to be like Jesus in every way that a creature can be. This means that we are becoming people controlled solely by the Spirit of the living God, not by our private passions. True humanness is being able to say "no" to ungodly passions even when it hurts.

Reckless self-indulgence and bondage to sinful passions are simply not what God intended for human beings. Such behavior has much more in common with a dog than it does with God's design for us. When we indulge ungodly passions, it is as if we were sub-human, licking our own vomit or eating our own feces. These actions might be acceptable in dogs, but they are shameful and disgusting for people created in God's image. So it is when we are controlled by our ungodly desires. We were created for something much more noble than eating feces. We were created to have passions that are directed to the glory of God.

If you have put your faith in Christ, your destiny is that you are going to be absolutely sinless someday. Now is the time to start acting like the person you soon will be.

Develop a Clear, Publicized Strategy

These are the theological nuts and bolts to the biblical teaching on self-control. Almost everything else is the application of these points. One application, for example, is that the desire for self-control must be accompanied by a plan. If self-control demands thoughtfulness, and if it is ultimately a declaration of war on both our own flesh and Satan's temptations, then there must be a strategy. If our battle were against an insignificant foe, there would be no need for planning. We could simply show up and win. But when the enemy is subtle and crafty, a strategy is essential.

The lack of a strategy is one of the main reasons why New Year's resolutions wind up on the scrap heap. After we've eaten too much, we feel bloated and make a resolution to eat wisely. But our decision usually lasts no longer than lunch the next day. Or, having been caught buying drugs, we figure that our vague sense of remorse will engender abstinence. We don't even think about next week, when we will be feeling the same drug cravings and have access to the same drug users and dealers. In these situations, there was no thoughtful plan, no consideration of the spiritual dominion involved, no calling out for the grace of God in Christ, no real desire to take one's soul to task, and no pleas for help and counsel from other brothers and sisters.

A good indicator of whether or not you want to grow in self-control is this: Do you have a clear, *public* strategy? If anyone says, "I am really going to change this time—I don't think I need any help," that person has yet to understand the biblical teaching on self-control. It is one thing to make a resolution; it is something completely different to repent, seek counsel, and develop a plan with the help of others that is concrete and Christ-centered.

The heart of any plan must, of course, be Jesus Christ. Self-control is like any other feature of wisdom: it is learned by contemplating a person. Strategically, this is unprecedented. We would expect God to simply yell at us and tell us, again, to shape up. But God's ways are much better than our own and rarely predictable. Rather than giving us twelve steps on which to rely, he gives us a person to know. As Jesus is known and exalted among us, self-control becomes more obvious. The double cure for sin is the foundation for all change: in the gospel, we have been released from both the condemnation and power of sin. We have been freed "to serve the living and true God, and to wait for his Son from heaven, whom he raised from the dead—Jesus, who rescues us from the coming wrath" (1 Thess. 1:9–10).

To place this in the context of the book of Proverbs, the fear of the Lord is the beginning of wisdom. What is the fear of the Lord? It is walking with reverence and joy with the God who is with us. It is our response of obedient love and devotion to the Holy One who has pursued us, loved us, received the wrath of the Father on our behalf, and is with us by the Spirit. As mentioned earlier, the fear of the Lord is knowing that we live *coram deo,* before the face of God. It is knowing that the Holy God sees every aspect of our lives. This "seeing" is a curse to those who try to avoid him, but for those of us who have come to know Jesus Christ, it is a wall of protection, enabling us to discern and do God's will, doing the important thing rather than the thing that feels urgent.

PRACTICAL THEOLOGY

In Western culture, our legal right to personal freedoms tends to infiltrate our theology. Anything that feels like restraint seems legalistic. Self-control, however, is a wonderful gift from God. It is a blessing. It is a chief characteristic of a wise person.

As You Face Your Own Addiction

1. Can you remember a time when you actually said "no" to sinful desires? It is not unusual to remember few, if any.

2. As a way to practice saying "no," consider small fasts. You could give up food, desserts, computer games, or other activities important to you. This is not a way to punish yourself for what you have done. It is simply a way to have more practice at self-control. Remember that self-control is a skill that develops with practice.

3. Are you spending time with wise people? Read through Proverbs so that you know what they look like. Spend time with them. Ask them how they have found blessings in self-control.

4. If you would like some other reading on self-control, get *A Hunger for God,* by John Piper. It looks especially at food, but it has immediate application to all addictions.

5. Read through this chapter more than once. Read it every week for a year. A wise person keeps wisdom in focus.

As You Help Someone Else

1. Wisdom comes when we keep important teachings of Scripture in view. Don't pass through this teaching too quickly. Keep reading it. Talk about it. Share how self-control has been a blessing.

2. When there is lack of self-control in one area, you will find it in others. What about the tongue? Is it also out of control? If so, read James 3 together.

3. Proverbs is the best-known book on wisdom, but James

might be easier to study together. You will find the theme of self-control throughout the book, but there are others too. Don't be too concerned if you spend less time on self-control and more on these other themes. If you grow in any area of wisdom, it will affect self-control.

4. If you are helping someone and she would like to try some mini-fasts, do it with her. It will be a good refresher course for you.

11

Staying Violent

From the days of John the Baptist until now,
the kingdom of heaven has been forcefully advancing,
and forceful men lay hold of it.

MATTHEW 11:12

If your hand or your foot causes you to sin,
cut it off and throw it away.

MATTHEW 18:8

There is a mean streak to authentic self-control. Underneath what seems to be the placid demeanor of those who are not ruled by their desires is the heart of a warrior. Self-control is not for the timid. When we want to grow in it, not only do we nurture an exuberance for Jesus Christ, we also demand of ourselves a hatred for sin.

So think again. When was the last time you said "no" to something out of obedience to Christ, *when it actually was hard to say "no"?* Maybe you can say "no" quite easily to cocaine, but you linger over salacious advertising. Maybe you can say "no" to the second or third drink, but you will never miss a dessert (though you vow weekly to change your eating habits). Any earthly desire that doesn't take "no" for an answer is a lust that surpasses your desire for Jesus himself. With this in mind, we quickly realize that self-control is not simply an exercise in self-improvement. It is an essential discipline in a high stakes spiritual battle. The only possible attitude toward out-of-control desires is a declaration of all-out war.

Actually, the war has been declared. The enemy has already made a preemptive strike; sinful desires already "war against your soul" (1 Peter 2:11). We simply need to be awakened by faith to engage in a counterattack.

Be very careful, then, how you live. (Eph. 5:15)

Put on the full armor of God. (Eph. 6:11)

Prepare your minds for action. (1 Peter 1:13)

Make every effort. (2 Peter 1:5)

Be self-controlled and alert. (1 Peter 5:8)

These are battle cries, and Scripture is full of them. But unlike our old conception of warfare, where battle lines are clear and the times of battle can almost be predicted, this is modern warfare in which you are not always sure where the enemy lurks. It is guerilla warfare. There are strategically placed snipers. You let down your guard for a moment and the village you thought was safe suddenly opens fire on you.

DECLARE WAR

There is something about war that sharpens the senses, especially when the enemy constantly hides. Issues of life and death will do that. You hear a twig snap or the rustling of leaves and you are in attack mode. Someone coughs and you are ready to pull the trigger. Even after days of little or no sleep, war keeps us vigilant.

The problem is that as Christians, we often forget we are

in a war. Or worse, we don't even know that there *is* a war. Unlike most warfare, where at least we know that there is an enemy *somewhere,* spiritual warfare tends to be especially covert. No one is getting shot and many people—even addicts themselves—seem to be managing their lives fairly well. It all looks like business as usual. Add to this the fact that we actually *like* the enemy, and it is easy to understand why many of us act as though we were on vacation.

A vacation is even more serene than times of universal peace. During peacetime, people still work and go about their normal duties, but on vacation, it is pure rest and recreation—nothing taxing. The idea of doing anything until it hurts is absolutely taboo. "Reduce stress in your life" is the watchword.

Scripture understands that life is hard and busy. In fact, God himself is the author of Sabbaths and times of rest. (The difference between a Sabbath and a weekend is that the Sabbath reminds us that we ultimately find our rest in God alone.) God himself is also the one who announces "comfort" (Isa. 40) and "peace," and he invites us to a place of rest. In fact, his peace is even more profound than we can imagine (Phil. 4:7). But when you examine Scripture as a whole, it says more than "peace." It is as if peace comes in installments. If we have turned to Christ in faith, we have peace with God and a conscience that is no longer troubled. Yet we are guaranteed that we will not, at this moment, have complete peace in all our relationships (Matt. 10:34), and we certainly do not have peace either in our battle with our own sin or with Satan. Instead, when we turn to Christ by faith, we are freed from the slavery of sin and empowered to fight.

"The violent take it by force" is how the King James Version puts it (Matt. 11:12). That is the way the kingdom of God advances. With persecution outside, Satan fighting us through temptations, and our own lusts within, every disciple of Christ is in a battle, one that demands spiritual strength and ongoing vigilance.

SHOW NO MERCY TO YOUR SINFUL DESIRES

The apostle Paul uses athletic imagery to exhort us to fight.

> Do you not know that in a race all the runners run, but only one gets the prize? . . . Everyone who competes in the games goes into strict training. They do it to get a crown that will not last; but we do it to get a crown that will last forever. Therefore, I do not run like a man running aimlessly; I do not fight like a man beating the air. No, I beat my body and make it my slave so that after I have preached to others, I myself will not be disqualified for the prize. (1 Cor. 9:24–27)

Paul is not a gnostic dualist who is teaching that our bodies are bad and our spirits or souls are good. He is using the body to talk about our appetites—natural bodily desires that dominate us when unchecked. He is talking about eating, drinking, and sexual desires. He is not suggesting that these desires are necessarily evil in themselves. They simply need to be watched carefully. Or, more accurately, since our sinful tendency is to carelessly indulge these desires, he implores us to have a battle-like, aggressive, rigorous, take-no-prisoners style of life. When your desires start growing into ungodly proportions, beat them into submission, says Paul.

This is where a disease metaphor is weak. It doesn't lend itself to violence—vigilance perhaps, but not violence. When you are doing battle with sin, it requires preparation and a desire to absolutely eradicate it from your life. To settle for a truce or a peaceful coexistence is a thinly veiled commitment to fall back in love with the desired substance.

Here is a good model. A thirty-five-year-old husband and father wakes up each morning with the same refrain: "I am going into battle today." When he envisions the enemy, however, it is not necessarily the person telling dirty jokes during a coffee break or the drug dealer who works in shipping (although he must be careful when he is with them). Instead, he envisions *himself* and the temptations that come from within him as the enemy.

FIGHTING THE TEMPTATIONS WITHIN US

All temptations are a kind of lure, dangling in front of us, waiting to ensnare us. We are exhorted to do battle with them all. Yet not all temptations are the same. Some come from within us, and some from external sources. When we are doing battle, we need to know the source of the temptation. Otherwise, it is easy to overlook the contribution we bring to the cycle of temptation and sin.

A popular biblical image of temptation is that of Joseph and Potiphar's wife. It is the picture of the alluring woman waiting to seduce. This narrative is, indeed, an excellent illustration of temptation that is *presented* to us. It comes to us when we have not called for it. However, other temptations arise from our own hearts and imaginations. They are described in the book of James.

> When tempted, no one should say, "God is tempting me." For God cannot be tempted by evil, nor does he tempt anyone; but each one is tempted when, by his own evil desire, he is dragged away and enticed. Then, after desire has conceived, it gives birth to sin; and sin, when it is full-grown, gives birth to death. (James 1:13–15)

How can we pray that God would not lead us into temptation (Matt. 6:13) if we also believe that God doesn't tempt? How can we say that Jesus was tempted like us (Heb. 4:15) but that he never even entertained the "evil desires" that James associates with temptation? These seemingly contradictory teachings are clarified when we realize that Scripture is talking about two different temptations.

James makes it clear that the desire for anything that Scripture prohibits is an evil desire that comes from our own hearts. We can quickly identify these temptations by asking ourselves which of our desires prefer to stay in the dark. Which desires do we want to hide from certain people? Illegal drugs? "Just one drink" when we know that "just one" will open the door to "just one more"? Internet sites? Pornography? More pain medication than we need? More ice cream than we'd like people to know we ate? We can't blame these temptations on anything outside of ourselves, so "fleeing temptation" is not a sufficient answer. If someone can actually flee something that he deeply desires, then, once removed from the external temptation, he must follow through by taking his soul to task. We are attracted by the temptations outside us because of the sinful desires we harbor within.

PROGRESSIVE SANCTIFICATION

The process of doing battle with internal temptations, or taking our souls to task, is called progressive sanctification. It means that the battle with our own sinful desires will gradually progress over time. In God's sovereign plan, conversion does not bring about instant moral perfection. Instead, sinlessness waits for the return of Christ. Meanwhile, God's plan is that we fight indwelling sin. Since it is God himself who makes the declaration of war, there is something praiseworthy about the fight as we participate in it. The fight itself brings glory to him.

This is a very important point: *the battle is good.* It is not a sign of failure; it is a sign that the Spirit is on the move. It is a sign that we are spiritually alive and engaged in the process of sanctification. Some addicts are led to believe that the battle against sin is over after a short, name-it-and-claim-it skirmish. They claim victory. The battle, they think, is largely over. Then, when the inevitable temptations arise, they don't fit the addict's interpretation of what should happen, so they are either ignored or denied. Eventually, the addict begins to question whether the Spirit is really powerful enough to conquer his addiction, and Scripture gradually becomes something impractical, increasingly separated from daily life.

The real spiritual battle, biblically understood, is similar to the way the Israelites were delivered from Egypt and taken to the Promised Land.

> "I [the LORD] have come down to rescue them from the hand of the Egyptians and to bring them up out of that land into a good and spacious land, a land flowing with milk and honey." (Ex. 3:8)

This was God's promise. He said that he would bring his people out of slavery and give them a land that was their own. *The land was theirs.* Those who trust in Christ have gone through an even more dramatic deliverance. Through the wonder of Spirit-wrought faith, we are united to Christ, so that what was his is now our own, and the sin that was ours has been placed on him. We died with Christ to the penalty and power of sin, and we are raised with Christ to live for God as his beloved children.

Scripture then makes very bold statements about our life in Christ. It almost seems to suggest that we don't sin anymore. For example, Romans 6:6 says that "our old self was crucified with him so that the body of sin might be done away with, that we should no longer be slaves to sin." This, however, is similar to God saying that the land belonged to Israel. They were promised the land, but *they still had to fight for it.* Furthermore, not all the battles were successful. There were times when Israel fought without the Lord himself leading them into battle. We, too, have been promised something truly remarkable.

We are promised a holy and blameless life, and then we are told to fight for it (Fig. 11.1).

FIGHT WITH HOPE

History and film are filled with stories of battles in which a small band of men tries to hold off a much larger and more powerful army. From "Remember the Alamo!" to *Saving Private Ryan,* such stories are part of our cultural psyche. In the early stages of the battle, the outnumbered force might show amazing bravery in one heroic stand after another. However, everyone knows that the end is inevitable. The heroic band will be crushed by the enemy. In fact, all hope was lost before the fight began. It is simply a matter of time before the foregone conclusion becomes a reality. Gradually, the men begin to lose their zeal for the battle. As one buddy after another is killed, soldiers begin to go through the motions, hoping, at best, that the end is quick and merciful.

FIGURE 11.1.
THE PROCESS OF CHANGE

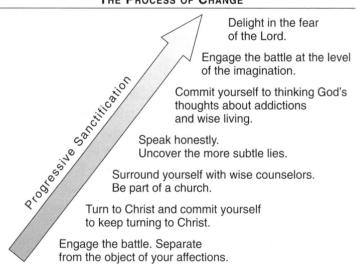

Progressive Sanctification

Delight in the fear of the Lord.

Engage the battle at the level of the imagination.

Commit yourself to thinking God's thoughts about addictions and wise living.

Speak honestly.
Uncover the more subtle lies.

Surround yourself with wise counselors.
Be part of a church.

Turn to Christ and commit yourself to keep turning to Christ.

Engage the battle. Separate from the object of your affections.

So it may seem with our lusts and sinful desires. Many people put up valiant efforts against them, but it always feels like a losing battle. We are trying to postpone defeat more than maintain any hope of victory. In Christ, however, there have been extraordinary changes. Satan has been defeated, we are no longer condemned, and sin is no longer our master. We are united with a new Commander, who wages war with the Spirit of power who raises the dead.

SATAN IS DEFEATED

Does it sound odd to talk about Satan? Usually, it only sounds odd to someone who has never experienced the true bondage of addiction. There are many sins in which Satan's lordship is hidden—the subtle lies of polite conversation, the fudging on our income tax. But it isn't hard to detect Satan's oversight when it comes to addictions. The bondage, lies, and accusations are blatant.

Satan's power is evident in the Old Testament, particularly in the book of Job, but it is with the coming of Christ that his dark kingdom is especially exposed. The New Testament mentions a number of encounters between Jesus and people who were possessed by demons. Each of these encounters was evidence that the kingdom of God that Jesus was inaugurating overpowers the kingdom of Satan. At one time, all people were easy prey, susceptible to Satan's devices. But now "the prince of this world" stands condemned (John 16:11) before Christ. He cannot dominate Christ or those who have his Spirit.

As a result, although Scripture certainly warns us to be alert to Satan, it stresses that we can "be strong in the Lord and in his mighty power" and we can "stand against the devil's schemes" (Eph. 6:10–11). We can "resist him, standing firm in the faith" (1 Peter 5:9). Even more, we can resist him and he will flee from us (James 4:7). Jesus has ushered in a new era in which Satan no longer has the power to blind the nations in the way he once did.

This changes the way we do battle. Instead of assuming that the battle will be lost, instead of just trying to last long enough to slow the inevitable onslaught of the enemy, in Christ we have been promised victory. We are given all the resources of Jesus Christ in our fight. Victory is assured. Yes, the battle must be waged, but it is now waged with the passion of an army that knows the momentum has shifted. The fighting may be fierce, but those who know they can and will win can fight with abandon.

WE ARE NOT CONDEMNED

When Satan gets desperate, he frantically tries to accuse us, suggesting that with every single slip we make, we are further condemned. His goal is to take us out of the battle, incapacitated by despair. Like an enemy using false propaganda to demoralize its foe, Satan will tell us that we have been abandoned by the commanding officer. We are told that our superiors thought we were hopeless and have decided not to send in reinforcements. Addicts are easy prey for such accusations.

There is pride, arrogance, and an unwillingness to hear counsel among addicts, but there is also a sense of hopelessness and uselessness. Addicts feel like they are getting what they deserve. Of course, even this despair can be used as an excuse for continuing their addiction, but it is also what they genuinely feel. Every addict lives with the experience of inner condemnation.

This is one reason why so many addictions counselors avoid any discussion of sin. They have spent time with addicts; they know that they already feel horribly guilty. To heap judgment on them (which is what Christians are perceived to do) just makes it worse. Every experienced counselor, secular or Christian, knows that change will not take place under a load of guilt and condemnation. Sobriety and guilt *are* incompatible. To address this guilt, counselors might teach that addicts are not responsible for what has happened to them. Instead, they have a disease.

Some addicts are not easily persuaded that this is true, but most will eventually succumb to the pressure of the addictive community. Once they do, everything feels different. Addicts feel liberated. Why? Because they have been offered a way to deal with their guilt. All this time, the addict was laboring under guilt and shame, and change is impossible under such a load. Now, with the news that they are not guilty, they feel free. They have hope, perhaps for the very first time.

No wonder any counsel that mentions sin is so widely disdained. Guilt and change *cannot* coexist. Guilt will stifle any attempt at self-reformation. So when Christians mention sin, we can understand why so few people are listening. The fact is that if mentioning sin only intensified guilt, we would not be listening either. But this is not a fair, biblical portrayal of the doctrine of sin. As we have seen earlier, sin is simply a reality. But Scripture does not offer a sin-based model of addiction. Instead, it invites us to adopt a grace-based model. Its emphasis is not so much on our sin as it is on the grace that comes from God through faith (Eph. 2:8). Our knowledge of our own sin is intended to point us to the redemptive grace we can receive through Jesus Christ.

Grace communicates two important truths. First and foremost, it reveals the character of God. God delights in showing grace to those who turn to him. So much so that the apostle Paul anticipates a question: "Shall we go on sinning so that grace may increase?" (Rom. 6:1). The answer is "By no means!" Grace *liberates* us from sin. How could we then use it as an excuse to go back to our old master? The point is that Paul reveals God as one who surprises us in his eagerness to show grace.

The second feature of grace is that it says something about us. It says that we can't pay God back for our sins against him. Scripture has clear teaching about restitution: if you sin against someone, you pay that person back, plus a fine. This, however, only works in human transactions. If you steal someone's bike, you repay a bike and more. We cannot, however, repay God. To consider such a possibility is to minimize the nature of our sin and minimize the cross of Christ. *Grace* reminds us that what we could not repay, Christ himself paid on our behalf. In this context, grace-based counsel talks about sin, but quickly points to the One who has taken our sin away. Contrary to what many think, when we see our sin clearly as the rebellion against God that Scripture says it is, it can actually lead to greater joy.

> "Two men owed money to a certain moneylender. One owed him five hundred denarii, and the other fifty. Neither of them had the money to pay him back, so he cancelled the debts of both. Now which of them will love him more?" (Luke 7:41–42)

To expose sin without grace does bring greater condemnation, but to expose sin in light of the free offer of forgiveness is a great joy that leads to thanksgiving and praise.

Yet grace has a certain price. To receive it is to acknowledge that we have no righteousness of our own. As a result, our human instinct is to choose to be miserable and full of self-loathing as a way to do penance before God. This might seem religious on the surface, but such self-loathing is actually sin. It basically calls God a liar. It says that we must do some kind of atonement for our own sins before we can experience the grace of God. Given the seriousness of our sins, it is understandable that we would look for a repayment plan, but in light of the grace of God shown us in Christ, it is unthinkable, and an insult to what God has done.

In Susan's case, this cycle would begin when she would go on a bulimic binge and then feel utterly condemned. To cleanse herself, she would vomit and then fast for the next few days, hoping that at some point she would be clean enough to please God and appease his anger. But before she ever felt like God was pleased with her abstinence and self-condemnation, she would get hungry and go through the cycle again. This is typical of many addictive cycles.

How can you reach Susan's heart? The best way is to simply remind her of what Christ has done.

> Susan, you profess your faith in Christ. You believe that Christ has taken all your sin and you have received all his righteousness. But you aren't living like that. You are still living like a slave who has to do extra work if she breaks a dish, not like a child who has been given the greatest of all gifts. You live like someone under the law rather than grace. You have forgotten that you have been cleansed from past sins (2 Peter 1:9).

> Don't fast and practice hating yourself. Instead, remember what Christ has done. Remember that he asks nothing more of you than to turn to him by faith. Faith means that you must bring *nothing* to him—no fasting, self-mutilation, or anything. To bring something is like saying that we can pay God back for our sins—and that minimizes sin. In fact, it is actually pride, and another example of how we try to do things independently of God. Jesus tells us to bring nothing so that he can be the One to give us everything. It is this true grace that brings glory to God.

> If you want something to do, here is one of the hardest—believe. Believe the gospel of grace and be thankful.

The reason the world avoids any discussion of sin is that it knows very little of the astounding grace of God.

Sin Is No Longer Our Master

When we have a weak and limited view of grace, we assume that we have to pay God back for some of our sins. This is a common misunderstanding. Another is that grace frees us so that we can do what we want. When grace is mingled with a heart that craves independence, it can be misinterpreted to mean that we have no master. We are freed from Satan's domain, and now we serve no one but ourselves. Yet independence is not an option. We are either mastered by our desires (and Satan) or by Christ. We were bought out of slavery at the greatest cost possible. We were not set free to serve ourselves, but to serve and love the living God.

> "Everything is permissible for me"—but not everything is beneficial. "Everything is permissible for me"—but I will not be mastered by anything. (1 Cor. 6:12)

It is certainly true that when the Spirit was given to God's people, certain applications of the law were no longer binding. But that freedom was intended to lead us into more wholehearted service of Christ, not into license to satisfy our own desires. Knowing our penchant to twist God's truth into something self-serving, the apostle Paul reminds us that freedom can quickly drift into license, and license leads to slavery. He urges us not to be mastered by our appetites. Why? Because we were not freed from sin to pursue our own desires, which simply enslave us again. Instead, "you are not your own; you were bought at a price. Therefore honor God with your body" (1 Cor. 6:19–20).

The reason we can fight with confidence against our sinful desires is that we belong to the One who is righteous. He has given us his Spirit, who leads us into righteousness. Sin no longer has the right to tell us what to do.

TEMPTED BUT WITHOUT SIN

The freedom and power not to sin does not mean we can anticipate a heaven on earth. Sin is no longer the master of those who put their faith in Jesus Christ, but that doesn't keep the conglomerate of sin, Satan, and the world from wanting us back. Temptations are guaranteed, but not the temptations that come from within. The temptations we entertain in our own imaginations are on their way out. They might persist as something unwanted, even detested, but they are being put to death. It is the temptations outside of ourselves (also called testings) that will continue. In fact, God himself allows them. These are the temptations that know where we live, how we go to work, and what we do on weekends. We don't beckon them, but they still know where to find us. For those who struggle with food, the temptations from the outside will certainly persist. Not only do we have to eat every day, we also have more advertisements exalting self-indulgence with food than we do with sex. For those who have wrestled with drugs or alcohol, there are ways to avoid old haunts, but nearly every nook and cranny will contain some reminder of the previous obsession. And sexual temptation is everywhere.

It is the ongoing saga of the Serpent in the Garden. We are walking along, minding our own business, when temptation appears from the most unlikely source. We can anticipate some temptations, but not all of them. We have distanced ourselves from old drinking buddies, bars, certain parties, and places where we might "coincidentally" run into a drug supplier, but who could anticipate the article in the paper, the song on the radio, the sudden emergence of a good memory (or a bad one)? Maybe we haven't given into the temptation, but we are dialoging with it rather than rebuking it. When a serpent comes across your path speaking lies, you should run from it or kill it. You shouldn't sit around for a friendly chat.

Addictive sin doesn't just show up and dominate us (James 1:13–15). It sneaks in quietly. It gently appeals to our imagination. It shows the best commercial you will ever see, falsely advertising itself in such a way that you are amazed that you have been able to live without it. This is where the battle is fought.

When temptations come, we live mindfully. We look past the façade of temporary pleasure and notice the smell of death that goes with it. If the temptation hooks our desires, we go public. We confess it to a friend, we confess it to the Lord, we get other people praying for us, we ask for counsel that helps us to see that the Serpent is dangerous. Above all, we remember that God's commands are good. They are intended to bless us.

Notice the strong pleas and exhortations to us from Scripture.

> You were once darkness, but now you are light in the Lord. Live as children of light (for the fruit of the light consists in all goodness, righteousness and truth) and find out what pleases the Lord. Have nothing to do with fruitless deeds of darkness, but rather expose them. . . . Be very careful, then, how you live—not as unwise but as wise, making the most of every opportunity. (Eph. 5:8–15)

Why would God allow temptations? They are divine testings that reveal our hearts. Isn't it true that we really don't know ourselves until we are put to the test? Some mild-mannered people display heroic courage and strength, while the person who seemed to be tough as nails freezes at the first gunshot. Our true natures are revealed when they are tested. Anyone can be kind when shown kindness, but what if someone cuts you off while you are driving or slanders you behind your back? These are not pleasant experiences, and some of them come at the hands of evil people who should be rebuked. But God is over them all, revealing us so that we can be led in more wholehearted trust in him. For the person whose heart does not pursue the temptation, there is joy and thankfulness that the Spirit of God is doing his good work. To the person whose heart is attracted to the temptation, there is the opportunity to know forgiveness and be strengthened for future battles.

The reason we are not immediately judged when our hearts embrace these temptations is that our advocate, Jesus Christ, *was* successful in his time of testing. By faith we have his record rather than our own (Matt. 4:1–11). Jesus is quite sympathetic to the testings and external temptations we face daily. He knows precisely what it is like to be surrounded by them.

As a result, Scripture emphasizes that Jesus is eager to give grace and mercy in times of special need (Heb. 4:15). This grace and mercy will most likely *not* come in the form of an easy battle. We don't expect to be able to arrogantly mock the temptation. Instead, the grace comes in the form of a way out (1 Cor. 10:13). God's Word could not be clearer: there is no temptation that can irresistibly lead us into sin.

FROM AFFECTION TO AFFLICTION

How long do we fight? We fight against the desires that wage war in our soul throughout our entire lives. This is the normal Christian life. It ends when we have been made perfect either through death or Jesus' return. But in the same way that there are steps into addiction, there are steps out of it. It can be very discouraging to wake up every morning and encounter the same old battle. It can be hard to recognize that the battle actually changes over time. One of the tasks of the body of Christ is to point out these changes, so that one-time addicts can be encouraged as they see that the Spirit of God is changing them.

With regard to addictive sins, the sanctification process may loosely follow this pattern. At first, we are in love with the addictive substance. We cannot understand how we could live without it. Since we know that it is so attractive to us, we make clear plans to separate ourselves from any external temptations.

As the battle is waged, the focus becomes our own heart more than the external barriers we have erected. We commit ourselves to be ruthless with our covetous imaginations. As we do, the things that were once affections gradually feel more like afflictions. That is, we still notice our heart's desire for the past idols, but these desires feel like a nagging salesperson more than an object of great love. We wish the desire would disappear, but it still occasionally shows up. When we encounter it, we groan, anticipating the day when we will be fully perfected.

Let's say a husband and father is dominated by anger. When he gives into his rage, he verbally abuses his family and destroys property. Rage is his addiction; he wants it. When he begins to take his soul to task, it is unlikely that he will immediately wear a cheerful grin in all circumstances. He might still have times when he gets very angry. However, he won't vent it on people or property, and he will be truly contrite about it. This is evidence of progressive sanctification. More change is needed, but we encourage him nevertheless that the Spirit is doing a powerful work.

A few months later, he leaves the house for half an hour rather than spew his anger on anyone. This is another step forward. He sees his anger more accurately, and he wants to avoid it rather than nurture it. Six months later, he listens quietly—without screaming—when his son explains why he came home late. The family has reason to praise God; they have witnessed the Spirit's power. A year later, his wife can tease him lightheartedly about the red face he had over a botched home repair. It is time for celebration.

This is the course of progressive sanctification. As with a young child, growth is not always apparent over a twenty-four-hour period. Only when last season's pants look like knickers do you realize that the child has grown. So it is with those who are leaving addictions. Unless you are looking very closely, day-to-day changes are not always apparent. But if the person has truly put his faith in Christ, there will be change. Look for it. Point it out when you see it. As you do, everyone can be encouraged by the work of God's grace even while the battle continues.

What about those who seem to be stuck or regressing? For example, what if the addict is caught returning to his addiction? Is this just a slip in the sanctification process? Or is it evidence that the person craves the darkness of the addiction and is once again actively worshipping an idol? It's hard to know for certain at first. But there is enough that we do know. Both the means of escape from bondage and the way to get up after a slip are the same: we repent; we remember who God is and what he has done in Christ; we learn more about our hearts' vulnerabilities; and we get help to revise our battle strategies.

What if someone has turned to Christ and really seems to have engaged in the battle, yet change feels slow? Sit down and review the strategies for growth and change. Are they clear? Does he feel like he needs more help? Does she still believe lies about God? Does guilt control him? If the person is truly willing to change, and if this desire is rooted in a growing fear of the Lord, God's power is certainly able to transform. If transformation is not evident, the problem is either in the person's heart or in the lack of suitable help in the body of Christ.

PRACTICAL THEOLOGY

Telling addicts to fight is like telling hysterical people to calm down: it might be good advice, but it goes against everything in them. Addicts have been running away from hard things, and now we say, "Fight." It is not that simple. Such a lifestyle change will take months to develop. This, of course, doesn't mean that addictions will continue through that entire time. But it does mean that addicts are not battle-ready. They will initially need more barriers between themselves and their addiction than the ones they set up themselves.

As You Face Your Own Addiction

1. Your interest in God's Word will be a barometer for how you are growing. One passage that should come alive is Matthew 4:1–4. It is the story of Jesus being tempted by the devil.

> Then Jesus was led by the Spirit into the desert to be tempted by the devil. After fasting forty days and forty nights, he was hungry. The tempter came to him and said, "If you are the Son of God, tell these stones to become bread." Jesus answered, "It is written: 'Man does not live on bread alone, but on every word that comes from the mouth of God.'"

As the Israelites were led into the desert, so was Jesus. But when they were tested, they grumbled, complained, and pursued idols. When Jesus was tested, he knew that life was found in knowing, trusting, and believing all the words of his Father.

What is your wilderness? What do you see when you are tested? Don't despair if you have known failure. Call out for the Spirit of Christ, and ask him to help you know God in such a way that life apart from him cannot compare to life with him.

2. This chapter began with a passage from Matthew 18:8–9.

> If your hand or your foot causes you to sin, cut it off and throw it away. It is better for you to enter life maimed or crippled than to have two hands or two feet and be thrown into eternal fire. And if your eye causes you to sin, gouge it out and throw it away. It is better for you to enter life with one eye than to have two eyes and be thrown into the fire of hell.

Is your method of waging war against your addiction pretty tame? If so, it is because you think you are fighting with a friend. You don't have the heart for it. Are you afraid to fight the way

Jesus teaches you for fear that you will no longer have addictions as an insurance policy? Something that is there "just in case"?

3. What is a good and wise thing to do that you nevertheless have a hard time doing? Going to meetings? Attending a good church regularly? If you don't want to do it, then you should do it. This is the battleground. This is what temptations feel like.

As You Help Someone Else

1. This chapter says that the process of change—progressive sanctification—is bumpy. This means that some weeks will be marked by more severe struggles, some by less. It does *not* mean that you deal casually with serious sin. For example, if a murderer only commits one murder a month instead of two, that is no reason to celebrate. If a drug addict with a daily habit gets sober and then smokes crack only occasionally, that is not evidence of progressive sanctification.

All sin is against God, but some sin is more serious than others. Indulging in actual addiction is more severe than indulging thoughts of the past idolatry in a private fantasy. Both are wrong, but one has more consequences. Adopt a zero-tolerance policy for actual drug use.

2. Are you willing not just to be pursued but to pursue? Are you getting a sense of how hard it is to fight this battle? Sometimes a person who needs help won't ask because she feels like she has already asked a thousand times. Other times she won't want to ask. Be someone who is willing to be involved for the long haul.

12   Being Part of the Body

Now the body is not made up of one part but of many.

1 Corinthians 12:14

Let us not give up meeting together, as some are in
the habit of doing, but let us encourage one another—
and all the more as you see the Day approaching.

Hebrews 10:25

Spiritual battles cannot be fought alone. Even though it seems much easier to keep our struggles private or to reveal them only to those with similar ones, we need the diverse ministries of the church of Jesus Christ. This is God's intent.

If you could interview a large number of people who struggle with addictive behaviors, you would find that they tend to cluster into two groups.

One group goes it alone. They tried an AA meeting and didn't like it, so they plan to handle their problems themselves. This group is probably much larger than we think. Also, in terms of sobriety alone, this group probably has more success than we think. If you want to get sober or gain some sort of control over an enslaving sin, it is not essential to go to meetings. Many people can testify to this.

The second group values the accountability of consistent

AA meetings. In fact, they believe that without AA they would be right back where they started. AA becomes their family, their church, and their job.

When either group thinks about the Christian church, it is usually with a sense of inferiority, superiority, or both. They feel inferior because they know that they have acted wrongly, and the mention of church activates their guilt. But they often feel superior as well. They are quick to judge the church as being hypocritical, judgmental, or ignorant of the nuances of addictions.

Is there a third group? Only a small one right now. Does there even *need* to be a third group? Yes indeed. If the battle against addictions is a true spiritual battle, then we need all the spiritual resources available, foremost among these the church of Christ. Regardless of the church's perceived weaknesses, it remains God's primary agent for change. Even the world hints at this when it diagnoses addictions as spiritual problems.

The church, of course, is *the* hospital for spiritual problems. Addictions counseling uses the word "spiritual" frequently, but it does not teach that the addictive struggle is a Godward struggle requiring the Holy Spirit's work in our hearts. Instead, addictions are popularly understood as quasi-medical problems. Addicts may not need expert medical help, it's said, but they *do* need assistance by addiction specialists—and pastors and church members are never considered to be experts. As a result, the church is rarely the place where addicts look first for help, and the church rarely thinks of itself that way either.

But think of the possibilities.

- When addicts look for help, the word on the street would be that the local church really loves people.
- When addicts look for help, the word on the street would be that the addicts who have gone to the local church have changed.

- Every church would have enough members who have struggled with addictions to have weekly prayer and accountability meetings.
- Churches would pray that they would attract men and women who have struggled with addictions because their strengths could bless the entire congregation. They tend to be practical, quick to help others who struggle, and able to speak the truth in love.
- Every church member would see the idolatrous bent to his or her own heart. As a result, we would all see addicts as no different from ourselves.

In theological terms, the category here is called ecclesiology—the doctrine of the church. Through the second half of the 1900s, the church lost its voice as the resource for addicts. Yet, with addiction problems growing, there are new opportunities for the church to be *the* ministering body, and more and more churches are getting serious about being instruments of change in the lives of addicts.

WHAT IS THE CHURCH?

Simply put, the church is people—people who say that Jesus is Lord and are growing in their love for God, each other, and the world. Think of it as a nation rather than a particular building to visit on Sundays. As a nation, it includes people of faith who came before us, and people throughout the world we will never meet this side of heaven. But it is a true nation with Jesus Christ as the King.

What does the church actually look like? In the New Testament, the church refers to local congregations that meet together. "Church 'emerges' whenever the Holy Spirit brings believers in any location to join together under Christ to be a people-in-relationship."[1]

Granted, individual churches can be a mess. The church, after all, consists of sinners. But they are sinners who have the

Spirit of God in their midst (Col. 1:27–28). In other words, we should expect things to be happening. Look for people changing. Look for people doing things that don't seem quite "normal," like loving and serving others. Look for people who are learning how to have joy in Christ even when life is hard. It's all there. And remember that God has actually entrusted his church to people. In other words, even though it is easy to see all the problems, and AA can seem much more welcoming at times, God has determined to use the church to accomplish his purposes in our lives.

THE BENEFITS OF THE CHURCH

Why make a big deal out of the primacy of the church? Why not go it alone or be helped by other addicts, whether they are believers or not? As is true with all theology, if we neglect what Scripture says about the church, there will eventually be bad fruit. Your chosen instrument of change, whether it is yourself, a Twelve Step program, or the church, will have a significant impact on how you see yourself and how you understand the process of change.

The church changes our identity. Notice the difference between "I'm Jim. I'm an alcoholic" and "I'm Jim. I am part of the body of Christ. I am part of 'a royal priesthood, a holy nation, a people belonging to God' (1 Peter 2:9)." For those who have put their faith in Christ, it is Christ himself who unites us and defines us—not race, financial status, hobbies, interests, or particular problems. Our family—those closest to us—are those who have put their faith in Jesus Christ. When our core identity is "alcoholic," "drug addict," or "sex addict," we are saying that our problem defines us, and our church consists of the people who share that particular problem.

The church teaches us to remember. It is very difficult to remember what is most important. On the surface, not getting caught, avoiding pain, and having our independence seem most important. With growing wisdom, we find that sobriety and self-control are very important. But it takes special revelation from God and the reminders of his people to teach us that God is most important. The church exists for the sake of God's glory. This is the purpose of all creation (Ps. 19), but it is especially expressed through the church.

This is demonstrated most clearly in preaching, corporate singing, corporate Scripture reading, and corporate prayer. These are all means by which we are reminded of our identity and purpose. What does this have to do with addictions? Addictions are ultimately a disorder of worship: we worship our desires over God. We desire the things of earth more than the One who rules it. This being so, worship is the true deepest need for addicts, as it is for all people. It is during worship that we are most fully human.

As we worship, the Spirit changes us. Sometimes this change is the more ordinary, imperceptible, and gradual change that is similar to the growth of a child. At other times, worship changes us more dramatically. Either way, when our hearts are pointed toward the risen Christ, we can't help but be changed in some way. This change, too, teaches us to remember. When we hear the stories of how God transforms people, it reminds us that God is making us to be "like God in true righteousness and holiness" (Eph. 4:24). It reminds us that he is truly the *living* God.

What are some of the best stories you will ever hear? To me, they are the stories of people who were in bondage to addictions, and by God's grace have been fighting the battle. Just as the stories within the church will help addicts to change, so the stories of addicts will help sanctify the church.

The church has everything we need. When Jesus ascended into heaven, he showered spiritual gifts on his people. He gave the church everything it needed to accomplish his purposes until he returned (1 Cor. 1:7). The grand purpose, of course, is that we would glorify God. Yet this purpose is expressed in a number of different ways, one being that we can fight sin more and more effectively.

In our battle with sin, we need a team of people. We need teachers to help us understand Scripture, prophets to help us apply it, interceders to pray for us, preachers to focus our eyes on Christ, encouragers to remind us of God's grace when we feel like failures, wise men and women to discern when we are making foolish decisions, and people of faith to tell us that everything God has said is true in Christ.

In other words, God's gifts to us are people—not just one person, but the church. This is how Christ meets us. The reason we need so many people is that we need Christ himself. Since his glory and gifts are so immense, we need many people, not just an individual person.

THE UNITY WITHIN THE CHURCH

All the gifts given to God's people are intended to glorify God by making us look more like his children, holy and pleasing to the Father. Yet this holiness should not be limited to the private working of the Spirit in our hearts. It is also a corporate holiness in which God brings glory to himself by uniting a diverse group of people who would otherwise never be together.

> [Spiritual gifts are intended] to prepare God's people for works of service, so that the body of Christ may be built up until we all reach unity in the faith and in the knowledge of the Son of God and become mature, attaining to the whole measure of the fullness of Christ. (Eph. 4:12–13)

In a nation of independent people, we don't naturally think about being united with a corporate body. Too often, we think about living our own lives and then doing our duty by going to church. Most people have a hard enough time finding some semblance of unity within their immediate family. To find unity in the church seems like the impossible dream. But God delights in doing what seems impossible. What better way to bring glory to himself?

The task, indeed, seems daunting, but we can take heart because Jesus himself has prayed for us.

> My prayer is not for them alone. I pray also for those who will believe in me through their message, *that all of them may be one,* Father, just as you are in me and I am in you. . . . I have given them the glory that you gave me, that they may be one as we are one: I in them and you in me. May they be brought to complete unity to let the world know that you sent me and have loved them even as you have loved me. (John 17:20–23)

Does this have implications for addictions? At first glance, it sounds true but seems to miss the point. "Why are you talking to me about the church and unity when my problem has nothing to do with the church?" Addictions, however, are not isolated from the rest of our lives. Attached to them are broken relationships, anger, lack of forgiveness, and a gamut of other social problems. In fact, many times in addictions the primary problem is relational—*between* addicts and other people—rather than simply within addicts themselves.

To compound these relational problems is the well-documented observation that addicts tend to be immature in their relationships. The longer the history of addictions, the more pronounced the relational immaturity. While other people were facing their interpersonal problems and developing more skills in relationships as a result, addicts were medicating their problems away. They avoided the God-given hassles of life that build character and wisdom into our lives.

For this reason, unity with God's people is especially

important for addicts. They can learn how to love, reconcile, and be loved. This is God's plan for all of his people. It is not easy, but since it is God's will for us, it will bless us in ways that we couldn't anticipate. In the case of addictions, you can expect cravings to loosen their grip as you focus on other people and the glory of Christ in the church. If we are following Christ in one area, it will benefit the rest of our lives as well. Godly change in any area cannot be isolated from the other struggles in a person's life. If there are changes in relationships, there will be changes in the addiction itself.

Needing Others

A simple way to practice unity in the body of Christ is to simply say, "I need you."

- "I need you to pray for me."
- "I need you to teach me how to live wisely."
- "I need you to rebuke me."
- "I need you to remind me about the gospel of grace."
- "I need you to tell me stories about the God who is to be feared."
- "I need you to pick me up at work so I don't go to a porn shop on my way home."

The list should be a long one. The longer the list, the greater the glory we give God. We are acknowledging that we are desperate people and that he alone has what we need.

And if an addict is not needy? Perhaps it is because:

- He does not want to turn from what he is worshipping.
- She thinks that needing the body of Christ is somehow selfish.
- He believes that by some kind of miraculous, divine intervention, while he is isolated from the body of Christ, God will take away all his addictive desires.
- She has already "tried religion and it didn't help."

Whatever the reasons, they will probably be mingled with Satan's lies. Satan's goal is always the opposite of God's. While God brings people together, Satan uses anger, guilt, and fear to separate. Such separation is the first step toward despair and the eventual domination by darkness. Addiction is not far behind. If an addict has not sought out the church—God's primary instrument of change—to bring its full resources to bear on his or her struggle, it is a danger sign. The pride, guilt, or resistance to living publicly that lies beneath this isolation from the body of Christ is a possible sign of an impending relapse, if the relapse has not already begun.

Reconciling with Those You Have Harmed

Another way to pursue unity in the church is to reconcile with those you have sinned against. Conservative estimates are that for every addict, there are at least ten people who have been seriously sinned against. Most likely this is a very low estimate, but it still suggests that addicts are some of the world's great offenders. Therefore, one of the most important steps in their battle is reconciling with others.

Reconciliation has been an emphasis in AA since its inception, and unresolved conflict with others has been noted to be a significant factor in relapse. In this, AA and the relapse literature are loosely following the biblical principle of resolving conflicts and righting wrongs as soon as possible.

Urgency in Reconciliation. Since fractured relationships and sinning against others are so contrary to the kingdom of God, it is no surprise that one clear principle of reconciliation is to do it *now*.

> Therefore, if you are offering your gift at the altar and there remember that your brother has something against you, leave your gift there in front of the altar. First go and be reconciled to your brother; then come and offer your gift. (Matt. 5:23–24)

The first thing to do is to make a list of the people who have been harmed. Who are they? Employers, co-workers, friends, people at church, parents, children, spouses. You might want to think back a few years as well. If the addiction has been long-standing, there is most likely an extensive wake of victims.

How far back do you go? There is a need for discernment here. If we list everyone who has ever been cross with us, the list will be endless. What about the junior high teacher, the one you constantly annoyed? The friend you picked a fight with in fifth grade? The neighbor you lied to? Perhaps you will want to focus largely on addiction-related sins. Also, you will want to focus on sins that are public, sins that other people are aware of. Certainly you don't need to confess every sinful thought you've had against another.

In AA literature, this is Step Eight: "Made a list of all persons we had harmed, and became willing to make amends to them all." It is a good, common-sense principle that has a long history of being crucial to the process of change. What it doesn't do is keep our attention riveted to the gospel as the foundation for all reconciliation.

> All this is from God, who reconciled us to himself through Christ and gave us the ministry of reconciliation: that God was reconciling the world to himself in Christ, not counting men's sins against them. And he has committed to us the message of reconciliation. (2 Cor. 5:18–19)

The Path of Reconciliation. We know from Scripture that we are ready to pursue reconciliation when we have thoroughly owned our sin. This means that there are no veiled attempts to spread out the blame.

> CHRISTIAN FRIEND: Jim, this may sound comical to you, but this is the way many people ask forgiveness.

"Sally, remember the day you were screaming at me and I got so upset I went out drinking? Would you forgive me?" Technically, this person did the job—he said his behavior was wrong and he asked forgiveness. But what he really said was, "Sally, if you weren't such a nagger, I wouldn't have gone out drinking."

JIM: But sometimes it may be true. Sometimes the problem really was with both people. Then what?

Certainly, other people can provoke us, but in the first step of reconciliation, the sins of the other person are not under discussion. They are not the issue at this stage. For now we examine only ourselves. Does this seem unfair? Remember that ultimately no one else can *make* us sin. Others certainly sin against us, and in so doing tempt us to a sinful response, but they do not have the power to force us to sin. At most, they can squeeze us to the point where our sin "pops out," but it still popped out of *our* hearts, not theirs. Therefore, never add a "but" or "because" to your confessions. No fishing for counter-apologies. Any riders immediately nullify the confession.

What if an addict doesn't even remember committing an offense? Heavy drinkers have committed murder while in a blackout and do not even remember—but they have still grossly offended God and others. Though this is a trickier situation, the principle remains the same. Neither people nor drugs can make us sin. Drugs can make us less alert, have amnesia, have poor reflexes, or be confused, but they cannot make us sin. They simply removed many of the normal restraints that hold back a sinful heart.

When Washington, D.C. mayor Marion Barry was arrested for cocaine possession, he was asked why he had repeatedly lied about his drug problem. Barry's response was classic: "That was the disease talking. I did not purposely do that to you. I was a victim." Needless to say, Scripture has a more realistic approach. It indicates that sin does not always have to be accompanied by conscious intent. Whether we were aware of it or not, we are responsible for our sin. On that basis, it is appropriate and important to ask forgiveness for sins we committed but don't remember.

Once we own sin without any "buts," we approach the person we have harmed. We begin by talking about the specifics of the past wrong and end by asking the person to forgive us. "I'm sorry" usually is not enough. We say "I'm sorry" at funerals. If we talk about our sorrow for what we have done (which is certainly appropriate), then we should follow it with "Will you forgive me?"

> CHRISTIAN FRIEND: How does this sound as an example of asking forgiveness? "Sally, I have been thinking about last week when I blamed you for my heavy drinking. I said that if you would be more supportive, maybe I wouldn't drink so much. Do you remember? I want you to know that I am very sorry for what I said. I was just plain wrong. It was another example of me trying to cover up and blame you. Will you forgive me?"
>
> JIM: That sounds hard.
>
> CHRISTIAN FRIEND: Bingo. You got it—you understand. It is humbling to ask someone's forgiveness. It is against our nature. It is definitely hard.

Yet the process of forgiveness doesn't stop with this question. For most victims, a simple "Yes" doesn't bring closure to the violation. It might be appropriate to add, "Sally, would you like to talk about this more? I know you must have been hurt by it." Give the victim of your sin an opportunity to share something about the damage done. Don't stop her until she is ready to move on.

Another step that might be necessary is restitution. This is particularly relevant if addicts have stolen, but it may be rel-

evant even if the sin did not result in financial loss. Such
restoration, however, can get complicated. What if the addict
robbed dozens of stores? What if the repentant addict has no
apparent ability to repay? What if the person is on probation
and reporting any past theft will put him back in jail? These
are just some of the questions. Once again, the wisdom of many
counselors is essential. This much, however, is clear: a repentant heart will desire to make restitution (Luke 19:1–9).

Pitfalls in Reconciliation. The spiritual preparation for reconciliation is straightforward, but actual practice is often riddled with pitfalls. The prospective repenter should be prepared
for several possible responses.

1. "I don't want to hear it." Some people will refuse to hear
any confession. They have heard it so many times, and there
have been so many broken promises, that the addict's words
are meaningless. If this happens, the addict must realize that
he bred that distrust. He must recognize that the only way the
relationship will change is if he demonstrates integrity. This
will take time.

2. "No." Some will simply refuse to forgive. They are angry. They don't want the addict to think that asking forgiveness can erase the years of lies and self-centeredness. Perhaps
they have heard confessions many times before. Too often former addicts have apologized even while they were planning
to continue the behavior for which they were apologizing!

When someone victimized by an addict simply refuses to
forgive, get ready for spiritual warfare. "It is hopeless. There
is nothing I can do," is one of the sure signs of Satanic deception. If the addict's goal is to rekindle the warm feelings
of a once-close relationship, then there may be reasons to feel
hopeless. It is possible, especially if the victim does not know
the gospel, that there won't be reconciliation. But the goal
should be much deeper than getting what we want. It is "to
seek first his kingdom and his righteousness" (Matt. 6:33). Such

a goal is far from hopeless. It is filled with daily purpose as well as the spiritual power to accomplish it.

What does this purpose look like? The possibilities are limitless. It could take the form of concrete expressions of love. It might be that the repentant person holds onto the relationship loosely and focuses on the war with temptations and cravings. Or the goal could be as simple as being faithful in one's job.

3. "Yes—if you do proper penance." Sometimes the person who was offended will grant conditional forgiveness. She will say "yes" but find opportunities to bring up past sins to punish or provoke guilt. "If I am still going to hurt because of what you did, you are going to hurt too." Or, "This is what it is like to be hurt. How does it feel?" Former addicts will feel like they are always under the law, trying to measure up.

This is a dangerous dynamic in relationships. In addition to the obvious result of further fracturing a relationship, living under the law can become very wearisome. Unless it is consistently countered with the more basic forgiveness we have received in Christ, it breeds hopelessness and makes the past addiction look more and more attractive.

This issue is particularly important when it comes to reconciliation with a spouse. Most likely, someone will have to supervise this. Contrary to what we might expect, spouses and families often experience *more* problems after the addict gets clean than before. If the addict was a husband and father, sobriety usually arrives with all sorts of promises: there will be no more problems at home and everyone will live happily ever after. This bubble, however, is burst almost immediately. Problems are still there; they are just different.

Another complication is that spouses' identities may be tangled up with the addiction. Although this sounds strange, sometimes spouses derive a sense of purpose from having the addict dependent on them. Sometimes the role of sacrificial caregiver is very meaningful to the spouse, and now it is being taken away. Perhaps spouses realize that they can no longer use guilt as a way to manipulate and control the former addict, now that he or she is clean. And sometimes the addiction very conveniently had kept spouses from intimacy. Now they have no excuses to distance themselves from the relationship.

All this may sound complicated, and indeed it is. Sin does that to our lives. But you don't have to be too sophisticated to be able to help. Just be aware that there may be a lot going on beneath the surface, and listen for it. Encourage families to be honest, and give them hope that God is in their very difficult situation.

Reconciling with Those Who Have Harmed You

Reconciling by seeking forgiveness is fundamental to pursuing the glory of God. We do this with humility and urgency, and in this way we point people to the God who makes all reconciliation possible. Another, often omitted feature of this reconciliation process is that one-time addicts should also extend forgiveness to those who have sinned against them. Since former addicts can be acutely aware of their own sin, they might think that they have no right to consider the sins of others against them. Yet this is a regular feature of biblical reconciliation: we ask forgiveness *and* we offer it. This is especially important with addictions because irritation with other people tends to trigger relapses.

There are a handful of biblical principles to keep in mind.

1. Remember the way Christ has forgiven you. Jesus has forgiven us past, present, and future. As we come to him by faith, we will never appear before a judge again. Instead, we have an advocate—a defense attorney—who lives to defend our case before the throne of God (Heb. 7:25). We live because of God's grace. If we are having a hard time forgiving someone, we have forgotten the way we have been forgiven.

2. Remember that God has forgiven you for a lot, not a

little. Don't slip into the trap of thinking, "I am a good person who occasionally does bad things." If we think we have been forgiven little, we will forgive little (Luke 7:36–50; Matt. 18:21–35).

3. Remember that you do the same things as the one who offended you. So confess your own sin to the Lord before you confront someone else (Matt. 7:3–5).

4. Remember that all sin is ultimately against God, and it is God's job to judge (1 Peter 2:23). It is God's law and his glory that are violated, not our own.

With these principles in mind, we forgive. We release the debt. We believe and act as if the one who sinned against us owes us nothing. Furthermore, since this can be done privately, we do this with the Lord before we go to the person.

The only question left is whether this attitudinal forgiveness (Mark 11:25) should proceed to transactional forgiveness; that is, should we lovingly confront the person who sinned against us? The Bible certainly doesn't demand that we confront every person who sins against us. But there will be times when, for the sake of the relationship, it will be wise to speak to the other person. When in doubt, encourage the person who was sinned against to get counsel from a Christian brother or sister.

If we do go to the other person, in gentleness and humility we should show our brother or sister the fault (Matt. 18:15). Former addicts can err in two ways at this point. On one hand, they can speak out in anger, in which case they have not really prepared themselves with the Lord. On the other hand, they can think, "Who am I to say anything, considering all that I have done?" Good relationships, however, include loving honesty that is at least willing to confront when sinned against.

Finally, wisdom suggests that if you have both offended and been offended by the same person, don't try to confess and confront at the same time. Confession should long precede your confrontation.

Loving and Serving Others

No discussion of our relationship with others is complete without the call to love and serve. One of the great blessings of following Christ is that it takes our attention off ourselves and directs our eyes to God and others. In this, we are led by Jesus himself. As he approached his own death, he washed the disciples' feet as a way to serve and teach them (John 13:1–15). In so doing, he concretely established the means by which the kingdom would grow: faith must express itself in love or service.

A man who recently completed an extended drug rehabilitation program wasn't so sure that love and the unity of the church were so important, at least right away. "What I learned [in the program] was that I have to deal with *me* right now. My sobriety is the most important thing." He had a point. There were dozens of disasters he needed to attend to, from his damaged relationships with his family to the repeated lies in the workplace that led to his firing. When he considered all these issues, he was overwhelmed. The only thing he could think about was getting high as a way of escape. Yet these things can't be avoided. There is no such thing as dealing with sobriety to the exclusion of relationships, especially this man's relationships with his family and the body of Christ. Since both are critical, God will give grace to attend to both.

A wise approach would be for this man to say, "I need you" to people in his church. He needed help prioritizing his lengthy agenda. He needed help to develop practical, Christ-centered plans to address each problem. And he needed help in remembering the forgiveness of sins, because he was going to take some heat from people who were very angry with him. This strategy is very different from ignoring his family and his church because he needed time "without lots of stress." According to Scripture, his true needs were to grow in loving God and others, starting with his family.

Loving others is essential to the process of change and

liberation from addictions. AA certainly has seen the value of this: it insists that people must give help in order to find it. AA, however, is not the originator of this principle. Christ himself established it as one of the ways the kingdom of heaven advances. We are to love as we have been loved (John 13:35), and serve as we have been served (John 13:14). In doing these things, we will be blessed (John 13:17).

What does this mean for someone who was once an addict? Does it mean teaching Sunday school? Giving testimonies to the entire church? Probably not at this point. It means taking small steps of obedience, being alert to the needs of others.

This can mean doing simple things like expressing appreciation, being courteous, keeping your word, and showing interest in people. These are immediate, practical ways to serve. They are applications of Scripture, which says that our Christian task is "to be peaceable and considerate, and to show true humility toward all men" (Titus 3:2).

Addicts can fool themselves into thinking that they are disqualified from deeply loving others. Like everyone else, men and women who struggle with addictions are natural sinners, not lovers, but they sometimes have the added disadvantage of thinking that they should just stay out of the way. They have hurt enough people already. They don't want to hurt any more. This, of course, is a variation of Satan's strategy to accuse and condemn. When we turn to Christ by faith, he pours out gifts on his people. No one has to wait and become an upstanding person first. We are given gifts to serve the body of Christ when we are given the Spirit. And the greatest gift is love.

PRACTICAL THEOLOGY

The local church is the prominent means by which God gives grace to us. It is an imperfect group that meets together for worship, teaching, prayer, and fellowship. There is no question that every local church can be critiqued for a number of reasons, and if you struggle with addictions, you will probably see many weaknesses immediately. This should make it that much more attractive, because it says that God welcomes imperfect people and he has purposes for them.

As You Face Your Own Addiction

1. One of the basic principles in AA is that if you don't want to go to a meeting, then you must go to a meeting. A similar principle exists for the church, except God himself has determined that we should meet with each other. If you feel like you don't want to be with God's people in church, then you must go to church.

2. What are some of your rationalizations for not meeting with God's people?

- "They don't understand."
- "I don't fit in there."
- "They are a bunch of hypocrites."
- "I just don't feel comfortable in church."

Be alert. This is warfare in progress. Satan starts with a kernel of truth (there is some truth in most rationalizations), and he uses it to hurt you. Be on guard against these lies and be prepared to combat them.

- " 'They don't understand.' Yes, they may not understand what I have been through. But I don't understand what they have been through either. I have to remember: this isn't just about me. It is about knowing and loving God, and knowing and loving others."
- " 'I don't fit in.' That's true; there may be no official, former addicts here. No one has my exact background. But this is a group of sinners seeking Christ, and the

Spirit is present when people meet in the name of Jesus. If I don't fit in here, I am in trouble."

- " 'They are a bunch of hypocrites.' I can't believe I have stooped to that excuse! I am losing my creativity! If there are some hypocrites here, then I should fit in just fine."

- " 'I just don't feel comfortable in church.' Of course I don't always feel comfortable in church. It's not a bar and it usually doesn't smell of stale cigarette smoke. But since God is the One who tells me to meet with his people, this is going to be one of the first times I do what I believe is right rather than do what I feel."

3. When you meet with Christians, remember that these are your brothers and sisters. You will be spending eternity with them.

As You Help Someone Else

1. People who have struggled with addictions can be great blessings to the church. They are open about their past struggles. They know they are sinners, and they are usually willing to tell you the sins with which they presently struggle. They want practical teaching. They are real and down-to-earth. Since they once wore masks and hid behind lies, they can usually tell when you are. And they know they need Jesus.

As you help someone, have a vision for some of the many gifts he will bring to the body of Christ.

2. One of your goals for those who struggle with addictions is that they have a clear conscience. This doesn't mean that they have no more sin. It means that they know they have been forgiven for past sins, they have appropriately owned their sin, and they are doing what they believe God calls them to do. "If it is possible, as far as it depends on you, live at peace with everyone" (Rom. 12:18).

You want the person to enjoy walking in the light, living publicly without having anything to hide or cover up.

3. If someone has had a long-term addiction, she will be unskilled at reconciliation. Prepare her as specifically as you can. If it is appropriate, be with her when she seeks to reconcile.

4. If the person is a member of the church, set aside time to prepare for the Lord's Supper. The Lord's Supper is a time when we remember that Christ's death has made us one body. Is she "discerning" the body of Christ? Is she at peace with other people? If not, make a plan to deal with it.

CONCLUSION

Where Two or Three Are Gathered

"For where two or three come together in my name, there am I with them."
(Matt. 18:20)

If we are convinced that we need the body of Christ, if we are persuaded that we need to pursue relationships with God's people, if we believe that we must meet together often, what does this look like? What should we do when we meet together? What should be the essential features of our meetings? The list is a familiar one.

- We worship.
- We remember what Jesus has done.
- We remember that we are in a battle.
- We remember to love one another.
- We remember that there is great joy ahead.
- We pray.

Whether we are meeting with a Christian friend for breakfast, in a small fellowship at someone's house, or with a group of ex-addicts for mutual encouragement and accountability, these are the recurring elements. These are what we do when we meet in the name of Jesus.

REMEMBER WHAT CHRIST HAS DONE: WORSHIP

Addictions are all about what we desire. Will we desire God more than anything else? As an antidote to addictions, worship is always central. This might seem out of place on the battlefield of cravings and daily temptations, but it is absolutely essential. Without it we are defenseless.

Consider one typical Old Testament battle (2 Chron. 20). The Moabites, Ammonites, and Meunites had just banded together into "a vast army." God's people were overcome with fear. Even the king was alarmed, and immediately moved into action as a result of the threat. But instead of rousing the nation to battle, he "resolved to inquire of the LORD." His resolve was then imitated by the people, who came together to seek the Lord. Worship had begun.

A standing feature of all worship is prayer, and this was the way King Jehoshaphat proceeded. He did not offer a perfunctory public prayer. Instead, he cried out to the Lord. He addressed God as "our God," the One who kept his promises of love and ruled over all the kingdoms of the world. His prayer was the cry of a humble and needy servant, but it was laced with a confidence that came from knowing the grace of God. After prayer, the Spirit came on Jahaziel, who prophesied God's deliverance of his people. In the light of such promises and love, all the people bowed down in humble gratitude before the Lord. In other words, their worship continued by believing the promises of God. When they got up, it was to praise the Lord "with very loud voice." The people were stirred with holy affections.

Early the next morning they prepared for battle. With a keen awareness that it was God himself who commanded the armies, the people were led onto the battlefield by men who spoke together to the Lord and praised him "for the splendor of his holiness." They sang, "Give thanks to the LORD, for his love endures forever." As they were singing, the enemy armies turned against each other, leaving only dead bodies on the ground. No Israelite warrior unsheathed his sword.

To be sure, not all battles are the same. There are times when God goes before us and foes seem to melt away. There are other times when he goes before us and the fighting is fierce and long. But what is common to all battles is that God is with us, and when God is present, we worship.

"Worship is the work of acknowledging the greatness of our covenant Lord."[1] It can certainly be done privately, but worshipping corporately is more in keeping with the greatness of God's worth—it is more aptly proclaimed by a choir of people. When we proclaim God's great worth together, songs of praise are most frequently associated with worship, but they certainly are not the totality. Some of the greatest times of worship are words of praise that are spoken rather than sung (cf. 2 Chron. 20:21; Isa. 6:3). The key is that worship proclaims the greatness of God as he has revealed himself in Jesus Christ.

IDEAS FOR PUBLIC WORSHIP

Here are some ideas to consider.

1. When meeting with God's people, come prepared with a passage of Scripture about the greatness of God. Be able to talk about the connection between the passage and its culmination in the cross of Christ.

2. Pick up a traditional hymnbook. Use the words of the hymns to lead you into worship.

> Make me a captive, Lord,
>   and then I shall be free;

> force me to render up my sword,
>   and I shall conqu'ror be;
> I sink in life's alarms
>   when by myself I stand;
> imprison me within thine arms,
>   and strong shall be my hand.²

3. There is a difference between thinking truth and saying it. Read a passage of Scripture together, sing songs together, recite creeds together.

4. During corporate prayer, focus especially on the glory of God being known throughout the world, and ways in which that glory is expressed most clearly in the cross of Christ.

5. If you are meeting as a group, invite people to come to Christ. The Christian life begins with people coming to Christ, but it also continues as a lifestyle of daily turning to Christ and away from sin. During this time there should be people who want to be converted.

6. When you hear preaching, take notes on the message and develop action steps to apply it to your life. When we hear God's Word preached, it is a time of responsive worship.

Ideas for Private Worship

1. Write when possible, including your prayers and the things you have learned from Scripture.

2. Start your day with a hymn.

3. Read the book of Daniel. What does it say about God? How did the knowledge of God affect Daniel's life?

4. Read Psalm 63. Notice the immense satisfaction available to us in the Lord. What does this have to do with addiction? What kind of answers does it give?

5. Can you give a description of the fear of the Lord? Do you have a desire to delight in it?

6. Develop a daily habit of starting each day by saying, "I need Jesus." Consider *why* it is that you need him.

7. Pray the Lord's Prayer. Read its explanation in *The Heidelberg Catechism* or *The Larger Catechism* of *The Westminster Confession of Faith*.

8. What music is most meaningful to you when you struggle with temptation? Develop a worship library. Consider "fasting" from popular music for a time and listen to worship music and good preaching instead.

REMEMBER WHAT CHRIST HAS DONE FOR *YOU*

Worship often takes our attention off ourselves completely. It isn't necessary to relate our worship of God to what he has done for us. God is great and worthy of our worship *regardless* of what he has done for us! Yet, having blessed the name of the Lord together, it strengthens our faith to remember what God has done for us, and also to hear what God is doing in other people.

The community of God can build each other up by remembering the blessings we have been given in Christ. Read Ephesians 1 together. Notice the long list of benefits we have in Christ.

- We are given grace and peace.
- We have been chosen by God.
- We have been forgiven because of the blood of Jesus.
- We have been given a new purpose—to be holy and blameless.
- We have been given insight into the great mystery of the gospel.
- We have been made children of the living God.
- We are God's beloved possession.

These blessings are even more vivid when set in contrast to our condition apart from Christ. "As for you, you were dead in your transgressions and sins. . . . we were by nature objects of wrath. But because of his great love for us, God, who is rich in mercy, made us alive with Christ. . . . it is by grace you have been saved" (Eph. 2:1, 3–5).

Take time to remember particular expressions of God's goodness. Have someone tell his story. Focus especially on God's pursuing love and "unlimited patience" (1 Tim. 1:16). If we are part of Christ, Scripture promises that God is now doing a good work in us and he will continue it. So we should be expecting to see the Spirit's work; we should be looking for it. Don't look just for episodes of deep joy and peace. Be alert to the less emotional but equally dramatic times when someone loves rather than rages, says "no" to temptation, or does something that simply isn't natural.

Figure 13.1, which also appeared in chapter 11, reminds us that the Spirit's work in our lives unfolds in small steps. As we meet together, we will find that the church has members at every point on the line. Each step can be filled with more

FIGURE 13.1.
THE PROCESS OF CHANGE

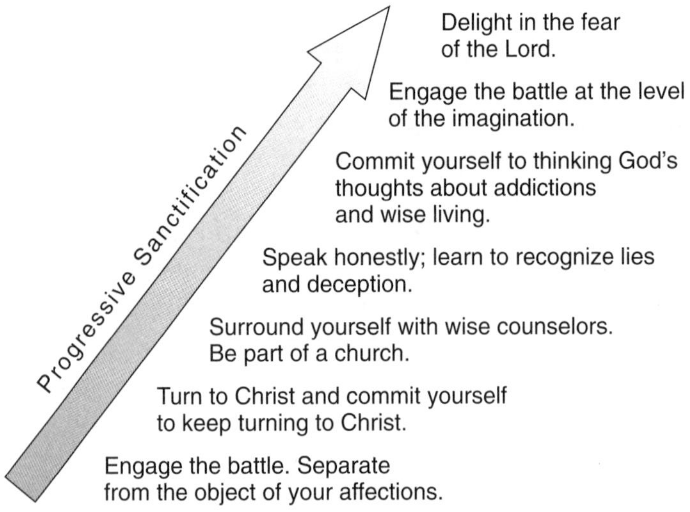

Delight in the fear of the Lord.

Engage the battle at the level of the imagination.

Commit yourself to thinking God's thoughts about addictions and wise living.

Speak honestly; learn to recognize lies and deception.

Surround yourself with wise counselors. Be part of a church.

Turn to Christ and commit yourself to keep turning to Christ.

Engage the battle. Separate from the object of your affections.

Progressive Sanctification

detail, and could have a different label. Nevertheless, these steps remind us that God himself is doing a good work in us.

IDEAS FOR REMEMBERING WHAT CHRIST HAS DONE

1. When you meet, have one person give a testimony of God's grace.

2. Remember that when people confess sin, it too is evidence of the Spirit's work. Be sure that your testimonies include more than spiritual success stories. Otherwise, some people will withdraw, and others will be tempted to be dishonest in order to match them. Remember that when the Spirit convicts of sin, it is also time to celebrate.

3. Remind each other that God is on the move (Phil. 1:6). Look for where that is happening and pray for more occurrences.

REMEMBER THAT OUR HEARTS ARE STILL DECEITFUL; REMEMBER THAT THE BATTLE CONTINUES

When we remember God's ever-present grace to sinners, we have the courage to look at our own hearts. Since Christian gatherings should focus more on Christ than our own sin, our own hearts will not be the central focus. But self-examination *is* a natural outgrowth of knowing God's holiness. His holiness exposes our sin, compels us to do battle with it, and makes a way for us to actually be made holy.

Sin should scare us. It is deceitful, blinding, and dominating. We should walk through life as if in enemy territory, always watchful, never traveling alone. If sin publicly announced its presence, there would be less reason for concern, but it lurks in the shadows and refuses to reveal itself. The danger, of course, is that we find aspects of sin very attractive at first. So, in a sense, it *does* parade in the open. It tempts and lures, being careful only to hide the fact that its goal is to curse and destroy us.

By God's grace, however, sin can be exposed. Since it doesn't just come out of nowhere and capture us, we should learn to be alert to signs that it is gaining ground in our hearts. Watch for signs like these:

- "I can deal with this one on my own."
- "I will *really* deal with this tomorrow. If I am still struggling, then I will talk with someone." This is usually a stalling tactic because we are not willing to part with the object of our sinful affections. The danger with the accommodation of sin is that tomorrow we will be even *less* inclined to deal with it! After all, nothing horrible happened, and our consciences are now a little quieter.
- We're angry and unwilling to forgive.
- We stop waging war at the level of the imagination. We are lax about our thought life.
- "I can't turn to God now. That would be hypocritical. I will deal with this problem first."
- "I am too far gone."

Fight these kinds of thoughts with the fear of the Lord principle: All aspects of my life are seen by God. Would I be comfortable having my behavior and my imaginations made public?

The Christian community should continually remind us *why* we are fighting a battle with sin. Just as Scripture does, it should remind us of the benefits of being strong in Christ throughout the battle. Sin tends to narrow our focus to the immediate pleasure; the Christian community can help us to see the larger story of God's plan for good.

Loving God's Law

Along with these warning signs, the Spirit uses our own conscience and God's law to sharpen our moral senses. Our conscience can be dysfunctional and out of practice, so it is not always reliable. But when honestly heeded, it typically says more than we would expect. For this reason, another way to expose sin is to ask, "What does my conscience say?" The law also teaches us about our own sin, so we can expose sins as we also ask, "What does God's law say?"

Sadly, the law has a bad reputation among many Christians. As the Psalms declare (e.g., Ps. 119) the law is a beautiful gift from God. When used as intended, it can reveal our hearts. However, it cannot help us change. Instead, the law provokes our worst instincts. For example, if you tell your kids not to jump on a bed, they will soon be dying to do just that, even if the thought had not previously entered their minds. Tell someone "you can't," and more often than not, the instinctive response is, "I will." In other words, the law doesn't seem to help us control our behavior.

The problem, of course, is not with God's law. The problem is that our flesh, the sin that lives in our hearts, wants us to be the center of the universe, and no one who aspires to be the center of the universe wants to be told what to do. In fact, sometimes we can be told what to do and—even if we believe that such a course would be the best for us—we will do the opposite simply to assert that *we* are in control.

The question is, How should God's law be part of the process of change? If it just makes things worse, why use it? There is much discussion in Christian circles today on the relationship between God's law and God's grace. At first glance, they seem to be two contradictory systems for living: "Do the right thing" versus "Trust the right person." And given a choice between the two, grace certainly sounds better. In reality, however, law and grace work hand in hand. One cannot be separated from the other. Law without grace is called legalism, and grace without law is called antinomianism (literally, against the law).

Addicts follow the norms for the culture and prefer

antinomianism. They have lived as if God had no say in certain areas of life. That is, they have lived as if some divine laws didn't apply to them. Although they may be quite moral in some areas, they have tried to avoid God in others. Like so many of us, they pick and choose the laws that suit them while avoiding those that don't allow them to indulge their favorite desires. Some might ignore God's law on gossip or complaining; others ignore what the Bible says about anger, honoring others above oneself, or generosity. Others bypass Scripture's teaching on sobriety and moderation.

Simply put, we don't like being told what to do, by God or others, unless it is something we want to do already. Too often our obedience to the Lord is a happy coincidence, where our desires and his commands happen to intersect. Yet God is God. He is not to be trifled with. When he tells us how we are to live, our bottom line response should be easy: "God is bigger, and he wins." A step better than that would be: "The sovereign God is our Creator and Father. He has the right to have us live any way he desires, and we owe him our obedience." But the goal, especially considering the fact that Scripture presents God's law as immensely attractive, is this perspective: *The wise and godly person loves to have God tell him what to do.* God desires something more than our mechanical obedience. He teaches us about himself so that our obedience can be in the context of a loving relationship between a father and child. He reminds us that he has loved us to the extreme in Jesus, and a father who loves us that much is not going to impose oppressive commands. Rather, his desire is to bless and prosper us as his children.

In this context, God gives us his law. He points us first to himself; then he teaches us how to love and imitate him. As we do, our paths are blessed.

Notice that this is the structure of the Ten Commandments. They begin with God revealing himself: " 'I am the LORD your God, who brought you out of Egypt, out of the land of slavery' " (Ex. 20:2). Immediately, we encounter the only true God who took a small, insignificant nation to be his own simply because he loved them. After such an introduction, whatever harshness people find in the Ten Commandments can only be attributed to their own sin, which wants no law at all. Both God and his commandments are holy, good, and beautiful. His law is beautiful in its manifestation of his character and pronouncement of his blessing.

Appreciating the attractiveness of God's commands is especially important for two reasons. First, we live in a Christian culture in which the law seems to have a bad reputation. Holiness is unpopular. If you were to take a poll of teenagers from Christian families, you would probably find that they see the law as something designed to limit their fun. It is intended to make them just a bit odd. For the rest of us, God's commands are considered antagonistic to grace. If we have to choose one or the other, we will certainly take grace. The church is more afraid of legalism than it is of licentiousness.

To make matters worse, there is the human tendency to believe Satan's lie that God is not good. Satan often whispers that the law is God's way of holding out on us, and we entertain these accusations far too often.

The biblical writers, however, were persuaded that the law demonstrated God's great love. They knew that there was no blessing apart from obedience to it. They knew that the law, far from being a rod to oppress, protected our capacity for pleasure.

> "Follow them [the laws] so that you may live . . . and take possession of the land. . . ." (Deut. 4:1; cf. Deut. 6:18; 7:11–15; 28:1–14)

> Blessed is the man
>   who does not walk in the counsel of the wicked. . . .
> But his delight is in the law of the LORD. (Ps. 1:1–2)

The law of the LORD is perfect,
reviving the soul. (Ps. 19:7)

Blessed is the man who fears the LORD,
who finds great delight in his commands. (Ps. 112:1)

Think about how different, how blessed, an addict's life would have been if he had considered the beauty of God's law. Think of how different relationships, jobs, and health would be. Think of how obedience would have been a blessing rather than an inconvenience. When Scripture says that "the LORD longs to be gracious to you" (Isa. 30:18), this "graciousness" refers to both the law *and* the gospel. God's way is not only right and necessary because he is God, it is also much more attractive.

We are prone to getting into trouble by making the law a system unto itself, as if it operates apart from the *fulfillment* of the law in Jesus Christ. When we follow the law without keeping Jesus and the cross central, we have simply developed another religion in which salvation is dependent on our own efforts. It doesn't matter whether that effort is a pilgrimage to Mecca, circumcision, or sobriety. If it is not centered on Christ, it is a false hope.

Ideas for Remembering That We Are in a Battle

1. Keep using the Lord's Prayer. It includes confession of sin.

2. Consider the quote, "The worth and excellency of a soul is measured by the object of its love."[3] What things do you love?

3. What do you tend to fantasize about? Have you wanted to go back to the bondage of Egypt? It sounds like a bizarre question, but it is a common tendency of the human heart (Ex. 14:10–12).

4. Expand your list of the ways you deceive yourself and others. Ask other people to help you think through the many ways we can be deceitful.

5. List recent situations in which you blamed another person for your actions, out loud or only to yourself.

6. Are you believing that God is good? If not, you are already deep in spiritual warfare. This is one of Satan's favorite entry points. He points to all your difficult circumstances—many of them a result of your own sin—and suggests that a good father would have made life easier by now. The answer is to go to the cross of Christ. It is there that God's goodness and love are irrefutable.

7. Study 1 Corinthians 10:11–14. It reminds us that there is no craving, no friend, no drug dealer, no miserable circumstances—no temptation—that can lead us into sin.

8. Have you spoken to a wise mentor this week? Scripture indicates that we all need daily encouragement from others so that we may avoid being hardened by sin's deceitfulness (Heb. 3:12–13).

9. Lying takes many forms. Look up these verses from Proverbs: 6:12–19; 10:9–10; 11:9; 12:19–22; 19:5; 20:17; 21:6; 26:18–26. Do they uncover ways in which you have neglected the truth?

10. Keep looking at sin and temptation accurately. For example, Proverbs suggests that the allure of the addictive substance is actually a path that leads to death (2:18); "an ox going to the slaughter" (7:22); "a bird darting into a snare" (7:23); and it "bites like a snake" (23:32). Your goal is to nurture a hatred of the past addiction (8:13).

11. What are your "high risk" situations or early warning signs? These are the times that precede your temptations and make you more vulnerable. Look carefully for these because, on the surface, they might seem unrelated to addiction. For example, anger, fear, pain, depression, frustrations in a relationship, or discouragement about a job can put us at risk if they are left untended.

12. How are your walls of protection (Prov. 25:28; 23:19–20)? Keep getting ideas from each other. What barriers

have you erected between yourself and the addictive object? Remember that it is easier to avoid an idol when we are far from it. When it is within reach, cravings will be much more intense.

13. Read and study Romans 7:13–8:17. This passage talks about the struggle with sin, deliverance in Christ, and no condemnation.

14. Is Christ always in view when you talk about sin? Commenting on Galatians 5:4, Luther asks, "What do you do when you are caught in some sin? If your answer is, 'I'll do better next time,' then you have no need of Christ." Luther then offers this alternative: "that you despair of your own righteousness and you trust boldly in Christ."

REMEMBER TO LOVE ONE ANOTHER

Sometimes, even when we are in a group of other believers, we still think that our faith is a private system of self-improvement. But the Christian life always looks in three directions: first at Christ, then at our own hearts, and finally at other people. Our meetings with other believers should stir us to love.

We were born in the divine house of love. The Father loved the Son; the Son loved those the Father gave him. Now, since we have been given the Spirit of love, it is only natural that we would love others. " 'My command is this: Love each other' " (John 15:12). In so doing, we will be a united body that brings glory to Christ. Also, we will display to the world the character of the God we serve. We want people to say, "If she believes in God and is so loving, then I want to know her God. He must be a God of great love."

If our gatherings are focused on addictions, remember that the call to love others is very relevant to our addictive tendencies. So far, addictions have been summarized as idolatry, lust, spiritual adultery, and bondage. They can also be summarized as selfishness, or a love for self that far exceeds the love for others. Think about it. The lies of addiction are against others, intending to mislead them. The broken promises are because we love our desires and, in essence, hate other people. No wonder that love is a treatment that goes to the very heart of addictions.

Part of the beauty of love is that it can take so many forms— a cup of water, a warm greeting, overlooking an offense, praying for someone. In any form, love and service offered in the name of Jesus honor his name, display God's character, and make even the angels take notice (Eph. 3:10).

Ideas to Serve in Love

1. Remembering the way that Jesus served us (John 13), what opportunities for service do you have today?

2. Seeking peace is a profound way to show love. Consider studying *The Peacemaker*, by Ken Sande.

3. Spend group time in prayer for other people.

4. Key features of love are patience and kindness (1 Cor. 13:4). In what situations do you react with frustration? What form could kindness take in your relationships?

5. Pray for the Spirit of love. Pray for opportunities to demonstrate love.

6. Talk about how you have seen the love of Christ in others.

REMEMBER THAT THERE IS JOY
SET BEFORE YOU (HEB. 12:2)

The battle is getting old. You are getting tired. Old desires start to exert themselves. What resources do you have then? The most obvious resource is other people. We were created to need other people, so we call out for help. This help might take various forms. It could be a compassionate reminder that you are not alone, a late-night meeting over coffee because temptations seem particularly strong, or verbal reminders of larger spiritual realities.

Perhaps the most relevant spiritual teaching for people who are tired is that Christ is coming. "In just a very little while," Jesus is coming (Heb. 10:37). When we think that each day is going to be the same as the last, life becomes drab and purposeless. We think that we might as well have as much fun today as possible, or we think of suicide. But when we realize that a deadline is approaching, it brings new strength and vigor to the battle. Like a boxer who can barely stand but unleashes a flurry of punches right before the bell, we are spiritually energized when we remember that we are on the verge of seeing Jesus face to face.

Think of it. We will see the One who has loved us from the beginning of time. We will be able to know him even better than we do now, and marvel at his being. All temptations—both cravings from our hearts and testings from the world—will be a vague memory. We will stand before the Lord as sinless children, united with him for eternity.

Such knowledge doesn't leave us dreamy-eyed and detached from our present life. It makes every moment more important. We take one day at a time because there might only *be* one day (Matt. 6:25–34; Luke 12:22–34). Given that time is short and the events to come so beautiful, we can certainly continue the fight a little longer.

Addictions live only in the moment, without the future in view. The gospel teaches us to see the future in a way that radically transforms the moment.

> Praise be to the God and Father of our Lord Jesus Christ! In his great mercy he has given us new birth into a living hope through the resurrection of Jesus Christ from the dead, and into an inheritance that can never perish, spoil or fade—kept in heaven for you . . . In this you greatly rejoice, though now for a little while

you may have had to suffer grief in all kinds of trials. These have come so that your faith—of greater worth than gold . . .—may be proved genuine and may result in praise, glory and honor when Jesus Christ is revealed. Though you have not seen him, you love him; and even though you do not see him now, you believe in him and are filled with an inexpressible and glorious joy, for you are receiving the goal of your faith, the salvation of your souls. (1 Peter 1:3–9)

Envision the prize (1 Cor. 9:27). There will be crowns, rejoicing, no sorrow, no broken relationships. Yet these in themselves are not the prize. Like the Old Testament Levites, we get something better than land. The prize is Jesus, God himself.

The battle is worth it.

Resources

The following resources are sympathetic to a Christian perspective. Some are committed to being biblical, others are Christianized AA programs. Check web sites for more information.

RESIDENCY PROGRAMS

AMERICA'S KESWICK—4-month residential program
601 Route 530
Whiting, New Jersey 08759
(732) 350-1187
www.americaskeswick.org

GOOD NEWS HOME FOR WOMEN—9–18 month residential treatment program for women 18 years and older
33 Bartles Corner Road
Flemington, New Jersey 08822
(908) 782-4132
www.goodnewshome.org

HEBRON COLONY—10-week residential program for men 20 years and older
356 Old Turnpike Road
Boone, North Carolina 28607
(828) 963-4842
www.hebroncolony.org

HEBRON-GRACE SANTEE, INC.—10-week residential program for women 20 years and older

P. O. Box 407

Santee, South Carolina 29142

(803) 854-9809

www.hebroncolony.org

HIS MANSION—MALE AND FEMALE, AGES 18-35

P. O. Box 40

Hillsborough, New Hampshire 03244

(603) 464-5555

www.hismansion.com

TEEN CHALLENGE—Multiple locations, long-term residential, adolescent through adult

P. O. Box 1015

Springfield, Missouri 65801

(417) 862-6969 or (417) 862-2781

TIMOTHY HOUSE MINISTRIES—Men only, 18-40, one year discipleship residency program

Bible Institute and Overcomer's Group included

715 Rothsville Road

Lititz, Pennsylvania 17543

(717) 627-1598

www.timothyhouse.org

WHOSOEVER GOSPEL MISSION—Men only, 21 years and older, minimum 6 months residential program

101 E. Chelten Avenue

Philadelphia, Pennsylvania 19144

(215) 438-3094

FURTHER INFORMATION:

Mr. Terry Livorsi, Crisis Care Counselor and Networker

(800) 895-5441

SUPPORT GROUP INFORMATION

ALCOHOLICS VICTORIOUS

9370 S. W. Greenburg Road, Suite 411
Tigard, California 97323

ALCOHOLICS FOR CHRIST

1316 North Campbell Road
Royal Oak, Michigan 48067

HARVEST, USA—Help for those with sexual addictions

P. O. Box 11469
Philadelphia, Pennsylvania 19111
(215) 342-7114

OVERCOMERS IN CHRIST

P. O. Box 34460
Omaha, Nebraska 68134
(402) 573-0966
www.overcomersinchrist.org

SUBSTANCE ABUSE VICTORIOUS

One Cascade Plaza
Akron, Ohio 44308

Notes

Chapter 1: Practical Theology

1. William Lenters, *The Freedom We Crave—Addiction: The Human Condition* (Grand Rapids: Eerdmans, 1985), 4.

Chapter 2: Sin, Sickness, or Both?

1. P. 47.

2. For example, Augustine, *Confessions;* Scott Peck, *People of the Lie: The Hope for Healing Human Evil* (New York: Simon & Schuster, 1985); Cornelius Plantinga, *Not the Way It's Supposed to Be: A Breviary of Sin* (Grand Rapids: Eerdmans, 1995).

3. D. W. Goodwin et al., "Alcohol Problems in Adoptees Raised Apart from Alcoholic Biological Parents," *Archives of General Psychiatry* (1973), 28:238–43.

4. D. J. Armor, J. M. Polich, and H. B. Stambul, *Alcoholism and Treatment* (New York: Wiley, 1978).

5. Martin Luther, *The Bondage of the Will*, trans. J. I. Packer and O. R. Johnston (Westwood, N.J.: Revell, 1957), 102.

6. J. E. Todd, *Drunkenness a Vice, Not a Disease* (1882).

7. M. Scott Peck, *People of the Lie: The Hope for Healing Human Evil* (New York: Simon & Schuster, 1985).

Chapter 3: New Ways of Seeing

1. "A Member's-Eye View of Alcoholics Anonymous" (New York: Alcoholics Anonymous World Services, 1970), 12.

2. B. Meehan, *Beyond the Yellow Brick Road* (Chicago: Contemporary Books, 1984), 175.

3. R. Weiss and S. Mirin, *Cocaine* (Washington: American Psychiatric Association, 1987), 55.

Chapter 4: The Descent into Addiction

1. The slow unfolding of addictions is now an accepted observation. E.g., M. D. Glantz and C. R. Hartel, eds., *Drug Abuse: Origins and Interventions* (Washington, D.C.: The American Psychological Association, 2000).

2. For example, *Drug-Proofing Your Kids,* by Steve Arterburn and Jim Burns. Also, although it doesn't speak specifically about drugs, see *Age of Opportunity,* by Paul David Tripp.

Chapter 5: Speaking the Truth in Love

1. D. Bonhoeffer, *Life Together* (San Francisco: Harper & Row, 1954), 112.

2. V. Johnson, *I'll Quit Tomorrow* (San Francisco: Harper & Row, 1980); *Intervention* (Minneapolis: The Johnson Institute, 1986).

Chapter 6: Respecting, Listening, and Inviting

1. G. A. Hemmings, "The Puritan's Dealings with Troubled Souls," in *Puritan Papers, Volume 1, 1956–1959,* ed. D. Martyn Lloyd-Jones (Phillipsburg, N.J.: P&R Publishing, 2000), 33.

Chapter 7: Knowing the Lord

1. Elizabeth Eisenstadt, "God, Wild and Tamed: Three Gifted Writers, a Trinity of Perspectives," *Philadelphia Inquirer,* April 4, 1999, H5.

2. For further discussion, see David Powlison, " 'Unconditional Love'?" *The Journal of Biblical Counseling,* vol. 12.3 (spring 1994).

3. See John Piper, *The Pleasures of God* (Sisters, Ore: Multnomah, 2000).

4. John Owen, *Works,* ed. William Goold, 16 vols. (Edinburgh: Johnstone and Hunter, 1850–53; Banner of Truth Trust, 1965–68), 3:370.

Chapter 8: Fearing the Lord

1. C. S. Lewis, *The Weight of Glory and Other Addresses* (Grand Rapids: Eerdmans, 1965), 2.

2. See also Robert D. Jones, "I Just Can't Forgive Myself," *The Journal of Biblical Counseling,* vol. 14.2 (winter 1996).

3. John Murray, *Redemption Accomplished and Applied* (Grand Rapids: Eerdmans, 1955), 111.

4. This definition has been sharpened by R. C. Sproul.

Chapter 9: Turning from Lies

1. D. Bonhoeffer, *Life Together* (San Francisco: Harper & Row, 1954), 20.

Chapter 10: Saying "No"

1. L. Robins, "Vietnam Veterans' Rapid Recovery from Heroin Addiction: A Fluke or Normal Expectation?" *Addiction 88* (1993): 1041–54.

2. Plato developed these four virtues in *The Republic;* Aristotle in *Nichomachean Ethics.*

Chapter 12: Being Part of the Body

1. Stanley Grenz, *Created for Community* (Wheaton, Ill.: Victor, 1996), 209.

Conclusion: Where Two or Three Are Gathered

1. John Frame, *Worship in Spirit and Truth* (Phillipsburg, N.J.: P&R Publishing, 1996), 1.

2. *Trinity Hymnal,* rev. ed. (Atlanta/Philadelphia: Great Commission Publications, 1990), #687.

3. Henry Scougal, *The Life of God in the Soul of Man* (Harrisonburg, Va.: Sprinkle, 1986), 63.

Index of Scripture

Edward T. Welch serves both the Christian Counseling and Educational Foundation (CCEF) and Westminster Theological Seminary. At CCEF he is, in addition to being a counselor and faculty member, the director of counseling and academic dean. At Westminster he is professor of practical theology. He joined both organizations in 1981.

In addition to writing *Blame It on the Brain* and *When People Are Big and God Is Small,* Welch has contributed to several books, including *What's the Brain Got to Do with It?, Our Smallest Members, Leadership Handbook of Practical Theology* (vol. 2), and *Power Religion.*

Welch has written more than ten articles for the *Journal of Biblical Counseling.* Other periodicals to carry his essays include *Journal of Psychology and Christianity, Journal of Pastoral Practice, Journal of Biblical Ethics in Medicine, Carer and Counselor, Modern Reformation, New Horizons, American Family Association Journal, Spiritual Counterfeits Project Journal, Reforma Siglo,* and *Westminster Bulletin.*

At meetings of such organizations as the Christian Association for Psychological Studies, American Association of Christian Counselors, and Pennsylvania Psychological Association, Welch has presented papers.

After earning his M.Div. degree at Biblical Theological Seminary, Welch received, in 1981, a Ph.D. in counseling psychology (neuropsychology) from the University of Utah.

Resources for Changing Lives

A series published in cooperation with
THE CHRISTIAN COUNSELING AND EDUCATIONAL FOUNDATION
Glenside, Pennsylvania

Susan Lutz, Series Editor

Available in the series: